Happy

All on

ti and Rob

It is not widely known that a group of All Blacks and top provincial players, seeking a fairer share of rewards from tours overseas, were responsible for starting professional football in Australia and New Zealand.
'All Blacks to All Golds' tells of their exploits, their tours of Australia and England, their successes and tribulations and their eventual return to New Zealand, bringing with them the Rugby League game they learnt to play so well in the north of England.

Cast out by the Rugby Union at their time of leaving New Zealand in August 1907 and being away for almost a year, they played six Test matches and countless other representative games against other top sides. Known, just like fellow players who had remained at home, as the New Zealand All Black Football Team, but dubbed 'The All Golds' by an Australian newspaper who decried their endeavours to earn gate-money, they were eventually to turn the name into a glorious one. To Englishmen they were quite simply All Blacks following on the tradition of the first All Blacks of 1905-06, some of whom were also in this 'professional' team. Only this time they played against the best and strongest clubs in English rugby, who had broken away from the Rugby Football Union twelve years earlier.

Award-winning author John Haynes draws almost solely for his material on previously undiscovered original documents.
He tells in lively detail of the clandestine way the players arranged the tour, setting it superbly into the context of the times. The result is a feast for lovers of sport and social history, and a ripping good read.

This edition published in 2007 by
League Publications Ltd
Wellington House
Briggate
Brighouse
West Yorkshire HD6 1DN

First published in New Zealand in 1996 by Ryan and Haynes.

A CIP catalogue record for this book is available from the British Library
ISBN 978-1-901347-17-3

Designed and Typeset by League Publications Limited
Manufactured in the EU by LPPS Ltd, Wellingborough, Northants

CONTENTS

ABOUT THE AUTHOR

JOHN HAYNES won the New Zealand Society of Authors Best First Non-Fiction Award in 1995 for his biography of Tom Fyfe, Piercing the Clouds. He first came into contact with football in the Waikato, and recalls as a youngster playing curtain raisers to matches in Hamilton that included the All Blacks Bob Scott and Ron Jarden. At university, Rugby League won out and he respresented New Zealand Universities in each of the three inaugural 'Tests' against Australian Universities in 1969. He was awarded a University Blue the same year.

The author's involvement with the All Golds began in 1984 when, following in the footsteps of Albert Baskiville, he organised the first New Zealand Universities tour of England and France. Then, while president of New Zealand Universities he interested other League nations in playing for a Students World Cup, and together with Bud Lisle and Barry Mitchell hosted the inaugural event in Auckland in 1986, New Zealand winning. In 1990 the New Zealand Rugby Football League honoured him with its Distinguished Service Award. He has a Masters Degree (Hons) in Political Science from the University of Auckland and taught history prior to his appointment to the Office of Ombudsmen in Christchurch.

AUTHOR'S NOTE

For most of this century rugby league has been the preferred rugby code of thousands of New Zealanders, yet its origins have not been the subject of significant historical research. This book is the result of my investigations into those beginnings. It tells of the tour of England and Australia by the first New Zealand football team to play both rugby codes on a professional basis. However, it is also a social history, because when rugby union players rebelled against the New Zealand Rugby Union in 1907, over compensation for playing, they challenged New Zealand's sporting and other structures. Amateurism, if not a practice, was strongly entrenched as an ideal. So closely does New Zealand identify with rugby, the challenge inevitably drew into the crisis both the government and the press, as well as public opinion reflecting different class values.

Up until 1939, both New Zealand's rugby union and rugby league national representative players were called 'All Blacks'. This can be confusing. For the purposes of this book, and to avoid any misunderstanding, I have referred to the 1905 and 1907 All Black teams selected by the New Zealand Rugby Union as the 'amateur' All Blacks, and the 1907-08 team selected by New Zealand's rebel rugby union players as the 'professional' All Blacks. The distinction is, in fact, an artificial one because all national players received monetary allowances; the 1905 All Black team was paid by the Rugby Union and the 1907-08 professional team received allowances from its players' committee.

Of other uses, Albert Baskiville's name is spelt as it appears in his birth and death records, and on his grave. For certain purposes Baskiville used Baskerville, but this was never formalised.

Authors of historical works never write in a vacuum. I am indebted to many helpful people. Geoffrey Moorhouse provided not only important information from England but also advice of inestimable value. My thanks also go to Ian Watson, a New Zealander in Brisbane, who threw open to me his vast rugby league archive. Bud Lisle in Auckland also gave valuable assistance with information as well as much needed encouragement. Many others played a part: Ian Heads and Ian Collis in Sydney, and George Smith's daughter, Edna Stansfield, in Oldham. For details on Bert Baskiville's early life, I must thank his niece, Margaret Henderson. Dan Gilchrist in Wellington provided several photographs. On a practical level, in addition to National Archives, access to newspapers has been granted by the British Museum, Mitchell Library of New South Wales, Canterbury Public Library, Dunedin City Library and the Wellington and Auckland Public Libraries.

My wife, Fiona, probably now knows more about these players than she might originally have wished, and Honor James re-typed the original manuscript.

John Haynes
MA (Hons), Dip.Tchg. Christchurch

FOREWORD

Rugby League has had a proud history since the Northern Rugby Football Union was created in the George Hotel at Huddersfield in 1895.

It isn't vital that a Rugby League supporter understands the game's historical development in order to enjoy the game. But I'm certain that anyone who studies how Rugby League developed over the years into today's high-speed and highly skilled collision game would have much to gain from understanding its history.

For journalists like me who cover the game, that knowledge is vital. As a Rugby League writer I am conscious that the journalist is someone who writes what is sometimes called the first rough draft of history. But without a knowledge of history we are unable to put today's events into a context that makes them meaningful and useful.

I first read 'From All Blacks to All Golds' when it was first published in 1996. It struck me then as being the finest book on the history of Rugby League that I had ever read.

I suppose that's a bold claim to make, but the reason for making it is because the book introduced me to the life and tragically early death of the man whose name deserves to be right up there at the very top when we think about the heroes of Rugby League.

Albert Henry Baskiville (he signed his name 'Baskerville', by the way) was a New Zealander, and a useful rugby player who was working as a post office clerk in Wellington when he heard about the new form of rugby that was being played in England. On learning more about the new game he resolved to take a touring party of New Zealanders to England, and what happened after that is what you will read about in this book.

Twelve years after the Northern Union came into being, the new code of rugby was experiencing many difficulties before Baskiville got in touch, and I believe that he secured the future of Rugby League. The fact that Rugby League became established in New Zealand and Australia was down to him, which is why, in my view, he can justifiably be called the greatest historical figure ever associated with the game.

I first met the author John Haynes when I was an official of the Student Rugby League and John, like Baskiville, brought a party of New Zealand tourists to this country (in his case it was the New Zealand Universities) in 1983. That early tour led to the first Student World Cup in New Zealand in 1986. Subsequently John went on to write this book, and I went on to jointly found 'Rugby League Express' in 1990.

I am delighted that League Publications is now able to re-publish this book in England, exactly 100 years after the arrival of the very first New Zealand tourists, and with their descendants also about to tour Great Britain.

Let those who drink the water remember with gratitude those who dug the well. Their story is told in this book.

Martyn Sadler
Chairman, League Publications Limited

The remarkable story of Rugby League's international pioneers

All Blacks All to Golds

John Haynes

LEAGUE
Publications Ltd

1. NEWS OF REVOLT

Professional Rugby! A *New Zealand Herald* report dated 13 May, 1907, stunned New Zealand. Over breakfasts and in hotels, in tramcars and on ferries, the country's sporting public learnt of plans by All Blacks and provincial players to play against professional rugby clubs in the north of England. Could it be true? The All Blacks bowed to no-one and in rugby the amateur ethic reigned supreme, or did it?

Many would have known at least something of the rugby revolution in England just twelve years previously. There, distrust and accusations about whether rugby players could be paid, and were being paid, had led the finest clubs in Yorkshire and Lancashire to split away from the English Rugby Union. Rooted in England's class and regional differences as much as anything else, the almost inevitable divorce had been an acrimonious one. Traditionally rugby had tremendous strength in the north, and the rebellious clubs formed a separate rugby union - the Northern Union. Enjoying its new freedom, the Union moved quickly, first legitimising compensation for players and then changing rugby's rules pragmatically, giving life to a new, faster brand of football - rugby league. Was the professional issue, now about to surface in New Zealand? The Herald's report continued - "Visit of New Zealand Footballers - a circular has been issued to the football clubs in the union by the Northern Union Committee respecting the proposed visit of a New Zealand team to the Northern Union Clubs next season. The Committee has had this matter under consideration, and they are very favourably disposed to the visit." [1]

Rugby was by then being played throughout New Zealand, and the New Zealand Rugby Union had been formed in 1892 to administer it on an amateur basis. The nation's representatives, the All Blacks, winning match after match, earned enormous respect and had not long returned from a highly successful first tour of Great Britain in 1905-06. At local level playing numbers surged and newspapers, reflecting the game's popularity, gave it extensive coverage. Also the profit to the New Zealand Union from the tour had improved their already sound financial position by £12,000. The game had never been in a stronger position. Yet could it be that the same All Blacks who had earned the plaudits of the nation, but little else, were no longer prepared to play for nothing? Further newspaper reports heightened speculation. Questions immediately followed on the implications of such a tour, both for the future of the game in New Zealand and for the players involved. Would Rowland Hill, the influential and fully paid Secretary of the English Rugby Union, and one of several powerful figures in the game there, seek to have New Zealand cast out on the grounds of professionalism? What should the New Zealand Rugby Union itself do? Should it do anything? If it did nothing would a more widespread revolt of players against the ruling authorities ensue? Would the amateur ideals encouraged and so widely accepted as a basis for playing the game, be lost? Discussion quickly followed on the likelihood of the tour taking place, the quality of any team's playing strength, who was organising it, and most curious of all, which players might join the team. For to do so would, under the stringent rules of amateur football, bring down the death-knell, spelling the end of that player's involvement with rugby union.

The very idea that such a tour could be arranged without anyone knowing seemed far-fetched, almost preposterous, and it was at first greeted with a fair degree of scepticism. The Rugby Union had history and tradition on its side. In both town and country, and also in the game's administration, amateur rugby had strong roots. The game had evolved over centuries. The Greeks had played a rudimentary game thought to have originated in China. It involved kicking a pig's bladder encased in leather. The Romans later codified this into a violent game, harpastum. Football, though popular during the Middle Ages, dimmed with religion's incursion into all aspects of social life in the post-reformation era. Much later, the great English public schools, Eton, Rugby, Harrow and Winchester played it in various forms. In 1867, a columnist of the *Pall Mall Gazette* observed: "Football is par excellence the winter sport of English youth ... the exercise is however the exclusive monopoly of the young"... but... "a great drawback is that it is not regulated by any uniform code. Each school plays its own peculiar game." [2]

New Zealand's earliest European settlers, coming at first predominantly from England, had football in their blood, and the game had grown from them. Football's formal constitution in New Zealand by the Christchurch Football Club in Canterbury in 1863, had seen several teams playing to the Eton rules, a combination of Association Football and Victorian Rules. In 1869 a match of this type was also staged on a wet pitch at the Albert Street Barracks in Auckland between a side representing Auckland and a team from two gunboats, involved in the Maori Land Wars, the 'Rosario' and 'Miranda'. Debate had raged in England between various footballers about how a game was best played. There were those who favoured handling the ball and those who did not. The issue had finally found resolution with the split in 1871 into two distinct football codes, soccer and rugby. The same columnist writing in 1867 of what he called the Rugbeian code described its attraction saying: "It, by a new rule, allows the ball to be held even when picked up off the ground: he who has it may at his peril run with it into the opposite base, with a view to "touch" and "try at goal". [3]

In New Zealand rugby drew many adherents. Between the first rugby games played in Nelson in the 1870s and the turn of the century, most footballers in this country decided they too preferred running with the ball in hand, even if it was "at their peril," or possibly because of that. *(See: Appendix 1 for details on different football codes).* But rugby was in an embryonic phase. In the first few years, games were organised on an ad hoc basis. It was more of a picnic atmosphere. Then once local teams were organised and had played each other, they began to look further afield. The mid-1870s saw Christchurch club teams travelling to South Canterbury to play clubs in Temuka and Timaru. In Canterbury the rugby clubs even refused to play a team of Australian Rules players who had come from Melbourne to try and establish that code in New Zealand. Some unruly players, displaying the peculiar parochialism for which the province is known, also burnt in effigy one Councillor Case, who had objected to games being played in Christchurch and we are told gave him 'three groans' outside his house.

The 1890s brought an explosion of interest in many different forms of recreation and sport, among them rugby, athletics, rowing, tennis, golf, cycling and mountaineering. When New Zealand spun into the twentieth century there were over 10,000 people playing organised rugby, far more than any other game, and double those playing cricket. It was from this vast reservoir of new players that any professional team such as the one now being speculated about by the newspapers would draw its strength. The game also probably owed some of its popularity and strength to the schoolmasters who supervised and coached sides in the primary schools, where attendance by then was compulsory. Starting the game young, the New Zealanders became instinctive players and rugby's dominance in turn was assured.

New Zealanders learned the game quickly and, as pioneers breaking in the land, were well suited to the fitness levels and hardness the game demands. With representative and international fixtures they developed experience and self-confidence. The possibility of being successful when playing against the professional sides in England was not a mere pipe dream. It was based on New Zealand's reputation for winning. At representative level the first rugby team to tour had been despatched from Auckland in 1875. Fifteen players played five matches in a fortnight. In 1876 Canterbury sent a tour as far as Auckland, captained by an old English rugby player WF Neilson. Otago toured New Zealand in 1877 and with Otago's decision in 1881 to form a Union, other provinces followed suit. International competition ensued in 1882 with the first visit of New South Wales, subsequently defeated by Otago one goal and two tries to nil.

The largest surge in numbers playing rugby followed the advent of overseas tours and the success they brought. New Zealand had first visited New South Wales in 1884. Then the visit in 1888 of the English team, captained by Stoddart, lifted the game's popularity, introducing the idea of passing the ball. Prior to this, players had run with the ball and when tackled kept hold of it until more players joined them to push it further up field, in a continuing maul. The next season the New Zealand Native Team visited England and games were played regularly in the 1890s between New Zealand and New South Wales, with New Zealand completely dominant in results. There were many great names, players like Tom Ellison, WT 'Tabby' Wynyard, Jimmy Hunter, Charlie Seeling and George Smith, to name just a few. In 1904, England's team captained by Bedell-Sivright

11

of Scotland toured New Zealand and the decision of the New Zealand Rugby Football Union to tour England in 1905 ensued. Money for players to join clubs in Auckland and Wellington had been widely rumoured. Even in times of high unemployment, positions with reputable firms had been found for players, but football was meant to be amateur.

There were reasons for the game's popularity, the most obvious being that it gave the new colony's men something to do on Saturday afternoon in winter. But there were more fundamental reasons. The country was underdeveloped and unsophisticated in comparison to England and rugby filled a vacuum in the lives of ordinary New Zealanders. Notions of social betterment and race were still strong and team sports provided an opportunity for mixing. A lawyer could find himself opposing, or playing alongside, an apprentice. A plumber played next to a clerk. Farmers packed down in scrums with labourers. Rugby had a leavening effect, and in an increasingly egalitarian society, a player's social position lent him no edge on the football field - in that arena every man had equal opportunity to excel. In many ways it reflected colonial life. This had telling results; one astute commentator noted the best New Zealand All Black teams owed their dominance to being comprised of "fierce farmers and fleet-footed Maoris." Early fixtures had also been placed at risk by unbridged and flooded rivers, but with the introduction of steamships, and railways running to timetables, games between the provinces, in particular, could be agreed in the knowledge that teams would reach their destinations and complete their engagements. For the less well off, the chance of All Black selection gave them an opportunity to travel internationally.

The game flourished at club level. By the turn of the century demand was such that mid-week business house competitions were being run in larger cities like Auckland, where there was also an organised secondary school competition. Rugby mirrored the standards and conduct of the times - there were rules to be kept, fair play was expected (but not always got). Newspaper reports emphasised the team and not the contribution of individuals.

Chosen to represent their country, New Zealand's All Blacks assumed special significance. The best players were household names. Clothed wholly in black, their uniform gave them a mystique entirely lacking in other teams. The nation recognised them as their representatives on the world stage. It was for these reasons that the All Blacks were important. There was a lot at stake. Would the professional tour mean the end of all these fine attributes? And what of professionalism anyway, why had it occurred in England, and were those elements present in New Zealand? These questions were high on the public agenda and a brief glance at what had happened in England may have provided some of the answers.

Rugby, while played in most parts of Britain, had developed strong grass-roots in the north and in Wales, where working people had embraced the game with particular fervour. Clubs in those areas drew in part on the resilience of miners and foundry workers. On the football field they excelled in the physical exchanges. But with a six day-working week, and with Sunday being set aside for religious observance, football could only be played on Saturday afternoon, and then only by those who did not need to work, or by workers who either sacrificed their wages or had lost wages made up by their clubs. A full-hearted approach to the game also brought injuries, and with miners being paid by the quantity of coal they extracted, time off work meant lower wages and doctors' bills to be paid. A cry arose that the compensation for the wages lost playing the game be legitimised - broken time payments. On this issue, in the 1890s, English rugby union split. The southern clubs saw it as professionalism, the northern clubs' perception was that broken time payments were generally occurring anyway, and that the situation needed to be dealt with by alterations to the laws of amateurism. At the annual general meeting of the Rugby Football Union in September 1893, representatives from northern clubs, Messrs JA Millar and M Newsome, had moved a motion that "players are to be allowed compensation for bona fide loss of time." The motion was lost 418 to 136. Encouraged by the size of the vote for the proposal, after several preparatory meetings, a meeting of twenty-one clubs at Huddersfield's George Hotel on 29 August 1895, had voted to form a separate Rugby Union - the Northern Union. The founding clubs were Oldham, Halifax, Leeds, Bradford, Hull, Huddersfield, Hunslet, Wakefield, Widnes, Broughton Rangers, Batley, St Helens, Leigh, Warrington, Tyldesley, Wigan, Manningham, Rochdale Hornets and Liversedge. Other clubs quickly joined.

A changed structure was soon reflected in new rules, the lineout being abolished and substituted by a kick in. A number of the more prosperous clubs were paying more than the 6 shillings a day that had been the agreed wages for playing in 1895. In 1898 the Northern Union adopted professionalism fully. The growth in popularity was marked by a membership in 1897 of 80 clubs, the inauguration of the Northern Union Challenge Cup and county matches between Yorkshire, Lancashire and Cheshire. The rule changes became focused on the value of scoring tries, goals being reduced to two points, and there was a consequent rise in spectators. With this huge industrial heartland supporting the game, that support was soon reflected in the gate money clubs received. The growth of professionalism was a natural consequence. By 1898-9 professional football in the truest sense was fully established, players being registered and only being able to transfer by agreement with clubs. In this way the professional Association Football game was being mirrored in Rugby. Players in southern England, and especially in Wales, could see the benefits of playing in a well-organised, paid competition, notwithstanding debarment for life from the amateur game. They moved steadily north.

In New Zealand, rugby football had moved on from the days of loosely drawn players forming up a team from the local country town, which was so much a feature of the game between 1870 and 1890. The country itself changed rapidly between 1890 and 1905. Industry had emerged. Railways had been laid. Mines were discharging coal for the steam engines and industry's machines. Large freezing works were being built and a sturdy commercial life in the large northern cities of Auckland and Wellington was well established. As government increased its role there were large numbers of civil servants and white-collar workers. Financial institutions were employing more accountants and clerks, and people worked in expanded technologies in the Post Office's telegraphic communications. Carpenters, bricklayers and labourers built housing for an ever-increasing stream of immigrants, and, instead of importing all their manufactured goods from Britain, New Zealanders were making them. There were iron foundries, clothing warehouses, and factories processing foods. Working people in all these industries joined rugby clubs. Many of the All Blacks came from these groups and this was the player base on which a professional team could now draw. New migrants, some of whom had come from the north of England, still had relatives there. They were aware of the rule changes and the move to professionalism in rugby in England and, amongst the All Blacks, their own success against the southern clubs during the tour in 1905, had sown the seeds of discontent. They had received the meagre sum of 3/- a day expenses while on tour (and even that was not divulged to their opposition unions for fear of repercussions) yet they had played before large crowds. The 'All Blacks' success in defeating all opposition except Wales had captured New Zealand's imagination. They acquired a special niche in the national psyche - the colonials had proved they were as good, if not better, than 'Mother England' and the Australians at one thing - Rugby Football. The Government of Richard John Seddon expressed the country's gratitude, reimbursing the Rugby Union the fares (£1,963.17/11) for the side's return home via America to a tumultuous reception in Auckland. It was a strange payment being made to an amateur game, which had profited by the equivalent of $12 million!

It may also explain why the professional tour outlined in the newspapers, and planned by a player from Wellington called Bert Baskiville, was getting support.

1   *New Zealand Herald*, 13 May, 1907.
2   *Pall Mall Gazette*, 14 November, 1867.
3   Ibid.

2. BACKLASH

Official opposition to the tour from the Rugby Union received extensive coverage. Reporters with close connections to the game made sure of that. They either openly opposed the tour, or panned its chances of success. The Rugby Union, through its relationships with newspapers, strove to sow doubt in the minds of players sufficient to try to bring the enterprise to its knees. The promoter in their view must be gaining at the expense of the players, the players would be gaining at the expense of the Rugby Union, and the team as a whole, if one was able to be got together, which in their view was unlikely, would ultimately be a disgrace to the country and the ideals of amateurism. The Rugby Union however was seriously underestimating both Baskiville's ability to administer the project, and also the level of commitment and involvement of George Smith and the other All Black players.

In the public arena much column space was dedicated to the supposed virtues of amateurism and the perceived evils of professionalism. The tour was cutting across some strongly held values that sport should not be played for personal gain. Its purpose was to edify the moral values of its participants, to build strength of character. It was feared that if money was earned somehow those ideals were undermined. Just why this was should be so was never stated, nor probably could be. It was taken for granted. The closest rational argument was that professional rugby would encourage gambling. Yet could this not also occur in amateur sport? No one saw, or if they did, they failed to mention, that in Britain that most loved of games, cricket, was played by both amateurs and professional players, and also that they played the game together.

Opposition to the tour came from many different quarters and attempts to undermine it took various forms. On May 29, 1907, the Weekly Press printed an interview its correspondent had had with Mr George H Dixon, the Manager of the 1905 All Black team, and an executive member of the New Zealand Rugby Union. Dixon said the players would only make £35 per head for a year's work after expenses. The reporter wrote "The margin of profit in the most favourable conditions does not strike Mr Dixon as being sufficient to warrant any person taking the very great risk that the undertaking involves." He took the view that: "If the professional team should not prove itself able to win matches (with the strength of the Northern Union football being an unknown quantity to us), their position will become a very serious one." The New Zealand Herald said, on 1 June, 1907: "The movement is naturally meeting with a good deal of opposition in Maoriland... Amateur football has worked very well so far, and it would be a matter for regret if a number of the best players in New Zealand - which may be regarded as the home of rugby in the Southern Hemisphere - were disqualified as amateurs." The Auckland newspaper when denigrating the tour's financial prospects, also added a parochial element to its opposition saying: "The venture

The NZRFU Management Committee in 1904
Back row: J O'Shea, R M Isaacs, D D Weir, A Laurenson.
Front row: G C Faches, A C Norris, G H Dixon, N Galbraith, W Coffey.

emanated from a speculative syndicate hailing from Wellington." There was other misinformed comment. The idea that Baskiville could only be doing it for personal profit would not die. Nor would the concept lie down now that there were several large promoters involved, putting up large risk capital with a view to reaping the profits from the players' efforts. The New Zealand Herald, on 22 May 1907, commented: "It is said two sportsmen in the North Island have personally guaranteed £500 towards the expense of the tour."

Yet the opposition of the Rugby establishment clearly could not reflect in full measure public opinion. People in the pubs and in the factories, on the wharves and in the timber mills, on the railways and in the iron foundries, could sympathise with the fact that responsible players could not be away from work for long periods playing football and not be taking money home to their families. It is now clear from the level of support Baskiville was finding that most players around the country endorsed these views, probably because teams were more often than not comprised of ordinary working people. It was the Rugby Union that was out of touch with the grass-roots sentiment.

There were precedents. Professional sport had already existed in several different forms in New Zealand for some time, horseracing being one, and there were also the well-patronised cycling and cash athletics circuits. In rugby football, too, there had already been the occasional player from New Zealand who had turned professional, having previously gone to England to join the Northern Union. George Stephenson, an Otago representative, had joined the

Warrington Club in the 1890s and played for a number of years before returning to Otago, and later he became an auctioneer in Gore. This outstanding wing three-quarter had, on his return to New Zealand, been given the mandatory life sentence ban from playing further rugby union. Stephenson had not, however, lost interest in the game and he was reported by the Canterbury Times of August 28, 1907, as saying that the New Zealand team would be a great success in England, "but would meet some pretty strong opposition from some of the Northern Union clubs." He thought the New Zealanders would probably win the majority of their matches "but it would not be without a struggle." Another New Zealand player had also recently already gone to play in England - the Petone and Wellington representative half-back, Alf Ramsden, was in 1907 playing for the strongest club, Hunslet - as a centre three-quarter, having already signed for the 1908 season. The northern clubs offered much, as in addition to wages for playing, Ramsden went to one of the big mills in England to learn his trade in woollen manufacturing under the aegis of his uncle. But these were isolated cases and the New Zealand Rugby Union had not yet had to face the prospect of a large number of its players wanting compensation for the time they spent playing the game, nor what would happen if that request was met with life bans from the game, and if players wanted to form both themselves and others into a professional code.

Amateurism in football also had deep strongholds in rural New Zealand where farms could be left in the hands of relatives for long periods, with profits still being made while the central asset continued to increase. It had, however, less appeal to those who worked for wages and who were pleased to accept reward for time spent playing sport and entertaining their fellow countrymen. The fact that some players were already being enticed to Auckland to accept payment for playing for Rugby Union clubs was not dealt with in the debate at all. New Zealand tended to copy closely attitudes in England. The idea that sport should be played as an integral part of one's life, but not as a means to sustain life, has proved hardy, being more pronounced in good economic times and finding less favour in more stringent decades like the 1930s and 1980s. These were the values that underpinned the Rugby Union's opposition and which in part explain what was to happen.

Cries immediately arose from several unions for the tour to be stopped - prominent amongst these were country unions, Hawkes Bay, Wanganui and Otago. One spokesman commented: "It was not to be expected that the governing body of amateur football in this country could stand idly by without making some effort to warn players under its control of the danger of dealing with a professional body. The New Zealand Executive now has a very good idea of what players are likely to remain loyal. As for the others, if they wish to become professionals, that is their own concern; they know the penalty, and Rugby football can spare them. The general body of the players in this colony are, I am sure, amateurs in spirit." [1]

Amateur in spirit or not, the New Zealand Rugby Union moved swiftly to try to bring the professional movement to an abrupt end. The attack was made, both on the possible players intending to join the team and on Baskiville. The showdown came with the run-up to the North Island v South Island game, an annual fixture, which also doubled as the trial for the All Black team to be chosen to visit Australia in July 1907. The Rugby Union, at its meeting of 21 May, 1907, resolved to require all the players nominated for the trial to sign a legal declaration. Its purpose was to identify the players so they could be expelled, and to kill the movement straight out. The document required the player to declare that he was an amateur and would have nothing to do with the proposed tour. They had to swear as follows:

"I .. of.... do solemnly and sincerely declare as follows:- (1) That I have never asked, received, or relied on a promise, direct or implied, to receive any money consideration whatever, actual or prospective, for playing football, or rendering any service to a football organisation. (2) And particularly that I have not asked, received or relied on any promise, direct or implied, to receive any money consideration whatever, actual or prospective, or to receive any benefit from, nor have I promised or asked to be permitted to take part in any manner whatsoever in, a scheme having for its object the sending of a team of Rugby footballers from New Zealand to play football against the teams of the Northern Counties' Rugby Union of England, and I make this solemn declaration, conscientiously believing the same to be true, under and by virtue of the provisions of the Justices of the Peace Act, 1882."

The Union also resolved that each player selected for the North v South Island match would be required to give the following undertaking:-

"I.. in consideration of the New Zealand Rugby Football Union having selected me to be one of its representatives to take part in the match North Island v. South Island, on 3rd June, 1907, do hereby promise and agree with the said Union - (1) That I will not form one of the projected team of footballers which is to leave New Zealand to play against the Northern Counties of England. (2) That I will not enter into any negotiation with any person with a view to my becoming a member of any such team. (3) That I will not actively or passively be a party to, or assist in any way, the promotion of any such team. (4) That if I am approached by any person or persons with a request that I should become a member of any such team I shall at once notify the said Union of the fact, and advise the said Union of the name of any person or persons so approaching me. (5) That I will, to the best of my ability, assist the said Union in its desire to put down any attempt to induce any footballer in New Zealand to make a breach of the rules as to professionalism, as adopted by the Rugby Football Union, and to this end will give the said Union all information bearing on the subject of the said projected tour to England." [2]

The Union's requirement was to have some far-reaching effects, but for the players the immediate problem was whether they would be committing a crime if they signed the declarations and then turned professional. The Rugby Union thought this would be enough of a deterrent to the players and that it would also satisfy the English Rugby Union that they had tried to stop tour. The New Zealand Herald, on 28 May, 1907, reported on the initial consternation it caused. Twelve Auckland players had been nominated in the North Island team for the All Black trial: George Smith, George Tyler, Charlie Seeling, George Gillett, George Nicholson, Bill Cunningham (all members of the 1905 All Blacks), Charlie Dunning, Alf Francis, Bill Trevarthen, Lance Todd, R McGee and Dick Wynyard. The men were summonsed to attend a meeting with the Auckland Rugby Union Management Committee in the Alexandra Park pavilion, then the headquarters of the game. A tense situation followed. When the Union Chairman, Mr Sheahan, explained the reasons for their signatures being required, and when the secretary, Mr V Langford, read out its contents to them - to a man they all refused to sign, even those who were not intending to tour, thus jeopardising their own futures and Auckland's participation in the All Black trial. In private, several of the players stated they had no intention of making the trip, and one newspaper reported: "the inference being that all were acting in unison, so those interested might not be known." [3] One of the players stated publicly that he objected to the principle of forcing amateurs to sign a declaration before a Justice of the Peace and thus "sell" any liberty they now had. He said: "For instance, I, like others, pay my subscription to a club to play football with the other members of the club. I also pay a shilling to go out to the grounds and why should I sign a declaration? I have been an amateur

THEY MAY STEAL HIS NAME BUT NOT HIS FAME.
The professional Rugby Team have adopted the famous All-Black name and costume for their Rugby tour.

The fact that the Rugby Union and not the players had benefited from the All Blacks' success was overlooked by this cartoonist.
Source: New Zealand Observer, Alexander Turnbull Library.

footballer for the past 14 years or so, and my status has never been questioned. Why should it be questioned now?" Continuing, he said: "The only money I have received for playing football was three shillings a day from the New Zealand Union when taking part in representative matches." He said he could not see "how one who played for the love of the game should be asked to go before a Justice of the Peace and sign something binding him over to a certain body, the penalty being that if at any time he broke it, he would be liable to imprisonment." [4]

Around the country more players refused to sign; Eric Watkins, the All Black and Wellington representative, joining H 'Bumper' Wright, Tom Cross and Con Byrne in opposition. The Auckland Rugby Union telegraphed the New

Zealand Union advising them of the stalemate in Auckland. In Canterbury, the much-discussed declaration placed another All Black, Duncan McGregor, in a difficult position. When he would not sign, he was told that if the Christchurch Club for which he was about to play his first game included him in their team for Saturday's game, they did so at their own risk.

The players sought legal advice on the declaration, which they naturally kept confidential. They learned that the threats of prosecution if they signed and then proceeded on a professional tour had no basis in law. The Union's administrators in Auckland cracked first. On 30 May, 1907, the New Zealand Herald reported a unique piece of diplomacy. The players had met the Rugby Union Secretary again and he was asked to amend the declaration, and did so. A face-saving compromise was reached. The 'All Black' players issued a statement that they had not signed the declaration at first because they had received monies from the New Zealand Union (3/- per day) when on the 1905 Tour. The other players said they had supported the members of that team. They then signed, and with the Auckland Union having satisfied its parent body by getting the declarations signed, the champion Auckland team was held together, at least for the time being. It was however too late for the trial - they had been banned from selection for the North Island, Wellington's players, in an example of inter-provincial rivalry, having been drafted in to take their places.

Canterbury nominated ten players for the trial, including Charlie Pearce, 'Jim' Turtill, and McGregor. Only McGregor did not sign. In Otago its four All Blacks, Booth, Casey, McDonald and 'Massa' Johnston, signed. Two Petone players nominated for the North Island side refused to sign. In Wellington, Wright, Cross and Byrne, who had originally refused, attended a meeting of the Rugby Union and explained that they had at first declined because they considered it unfair that a few should be singled out. They said that they considered that every player should be asked to sign, and that they had no intention of going with a professional team to England. They then signed the declaration.

The Rugby Union, and the newspapers, declared themselves the winners. Victory had been achieved. In one stroke the pestilence of professionalism had been put down, and they had retained the country's top players. Any professional side was now considered an impossibility. In Dunedin, The Star approved of the Union's action and patronised Baskiville saying: "The much cherished hope of a Wellington player who looked forward to becoming assistant manager of the team, advertising agent, press reporter etc. .... is doubtful of realisation." The Auckland selector, Gallagher, said on his return from the trial that in his opinion "there would be no professional tour" and that "the majority of players who would be a sufficient draw had definitely announced they were not going and, that being so, where was the team to come from?" [5]

The Australians had been watching developments closely. The New Zealand Rugby Union, confident in having killed the movement off, transmitted messages to Sydney. Oakes, a Member of the Legislative Assembly, said he was "glad to see that the first attempt to introduce professiona[l] had been shut down." Calvert, president of the New South [Wales] speaking at a reception for the Queensland team, said he [...] would resolutely set itself against professionalism [...] professionalism entered anything, behind it came that d[...] gambling spirit, and that was a thing they wanted to keep ou[t] game like football." [6] While the declaration had been [...] to have maximum publicity and effect, the only persons deluded were those who believed the declaration was legally enforceable.

It soon became evident that the New Zealand Rugby Union was fighting against an expertly organised and widespread player rebellion that had started to fight for the players' individual economic liberties, financial compensation - money. The organisation's public persona, Bert Baskiville, a mild-mannered, sober, quiet young man, and one well liked by his fellow players, was soon to feel the Union's lash. The New Zealand Herald headlined a story on 28 May 1907, about the New Zealand Rugby Union's letter, which had been addressed to Baskiville. The Union stated that it had reason to believe he had information upon the proposed tour of professional footballers to England. It addressed the letter to his employer, the Postal Department, knowing his mail would be opened and thereby putting his job at risk, so widespread was the opposition in the business community. He was summonsed as a member of a city team, to attend a meeting of the Wellington Rugby Union. Baskiville's reply was curt, he said - "he was bound not to divulge information" and, "as I have severed my connection with the Oriental Football Club on the 25th inst. and am also leaving the Postal Department, be good enough in future to post all communications to me at the above address." [7]

In his absence, the meeting applied the rules as to professionalism and banned him from entering any grounds under their control. But they were Council-owned grounds. Knowing Baskiville could issue civil court proceedings against them for the attempt to restrict his freedom of movement, it requested a monetary guarantee from the New Zealand Union against any losses it might incur through the suspension. This was duly given. In an interplay of local politics and sport, the Petone Borough Council decided, at its June meeting, to delegate to the Rugby Union the power to warn Baskiville off the Petone Recreation Ground on match days. The Wellington Rugby Union tabled Baskiville's swift and pointed reply at its next meeting. He asked for the specific by-law under which he was to be excluded from municipal reserves. His letter to the secretary dated 10 July, 1907 read as follows:

"Sir, - Be good enough to inform me as soon as possible whether I am prohibited from attending hockey and football matches held on the Petone Recreation Grounds on Saturday afternoons during the winter months, or am I an 'objectionable' person in the eyes of the Wellington Rugby Union and amenable to the authority given in the enclosed letter [from the Petone Borough Council to the Union]. I asked the Petone Borough Council for

...nformation on this subject, but though a motion was passed 'that I be ...ed with a copy of the exact resolution adopted at the previous meeting' ...de "New Zealand Times," June 25th) only a copy of a letter forwarded to your union came to hand. Other information re a by-law, asked for, was not given. From this I conclude that the Petone Borough Council has handed over to your charge the by-law, in addition to the 'dirty work.' Therefore, I would like you to procure, if possible, and forward to me with your reply, the by-law mentioned in my letter to the Petone Borough Council.

"*I am, etc.*" *A H Baskiville.*

The Wellington Rugby Union at its next meeting was faced with a dilemma. Should it align itself with the ban it had imposed, based on a by-law that the Council could not enforce, and which it had not yet been able to provide a basis for, or should it lift its ban and incur the public humiliation that would flow from its decision? It caused some debate. One of its officers, McIntyre, said the purpose of the New Zealand Union had been served, and the question asked by Mr Baskiville was a fair one. He took the view that "There was nothing to prevent him (Baskiville) from going to see hockey or other games being played. He had broken the laws of football and had to suffer the penalty therefore," and he (McIntyre), "thought the New Zealand Union had now gone a step too far, so that the suspension could be removed without any disadvantage." Another committee member, Mr Bogle, thought to lift the suspension would indicate weakness and that the committee would if it did so go back on its agreement to carry out a certain request made by the New Zealand Union, which had shown a sincere desire to put down professionalism. Mr McIntyre said Baskiville had not proved personally objectionable and the action taken by the New Zealand Union had resulted in alienating public sympathy from the object it had in view - the suppression of the proposed professional football team to visit England. The question of replying to Mr Baskiville was held over pending receipt of an answer from the New Zealand Union. [8] "Personally objectionable," or not to the public, Baskiville was portrayed by the press as the secretive organiser of a tour disloyal to the Rugby Union.

Later the All Black 'Massa' Johnston wrote of Baskiville saying: "It is a little difficult to figure him as the public knew him. He was a masterful man with big ideas, and wearing his life out in the routine of a Government billet must have chafed and hurt. A man like that always feels that he must 'do something'." [9]

1   *The Weekly Press*, 29 May, 1907.
2   Ibid.
3   *New Zealand Herald*, 28 May, 1907.
4   Ibid.
5   Ibid.
6   *New Zealand Herald*, 8 June, 1907.
7   *The New Zealand Mail*, 29 May, 1907.
8   *The New Zealand Mail*, 5 June, 1907.
9   *The Weekly Press*, 17 June, 1908.

3. BASKIVILLE AND THE RUGBY UNION

Baskiville was already a well-known figure in rugby circles in 1907 both as a player of outstanding promise and as the author of an authoritative text on how to play the game. Aged just 25, he was playing an audacious brand of football for the Oriental Club in Wellington, and was right on the verge of selection for the Wellington provincial rugby team. Alongside these achievements he held a national ranking in athletics specialising in middle distance running. The Baskivilles were of Irish extraction. Bert's grandfather, Walter Baskiville, a Chelsea Pensioner of the 17th Lancers, had been an early settler joining the Royal New Zealand Fencibles. He arrived in this country on the Inchimann in 1852 and his first wife had two sons, the first, Henry, was Bert's father. His forebears like many others who came to New Zealand had a sense of adventure; they wanted to better themselves but they also had an abiding interest in sport, and an ability to play it well.

Bert Baskiville
Test footballer, author and secretary of the professional All Blacks.

His mother's father, John Mace, had joined the exodus from England to the Australian goldfields in the 1850s. A cricketer and a Yorkshireman, he was the licensee of the Oddfellows Arms Hotel in Bedale before emigrating. This establishment, now known as the Mace's Oddfellows Arms, had been in the Mace family for five generations. The hotel still stands, and is much as it originally was. After their arrival in Australia, John, and John's brothers, Henry and Christopher, played cricket in 1860-61 for the State of Victoria, cricket then being by far the most popular summer team sport.

When news reached the Victorian goldfields of even richer finds in New Zealand, the Maces, and others like them, left to try their luck in a different country. They landed in Dunedin in 1863 en route to the barren tussock lands of Central Otago. But unlike many they were lucky; their claim yielded significant finds and Macetown, an historic gold mining area, is named after Bert

Baskiville's grandfather and his brothers. The Mace brothers continued playing cricket in New Zealand and were included in the Otago cricket team in 1864 that played in Dunedin against the first English XI to visit New Zealand. Later John Mace and his family moved from Otago to the goldfields of the Coromandel in the North Island. There his daughter, Maria, married Henry Baskiville, who was by then a trader and general storekeeper. Their eldest son, Albert Henry (Bert) Baskiville, was born in Waiorongomai, a small rural town on the outskirts of Te Aroha in 1883.

The goldfields area around Thames was at the time particularly strong at rugby and it is likely that Bert got his first taste of rugby there. Along with most young New Zealanders, Bert Baskiville would have first been encouraged into sport at school where rugby was played in the winter under the watchful eyes of schoolmasters who had learnt the game in England's public schools. Athletics was also encouraged. In 1895 when Bert was twelve years old, his parents left Waiorongomai for Northland and became the licensees of the Kohukohu Hotel on the beautiful Hokianga harbour. In moving to the secluded little pearl shaped bay that is Kohukohu, the Baskiville's were joining Maria's sister and her husband, who owned the general store and butchery business, but who had no children of their own. There was a sound small business tradition in Baskiville's family background.

Kohukohu was at that time an important settlement. Being on the western side of the North Island it was well situated to export Northland's kauri logs and gum to Australia and further afield in considerable quantities. Different sized vessels entered the port and among them the scows, with their shallow draft, could sail right up to the Baskiville's hotel and store to load supplies at the adjacent jetty. Rugby, in this area of New Zealand, found favour with most of the young men working in the timber industry as they felled and trimmed the giant trees before floating them down the river for loading. During the 1880s and 1890s, it became by far the most watched and played game. It was a source of entertainment and excitement in an area that was otherwise quite isolated and was not easily visited by travelling shows.

The teacher at Kohukohu School, James Eliot, first placed Bert in Standard 5; there were 70 pupils, ranging from 5 to 17 years of age. Then in July he moved him up to Standard 6. Promotion on merit to the school's senior class, known as Standard X, came in October 1896. By 1897 he was one of three boys in that class, and there he stayed until finishing his formal education, and leaving school at age 13. The family moved again when his parents took over the licence of the Royal Hotel at Kuaotunu on the Coromandel Peninsula. There was still considerable gold mining being done in the bush that had spawned the wild little settlement, which had two hotels and several shops. At 17, he started full-time government employment as a Letter Carrier with the Post and Telegraph Office in Auckland, with an annual salary of £50. On becoming a Cadet, this increased to £60 from 1 April, 1901. By 1902, with two years and 9 days service to his credit he earned a salary of only £85. He was then 19 years of age.

Being the eldest Bert probably took some degree of responsibility for his younger brothers and sisters. However tragedy struck in 1903, his father being killed when a drain he was digging in Auckland collapsed. This left Maria Baskiville on her own with seven children, the youngest, Kathleen, aged just seven. They moved to Wellington shortly after his father's death, purchasing 93 Kelburn Parade. [1] The house, a plain but spacious timber villa, still stands, and is currently owned by the University. The family had a little capital but with his father now gone, Bert became the breadwinner. Suddenly how much he could earn, and how that might be increased assumed extra importance. In 1904 he won promotion to a Clerk's position and at home began to share in family decisions with his mother. They were obviously difficult years, but shouldering his responsibilities he remained doing what must have been a sometimes tedious job. Had his personal circumstances been different, he may have already been travelling, or have gone into business.

In 1906 he was enjoying playing rugby at senior level in Wellington for the successful Oriental Club alongside the brilliant All Black halfback Fred Roberts. Baskiville quickly earned a reputation for scoring tries, having two prime assets - exceptional speed and size. He could play equally well either as a loose forward, or in the three-quarters. An early-season fixture had Baskiville's Oriental team playing Old Boys'. The local newspaper reported that: "Oriental opened with a fairly brisk attack, which closed by Buddle, just prevented Baskiville scoring at the corner." It continued: "Ultimately Baskiville headed a sweeping charge, a combined foot and hand passing onslaught by the forwards. Later in the match Baskiville was again unlucky just missing out scoring again in the corner." [2] Towards the end of that season another newspaper had nothing but praise for the way he played saying: "Baskiville is a rattling good player - fast and dashy - and at the business end of a forward rush he can fall on the ball with the best of them." The New Zealand Mail of 17 May, 1907, in a report of one of Oriental's games against Petone, went on to say that: "Baskiville went through the Petone backs and secured a fine try between the posts." [3]

In addition to his ability on the field, he also possessed other talents valuable to the game. Rugby was at the time enjoying exceptional popularity in New Zealand, in large part due to the success of the All Blacks in Britain but also because of the revitalisation of provincial football by the introduction of the Ranfurly Shield, played for on a challenge basis. At this time the two strongest provinces, Wellington and Auckland, were vying for the honour of holding the Shield. Baskiville's ability had been noticed and selection as a provincial representative seemed only a matter of time. He also studied the game, analysing how it should be played in great detail. He brought these ideas together in a book entitled 'Modern Rugby Football: New Zealand Methods'. Published in 1907 by Gordon and Gotch, it is one of the first written about how rugby was played in this country. It covers the game extensively, containing diagrams and advice on such diverse matters as the advantages of certain ways of packing a scrum, training methods as adopted in New Zealand, and even the best ways to place the ball to kick at goal. Of this aspect of the game he said: "Some stand it on end, with the top inclined towards them, but the majority now incline it with the top away from them, or pointing towards the goal-posts and with the lace side upwards." [4] His concise style reflected a good education and keen intelligence, attributes that proved of immense benefit when he was later faced with heavy demands on his organisational and journalistic skills. One reviewer wrote: "His book of 'Rugby Football' was widely read, his conclusions and conceptions of the game as therein expressed showing the master mind. Many of his literary contributions were published in newspapers in the Dominion, and in the Old Country, and as a writer his career promised to be a bright one." [5] The book was well received by the public, being both perceptive and readable. 'Modern Rugby Football' also meant he had a national profile in Rugby circles. But perhaps more importantly, Baskiville, although still only 25 years old at the date of the book's publication, had also demonstrated he could bring an innovative project to a successful conclusion.

Of the fact that Baskiville first conceived the idea of forming a professional team to go to England and then acted as its prime advocate and organiser there can be no doubt, but in putting it into effect he could not, and did not, act alone. Writing from Colombo on 11 September, 1907, on the evolution of the tour, Baskiville outlined how it had been organised, and his reasons for the venture. He said: "The possession of some money and a love of adventure and an article appearing in a London daily newspaper are, in the first place, responsible for a team of New Zealand Rugby footballers visiting Great Britain and playing combinations affiliated to the English Northern Rugby Union." He continued: "The article in the Daily Mail written by FW Cooper, a Northern Union enthusiast, indicated that there existed in the north of England a keen desire to see their clubs or players try to play the game against a team of New Zealanders." [6]

The correspondent to the Daily Mail had issued a challenge, saying: "What many old players like myself would like to see would be a match between a picked Northern Union team and the colonials. I have no hesitation in saying that I would pick 15 players who would willingly give their services to play such a match, the proceeds of which could be devoted to charity, and I have little doubt that my side would achieve victory. The wearers of the silver fern may not have been defeated, but they have not played the cream of English football. Such men play under the banner of the Northern Union." [7]

That article fired Baskiville's imagination, and clearly intrigued, he wanted to find out more, and he later wrote, "From a conversation with a returned 1905 All Black, I gleaned that the Northern Union authorities had actually held out a substantial guarantee for a match with the New Zealanders, but of course this proposal could not be entertained then. This set me thinking why shouldn't a New Zealand team play the Northern Unionists? Guarded conversations with prominent New Zealand players elicited information that, with few exceptions, they would be willing to join a team if one was formed with that purpose in view: so I set to work." [8]

It seems almost certain that the All Black who had told him of the Northern Union's interest when they had toured was George Smith, and that he and Lance Todd worked closely with Baskiville, and with a group of Wellington players, in forming the nucleus for those interested in the tour. The New Zealand Rugby League Annual, 1933, provides support for this view. Its writer states that en route back to New Zealand after the 1905 tour, Smith had sounded out friends in Sydney about the introduction of Rugby League, amongst whom it was said was Mr JT Giltinan, the well-known Australian cricket administrator. The Annual goes on to say that Smith finally said, interalia, to Mr Giltinan, "What about you getting Rugby League going in Australia, and I'll do my best when I cross the Tasman home." [9] While there is no evidence to suggest George Smith set about trying to establish the code in New Zealand, both he and Baskiville were connected through athletics as well as football. When he sought Smith's view on the possibility of a tour, Smith's connections in Australia were to prove very useful. George Smith's role in the organisation was to be crucial and has also recently been confirmed by Smith's daughter. He not only lent credibility to the project, but also could speak to players around the country on a first name basis.

Put simply, George Smith was the most respected and well-known sportsman in New Zealand at that time. There was no-one his equal, and there has probably not been since. He was an All Black, a world-class athlete and a champion jockey. Born in Auckland on 20 September, 1874, he went to the Wellesley Street School. Auckland was then, as it is now, basically a busy commercial centre with a temperate climate that encouraged sport. The city's commercial founders also played a significant role endowing the city with the open green spaces that are the Auckland Domain, and Cornwall and Victoria Parks. Young Smith showed early signs of an independent nature when he ran away from home. Being small for his age, he was apprenticed in the stables of Mr J Keen to be a jockey. He rode 12 winners on the flat and as he grew progressed to steeplechasing. National success came with the winning of the Easter and Autumn Stakes, and then the prestigious New Zealand Cup at Riccarton in 1894, when he rode Impulse, at a weight of 7st 9lb. The Smiths were a racing family. George, and Fred Smith, the then well-known Takanini trainer, were brothers.

Smith first played football at halfback for the stable boys' team, showing, even at that time, he possessed that enormous advantage - speed. He also practised side-steps and swerves, placing obstacles out in the horse paddocks and dodging through them. He was a natural sportsman, always keen, but he also understood the value of daily training and of staying in top physical condition.

When he began running in competitive athletics, it turned out he was world class, and at the same time he became an accomplished billiards player.

Nicknamed 'The Greyhound', Smith won the New Zealand l00 yards sprint championships five times between 1898 and 1904. He also took New Zealand titles for the 120 yards hurdles four times and the 440 hurdles five times. George Smith was the idol of New Zealand athletics, yet he loved all sport, and, in 1895 and at age 21, joined the City Rugby Club in Auckland. This brought instant success, and he first represented Auckland in 1896 as a wing three-quarter, and also North Island in 1897. When selected for New Zealand to tour Australia, with his speed, he made an ideal centre on the fast hard grounds in that country. On that All Black tour Smith scored 11 tries, five in one game against New England. The latter part of Smith's athletics performances ran parallel to his rugby commitments. In 1902, at the height of his illustrious track career, he travelled alone to England to compete solely in one race - the 120 yards hurdles, which he won, becoming the English Champion. He followed this in 1904 with an unofficial world record of 58.5 seconds for the 440 yard 3'6 hurdles. Many years later, in a press interview, he spoke of his involvement in athletics, saying: "While I was in the stables I became interested in running. I seemed to make astonishing progress... Altogether I won 21 amateur championships - 15 New Zealand, five Australasian, and one British. My best time for the 100 yards was 10 seconds dead, and quite early in my career I broke the existing world record for the 440 yards hurdles in the Australasian

George Smith hurdling his way to an unofficial world record.

Championship at Melbourne." He was never beaten at the quarter-mile hurdles. During the 1905 season he was again selected for the All Blacks, as they were to tour England for the first time. Although only 5'7" tall and weighing 11st 12lb he could play centre or wing.

Both on and off the field, George Smith cut a fine Edwardian figure, impeccably dressed, easy to talk to, and with a wide circle of friends and sporting contacts. He was also the crowd favourite with the rugby public in Auckland. The tour of Britain in 1905-06 with the original All Blacks had him in brilliant form. An elusive player, he could outrun any defence and also anticipate play. As a good football tourist should, he relished travel and the variety of conditions encountered on that tour, scoring 19 tries in as many games. Eight of these came quickly in the first three matches, and there were two tries against Scotland. In that Test he ran the length of the field, snatching victory for the All Blacks from what seemed certain defeat. Smith was by nature a competitive person and, after they first met, he must have found he and Baskiville had a lot in common. Baskiville, as well as being a fine footballer, had run the half mile in 2 minutes, 2 seconds and the mile in 4 minutes, 30 seconds. Like Smith, he was abstemious and kept himself in top physical condition with regular training, even when he found his time taken up with administrative duties. They formed a great team; Baskiville had the organisational ability and tenacity to bring a long project to a conclusion, and Smith, with his worldwide reputation and personal contacts, could influence other players to join their cause.

When they discussed the idea of forming a Professional All Black team with other players, All Blacks like Johnston, McGregor, and Gillett who already knew of the Northern Union game, the concept was grasped enthusiastically. Of the fact that the tour was both well planned and ably canvassed in its early phases, there can be no doubt. The New Zealand Herald of 21 August, 1907 reported that Baskiville was speaking of the tour with other players during the months of September and October 1906, twelve months before it was scheduled to take place. Secure in the support he received from what we now know to have been many of the country's best footballers, he took the first step to give effect to the tour by writing to each of the Northern Union clubs in January 1907. What then was the English response?

The Northern Union Clubs were convinced they had developed a game that had greater spectator appeal, and, being more open, that there were more opportunities for players to score tries. By 1902, the punt in from touch had been discarded in favour of scrums. The 1906/07 season had seen the number of players permitted on each side reduced to thirteen. Other rule changes ensured greater continuity of play, kicking the ball out of play on the full being discouraged by the rules. The problem which rugby union had, and which it still has, of what can be done with the ball after a player is tackled, had also been addressed by the Northern Union in 1906. It changed the rules. It became that: "The player in possession should regain his feet before the ball is put on the ground, but it is not imperative that he should absolutely stand erect before doing so. Further, it is not compulsory to actually place the ball, it may be dropped from the hands, so long as it is allowed to reach the ground and there next be played with the foot." This was later refined to permit the ball to be played in any direction. The distinctive differences between the rules of the two games had emerged.

Yet despite the appeal of the 'New Rugby', as it was called, its organisation, by the nature of the split, had some unresolved problems of its own - there was no international football, and along with that, a question as to its ability to survive without Test match gate receipts. Nor with the 'New Rugby' being confined mainly to the north of England could the Northern Union offer players overseas tours. There were no national honours to aspire to, yet these were the very same clubs that, because of their brilliant playing records before the split, had commanded the respect of all England. Not surprisingly, against this background, when Baskiville wrote to the Northern Union offering to take over to England an All Black team, or one of the same quality, for a series of matches, his letters to each of the clubs were greeted enthusiastically. At last the Northern Union, and its famous teams like Wigan, Hunslet, Leeds and Oldham, to name a few, would have an opportunity to play against some of the world's most highly regarded footballers.

The northern counties had traditionally provided many of the best players for English international teams before the split in 1895 from the southern clubs. Since then they had been in a kind of rugby wilderness, exiled for twelve years and not having played against international opposition since the tour of the New Zealand Native Team in 1888/89, still remembered by many in the north for their open play under Rugby Union rules.

The Committee of the Northern Union, on 26 March, 1907, advised its member clubs that it was "very favourably disposed to the visit provided they received an assurance as to the strength of the team and provided there were sufficient monetary guarantees from the member clubs." [10] They suggested that the New Zealanders be paid seventy per cent of the gross gate, with a guarantee from the Union that their share for the tour was not to be less than £3000. The clubs readily agreed with clubs having a Saturday or holiday match guaranteeing £100, and a Wednesday match, £50, as New Zealand's share of the gate. Displaying the financial caution for which the north is known, the clubs were required to deposit the guarantees in the Bank to the credit of the 'New Zealand Guarantee Fund' no later than 1 June, 1907, four months prior to the scheduled arrival of the team, and two months before it was due to leave New Zealand. When Baskiville and his team required of themselves that each person travelling pay £50 in advance, the actual costs of the tour, which amounted to £3852, including weekly payments to members, were adequately covered. These arrangements, while not eliminating the financial risk associated with the tour, meant it was effectively shared.

The Northern Union now cabled an excited Baskiville asking him to send the names of the players from the 1905 team who would make the trip. These were to be confidential to the President and Secretary to protect their identities. The Committee prohibited any club from approaching any player to transfer to their club prior to the termination of the tour lest they obtain an unfair advantage. They also formed a subcommittee to deal with the arrangements comprising: H Ashton, TW Wood, JB Cooke, JH Smith, WD Lyon and J Platt, the Secretary. All this was decided in March, six months before the tour was scheduled to commence. When Baskiville received the almost inevitable reply from the Northern Union favourable to the tour in March, he immediately advised the others involved. Yet the secrecy surrounding the venture was such that it was May before any detailed reports of what was taking place could begin to appear. It only needed the members to remain loyal to the venture and success seemed assured. But then news of the proposed tour reached New Zealand from England.

When the Rugby Union asked him to explain his actions and threatened to expel him on the grounds of professionalism if he did not, Baskiville advised them abruptly they would learn all in due course. By May 1907, the arrangements were starting to fall into place and Baskiville resigned from his position with the Post Office. He also wisely involved Jim Gleeson from the Hawkes Bay, who had studied law at Sydney University and who played at scrum half. Gleeson brought knowledge into the organisation that was to prove invaluable. So great was the secrecy, though, surrounding this tour, that the New Zealand Rugby Union did not know how advanced the preparations were, how well organised was the approach, and also how great had been the gulf between the officials of the Union and the players. They were trying to counter opponents, the names of whom were not even known to them, Baskiville excepted - a difficult task when faced with a united front.

With the declarations having proved impotent, the need for secrecy became less pressing and intense. The extent of the planning undertaken now began to unfold and opinion started to swing a little. The New Zealand public were astonished, as news item by news item, Baskiville told of what had been arranged at a much earlier time. The tour was in fact being financed on a very different basis to anything previously seen in the sporting world and that was to prove to be one of its greatest strengths. The Rugby Union was correct in one important matter - for the venture to be successful it needed top-flight players who could draw a crowd in England, carrying on from where the 1905 All Blacks had left off. The final selection of those players now began.

1   Biographical Notes of Mrs MH Henderson
2   *The Evening Post*, 1 March, 1907.
3   *New Zealand Mail*, 17 May, 1907.
4   AH Baskiville, Modern Rugby Football (Wellington, 1907).
5   Undated newspaper article, HS Turtill Scrapbook.
6   *Otago Daily Times*, 10 October, 1907.
7   Ibid.
8   Ibid.
9   *New Zealand Rugby League Annual*, 1933.
10   Letter of J Platt, Hon. Secretary, Northern Rugby Union, 26 March1907.

4. PLETHORA OF PLAYERS

May and June 1907 were crucial months. The team had to be selected and the final arrangements made for the tour. Baskiville now devoted himself entirely to organising it and, in having resigned his job with the government, was in a vulnerable position. That particular decision would only prove worthwhile if the tour went ahead. He was utterly reliant on the players who had said they wanted to go remaining committed. He had promised them total confidentiality. The players rightly feared that the life disqualification imposed on him by the Rugby Union would be widened to them and that, not only would their rugby be ruined, but their jobs could be threatened also, so close were the links between rugby and local business. In this hostile climate the whole selection process became shrouded in the utmost secrecy. A mere slip of the tongue, an imprudent interview, even a casual comment in the rugby clubrooms, or loose talk in a bar, could spell the end of a player's career. As it happened, everyone remained tight-lipped, even the players not going. For the organisers it was a case of self-preservation and they imposed a total media blackout. It meant no-one could be personally attacked, but the ban also had a negative effect. Impatient for hard news and thwarted in their attempts to uncover the details of the tour, newspapers grew increasingly frustrated and critical - they described the team as being "like a republic - answerable to no-one and self-interested."

Baskiville and the other selectors, McGregor, 'Massa' Johnston, Wright and George Smith, began thinking about the type of players they needed and they worked closely together. The requirements were daunting. To have even the slightest chance of competing with the professional teams in Great Britain, it was crucial they choose the best, and that those selected be personally suited to the faster game the new rules were known to encourage. Yet the very same players had to be prepared to face the threat of the lifelong disqualification from rugby union and the inevitable public reaction that would follow. That alone required special people, probably unorthodox, independent men, but not players who were so single-minded that they could not be relied on to work over an extended period for the common good of the team. They would be stepping off into a void, so it goes almost without saying that a tour with an itinerary of 10 months demanded they be physically durable as well as mentally tough. Added to this, they had already decided each member would have to pay £50, or nearly half a year's wages, towards the tour. It could prove difficult for some and prohibitive for others. Baskiville now made public how the profits from the tour were to be distributed. Each member of the touring party was to receive an equal share of all profits - it mattered not how many games they were to play. There were to be no bonuses, and if a man was injured, he received the same share as the remaining players.

As the co-operative nature of the enterprise became known, it struck a more

32

The Auckland Representative Team.
They had beaten in succession: Canterbury, Taranaki, Southland and Wellington.

sympathetic chord with the public. The newspapers, too, became a little less strident. It was as if they were in the meantime prepared to suspend judgement, and to wait and see whether or not the team was successful and whether the country was being well represented. There was still, however, none of the usual nationalistic, almost adolescent enthusiasm associated with an overseas football tour; their reports instead tended to be very factual: The Christchurch Star, 6 June, 1907 - "Notice was received six weeks ago that the £3000 now banked would be deposited for the expenses of the tour ... and a number (of the players) declare they have no intention of returning to New Zealand, but will remain in England either as coaches or as professional players under the auspices of the Northern Union." [1]

The Union soon lamented its arrogant and ill-conceived prediction that a sufficiently strong team would not be found. There were approximately 200 players involved in provincial and international football in New Zealand at that time and when the Evening Post reported, on 1 July, 1907, that: "No less than 160 applications were received for a place in the team", it was a major blow and a huge shock to the Rugby Union. The problem facing the selectors was not whether the team would be sufficiently credentialed, but which of the 160 players to select. There was an embarrassment of riches. Baskiville, who had sent out letters to all the well-known players inviting them to apply for a place, now went to the various towns looking at each player's form, assessing them against criteria he and his fellow selectors had developed based on what they knew about the game as played under Northern Union rules. With no lineouts, specialists in that area were not required. The ball not being permitted to be kicked into touch on the full would mean more continuous play and mobile players, especially in the forwards, would prove an asset, slow heavy-weights, a disadvantage. There were so many players wishing to go, not all of them could be seen.

The selections had their lighter moments. Barred from entering any grounds, Baskiville went to Athletic Park on Saturdays in disguise, even going to the length of dressing as an old women. [2] On another occasion he travelled to Christchurch with a party to see the England v New Zealand 'test' match but was stopped at the gate. The zealous gate attendant told him that the New Zealand Rugby Union would not permit him entry and, if he persisted, the Police would be called. The respectful but also resourceful Baskiville watched the match from the good vantage point of a tree near the gates. But with icicles hanging from the branches, this natural grandstand must have had its less convenient moments. The North Island v South Island trial he watched from the apple tree of a friend's house near the ground.

Some of the players who were now to be selected had been in New Zealand teams from 1900 onwards. With nine of these being All Blacks, one third of the team's complement had played international football. They had received no financial return during over nearly a decade of service to the game. While important, it is unlikely monetary considerations were the sole motivating force. The best footballers all want to play at top level, and they play first because they like the game. Those who had toured in 1905/06 had not played in Yorkshire and Lancashire against some of the greatest rugby clubs England had known.

For other players who had played against Australia so successfully, but who had not been included in the 1905 touring party, there was the chance to follow in the footsteps of their illustrious predecessors. England offered the prospect of playing against new opponents, and the tour would be another football experience. These players had learnt from the returning All Blacks of the vast crowds they had drawn. A trip to the Northern Union for these players would compensate for the fact that they had missed the earlier tour.

Provincial teams have long been the cornerstone of New Zealand rugby. They provided a rich storehouse of experienced players who were regularly selected to play for the Auckland A and B, and Wellington teams, closely followed by Otago, Hawkes Bay, Taranaki, Canterbury and Wanganui. The number of fine players in Auckland was such that the B team defeated the A by 11 points to 3, and Auckland A had been holders of the Ranfurly Shield. There were players like Mackrell, the 1905 All Black and McDonald, Todd, Rowe, and the two Wynyards, Bill and Dick. The report on the match says: "Hogan, Rowe and Wilson 'showed dash', especially Rowe"...and..."Todd was the most conspicuous of the five-eighths, but the Wynyard brothers played solidly and with dash." Of the forwards Mackrell and McCormack shone out well. Among the others Dunning, Hooper, and Trevarthen were the most conspicuous. Todd had many fine runs, one correspondent wrote: "No one who follows football can doubt Auckland's superiority in football in New Zealand as was shown last season." [3] On 10 August, 1907, Auckland defeated Hawkes Bay 12-3 and included in that side were WT (Billy) Wynyard and Charles Dunning. Prior to this, in July Auckland had defeated Buller, then a strong union, and amongst the players were R Wynyard, WT Tyler, W Trevarthen and Dunning.

Wellington formed Auckland's strongest provincial opponents and it was well known for the quality of its forward pack. Bred on a diet of wet days they had developed a forceful combination with a reputation for rugged play. The team's members had also forged a good understanding of each other's games during their tenure of the Ranfurly Shield. Fred Roberts, the All Black, was the unchallenged king of half-back play, and the forwards included HR (Bumper) Wright, Tom (Angry) Cross (an All Black), Con Byrne, Dan Gilchrist and Adam Lile, who represented North Island as well. Duncan McGregor, also an All Black, had been a prominent Wellington three-quarter before he moved to Canterbury. Also on the centres, they had the youthful Arthur Kelly and another All Black, Edgar Wrigley, who had been chosen for national honours at the tender age of 19 years, a record that was to stand many years, only superseded by Jonah Lomu in the 1990s. Wrigley was from the Wairarapa. J Barber filled the fullback position. EL Watkins the All Black and Wellington forward, was at this time playing in the Raetihi competition.

Canterbury's provincial team hosted several inter-island representatives including CJ Pearce in the forwards, HS 'Jum' Turtill at fullback, and J Lavery in the centres. For all these players, and the many more playing representative rugby, the chance of a tour of England, be it as an amateur or as a professional, would have been the fulfilment of their football ambitions. It also offered the chance of overseas travel, which most of them had not yet been able to experience. Some also had been frustrated by injury in taking part in the earlier tour. 'Opai' Asher, the great Maori back, born in Tauranga, but who played his rugby in Auckland, and who was called variously the 'Indiarubber Man,' or the 'Bubbler' by the Australians in 1903, had missed the 1905 tour because he was a fireman and, when injuries flared up, his leg was found to be full of glass. He was, however, to be disappointed twice. Of the professional tour he said: "George Smith wired me in 1907 to join with the All Golds, but I was laid aside with a broken ankle at the time and had to decline." [4]

Clearly, also, there was some frustration among top provincial players at All Black selection policies. While some in the top echelons had won national honours, there were those who laboured under the weight of having just missed national selection, or of being selected once and then being overlooked. In addition to these players, there were those who had ambitions of making a career out of professional rugby, and to do that by playing the game full-time in England. For these players, among whom George Smith could be counted, their predilection for meeting sporting challenges offered ever more personal challenges. Smith had done all there was to do in New Zealand, his record spoke for itself. For other players yet to acquire such a reputation, the chance to prove themselves in England, when they had been blocked in New Zealand, was definitely an attraction. In this category were the outstanding Auckland backs who played with George Smith, Lance Todd and Harold Rowe. Of the latter Baskiville was to write: "I cannot imagine how a player of his stamp failed to win his representative cap for Auckland. I have seen several under his standard playing in representative football." [5] A report in the Evening Post, dated 5 August, 1907, indicates they also saw the tour as heralding the start of a new era for football in New Zealand. It said they intended, when in England, to arrange a visit to Australia and New Zealand of a team representative of the Northern Unions. There could be only one game the Northern Union would be playing - rugby league.

By June, Baskiville and those working with him, were in a better position to release some of the broad detail on the tour, commencing with information on the numbers involved and how many backs and forwards had been chosen. Their reports mirrored very closely the final team selections two months later. The Weekly Press, on 17 July, 1907, reported Baskiville as saying: "The team is a strong one. There are sixteen forwards and nine backs, but probably two more players will be added to the list before the team leaves New Zealand. As at present constituted, the team comprises mainly North Island men. At least nine of the men selected have represented New Zealand, and several of them were members of the famous All Black team." In fact, fourteen of the All Blacks who toured England in 1905, had applied in written form for positions and an additional four made personal requests. [6] Eventually a side was chosen.

Of the final selection Baskiville wrote "Many other New Zealand forwards with good local reputations, no doubt excellent men if tried in a good team, applied for positions, but were passed over, in some cases reluctantly, by us, because we could not see them play or give an exhibition of their prowess." [7] Of the backs, there were too many for the positions offered and others may have been included if they could have been viewed by the selectors. There were also some restrictions. Some players had indicated at a very early stage, probably in 1906 when Baskiville was sounding out whether players were interested, that they would tour. Their initial loyalty to the concept was not misplaced - Baskiville wrote: "Certain players were promised the tour, and because they made considerable preparation and looked forward to it so enthusiastically, one could not turn around and disappoint them, even if they had lost form to an extent because better players came forward at the eleventh hour and offered their services." [8] This meant there was no place in the team for those who had held back awaiting developments. Of these restrictions, and of the philosophy behind the tour, Baskiville wrote: "Before proceeding further, it should be mentioned now that if a capitalist had promoted the tour with an idea of making money, he could have secured a team that would have satisfied many others by taking Home a few very prominent players as professionals - that is by paying them a certain sum of money and their expenses. But this would have spoiled the whole intention of the scheme. Our idea was to get players to travel Home as amateurs

- that is to pay their own expenses and divide the gate takings equally." [9] He explained the team's view of the difference between an amateur and a professional: "We hold that we are still amateur footballers because we do not intend to make a living by playing football. We are making a trip to England at our expense. The mere fact of our playing against teams which play a few professionals does not alter our status one jot." [10] He saw professional sportsmen as those who lived solely off their earnings.

Others also saw this as a commonsense approach to the issue of compensation for playing and this concept began to receive greater acceptance. The rugby writer for the Canterbury Times under the pseudonym 'Quidnunc', and as one who had previously panned the expedition, now wrote in respect to professionalism in Rugby, saying: "This is not a time for talking twaddle about the purity of the game, and the sordid spirit that calls for rewards. What is required (of a Rugby Union) is a sensible grasp of changing conditions, of the casting aside of old traditions, of the determination to have a different distribution of the spoils. The democratic spirit of the age demands a change for hoary-headed conservatism, born in England and transplanted here by descendants of the original conservatives." [11] He continued: "Cricket has its amateurs and its professionals playing together, and few people would dare to belittle cricket. Cannot professional and amateur footballers play together? Will the payment of individuals spoil the game? There is no reason why it should. Many men who play would play just as well for a fee as they can play without... by all means let the man who needs a little supplement of his wages receive it for his skill and energy in football." [12] Will McKenzie, a former great player himself; writing for The Dominion had this to say: "The Auckland Union is so rich that it does not know what to do with its money. Still it is asserted that George Smith became a professional footballer simply because he was disgusted by the treatment meted out to him by the Auckland Union. He was temporarily injured in a match, and sent in a bill to the Union for some nine shillings. George Smith in his time had probably brought in hundreds of pounds to the coffers of the Auckland Union, but that body refused to recognise his claim." [13] It is unlikely that Smith decided to involve himself with professional rugby for that reason solely; however medical expenses and payment for lost time away from employment were hip-pocket issues that had a direct bearing on players' attitudes. In fact Baskiville and his friends were in good company in attracting attention to the professional issue. No less a player than the great Tom Ellison, a former All Black captain and one of the first writers on the game, had, in 1898, suggested that players going on tours be paid a wage.

The team itself had, however, almost made this debate academic. They had seized the initiative by what they were doing and were by then a registered and legally incorporated body, their full title being: 'The New Zealand All Black Rugby Football Team.' Speculation regarding the identities of the players who would make the tour intensified and finally reached fever point. Certain players were noted as being absent from club play in Auckland, players like George

Nicholson, the Auckland and All Black forward, and George Gillett, a winger. Other likely members were seen as being 'Massa' Johnston and Charlie Seeling, the latter a great All Black and Auckland back row forward. This newspaper talk drew denials from Seeling. The statement he said: "was a gross libel. He was approached on the matter and that was all." Seeling also announced that his intention was to retire from football, and said he did not intend to take more risks. Yet a year later he joined Wigan and was to have a Rugby League career as brilliant as had been the case with Rugby Union.

England offered much that was not available to young New Zealanders - infinite variety, entertainment and history, all spoken of by their older relatives with great affection. England was a magnet, and for colonials who liked to pit themselves against their forbears it acted, in a way, as the ultimate challenge. While the motives of the 160 applicants for the tour may have been diverse, they had a desire to prove themselves worthy of selection, and, at the same time, represent the country they were proud of. New Zealand, desperate to renounce its parent country, was in the process of throwing off its colonial status and becoming a Dominion - a country that could act on its own behalf in all matters. A youthful independent spirit shone brightly among the plethora of players Baskiville and his fellow selectors could now choose a team from.

It was to be a professional All Black Team, their uniform being the same intimidating colour as other All Black sides - black jersey and black shorts, and, to the dismay of the Rugby Union, and some other adherents of the amateur code, the national symbol, the silver fern, would be emblazoned on their jersey. Their original intention had been for the team to sail direct to England via the Suez Canal. These plans were now changed. The momentous events that were taking place in New Zealand began to have an effect in Australia.

New South Wales and Queensland were the cradles of rugby union in Australia, but events in Sydney were soon to show the New Zealanders were having a direct and predetermined effect outside their own shores. The English Rugby Union inquired of the New Zealand Union about what was being done to counter the threat. The New Zealand Union, fearful of its position, felt it had to at least be seen to be doing more than it had done up till then. It was now common knowledge the amateur declarations were worthless documents; the players could not be held to them. Talk also began of a South African professional tour of England.

Opposition to the tour now came from the New Zealand Government's Agent-General's Office in London. This office was the forerunner of what is now the New Zealand Embassy. Mr C Wray Palliser was also the New Zealand Rugby Union's representative on the English Rugby Union. Using his contacts with The Times in London, he disseminated information contrary to the interests of the professional team. This meant a Government official was acting for the New Zealand Rugby Union in a capacity that he would not have been able to carry out if he had not been so employed. He labelled them the 'Phantom Team,' and confidently predicted the tour would not take place. His comments that

Baskiville was "hoodwinking the people," and that the players "would bring no sort of credit to New Zealand" were, in all probability, defamatory. The intention was to undermine the Northern Union's backing for the tour. The New Zealand Government, by not restraining Palliser, was seen to be acting in a manner contrary to the interests of the professional team. It was not to be the last effort by the Union to induce the Government to ensure amateur football was not overtaken by professional rugby.

1   *Christchurch Star*, 6 June, 1907.
2   *Auckland Rugby League Gazette*, 10 September, 1938, p.15.
3   *New Zealand Herald*, 15 June, 1907.
4   *Auckland Rugby League Gazette*, 16 September, 1903.
5   *Canterbury Times*, 18 September, 1907.
6   *The Athletic News*, 7 October, 1907.
7   *Otago Daily Times*, 10 October, 1907.
8   Ibid.
9   Ibid.
10 Ibid.
11 *Canterbury Times*, 17 August, 1907.
12 *Canterbury Times*, 5 August, 1907.
13 *Canterbury Times*, 6 November, 1907.

ouvenir of the

NEW ZEALAND

RUGBY

FOOTBALL TEAM

1907/8

AKE AKE KIA
KAHA

5. THE PHANTOM TEAM

By July the team had been selected but not announced. Eventually the public were to find out it included nine All Blacks, and fourteen provincial players, the majority of whom were among the top thirty to forty players in New Zealand. The forwards included four of the Wellington Ranfurly Shield side, Dan Gilchrist, Eric Watkins, Con Byrne and the durable Tom Cross, together with most of the Auckland Ranfurly Shield team and the well-performed Auckland B side. The backs contained, on the one hand, out and out stars in George Smith and Duncan McGregor, and on the other, several talented uncapped players. These latter included four Aucklanders, Lance Todd, Dick Wynyard and his brother Billy, together with Harold Rowe. They were accomplished provincial representatives but were untested in the international arena. There were some absentees who either did not make the side, or were not available to tour - notably two impressive All Blacks, AF (Bolla) Francis and George (Broncho) Seeling. Many thought the team surprisingly strong, given the restrictive circumstances in which it had been put together and that it contained a good mix of experience and youth.

Starting with the fullbacks, Turtill and Harold Rowe, the crucial last line of defence looked in safe hands. In Turtill they had a player well versed in wet-weather football, and Rowe had the advantage of being a fine tackler and possessing good speed. The transition to the new rules would require major adjustments for them, with the ball being kicked out on the bounce if at all. To have an impact on the game, and an influence on results, the fullback would have to run the ball with more vigour than was often the case in rugby union, where he could kick for the sideline.

Turtill was already an All Black, and a popular one, having played well for New Zealand in 1905 against Australia. He was also the only member of the side not born in New Zealand. His father had died in London, and when Turtill was three years old, his mother emigrated to New Zealand to be with relatives. He played rugby against his mother's wishes, joining Christchurch Albion, and by 1902 had cemented his place in the Canterbury provincial team. He played for South Island in 1903 and again in 1907. Turtill was an immaculate catcher of the high ball and seemed to excel in wet conditions, useful attributes for a full back on a tour of England. He practised a lot, catching the wet ball on his jersey from all different angles, and the dry ball in his hands. He said: "To endeavour to catch a greasy rugby ball with outstretched hands is to court disaster." [1] Aged 27 and weighing only 11st 5lb, Turtill's game was based primarily on confidence, courage under the high ball, and kicking skill. He was an ironworker and the chance of a trip 'home' offered him the opportunity of returning to his birthplace. He spoke later of his decision to sign the amateur declaration, and then to tour saying: "I attached my signature in all sincerity at the time, for then

H. J. PALMER, Esq.,
Manager.

I had not been asked, but like others, when I was invited to make the trip home, I took legal advice and was informed that the document was worthless, and I came." [2]

By contrast, his fullback partner, Harold Rowe, was a qualified accountant. From Auckland he played for the Newton Club. Bigger than Turtill at 12st 2lb and 5ft 9in, he possessed fine finishing qualities. Rowe's versatility and deceptive speed meant he could play equally well at fullback, wing or centre three-quarter. His value as a utility player was later to be a great asset to the team when injuries and the length of the tour forced players into unfamiliar positions.

The three-quarters brimmed with talent. McGregor and Smith had formed one of the fastest outside back All Black combinations ever. Both were household names. McGregor, a railway worker, first played for Wellington and later Canterbury. His place in the team was assured from the outset. He was one of the influential group of Petone players before his move back to Christchurch where he played in the red and black hoops of the Christchurch Club. In a memorable match in 1904, when Wellington defeated Auckland for the Ranfurly Shield, 6-3, it was McGregor who had opened the scoring with a try. Noted more for his attacking skills than his defensive ability, he played as an All Black in 1903-04-05. In 1904, against the, until then, undefeated British team, he had scored two brilliant tries in the second half, sealing the result of the Test match 9-3. During the 1905 All Black tour of Great Britain, as if to underline his

A. H. BASKERVILLE,
Secretary and Promoter.
Oriental, 1905   New Zealand, 1907

amazing speed, the British press dubbed him the 'Flying Scotsman' - truly appropriate - when he scored four tries in the Test match against England. Aged 25, he was prone to injuries, but on his day McGregor was among the greatest backs New Zealand had produced.

There are few players who, at age 35, merit selection in a national side purely on their football ability, yet George Smith's play was of such stature that he would have been an automatic choice even had he not been one of the organisers. A football genius as well as a world-class athlete, Smith constructed his play around tremendous speed, anticipation and elusiveness, and an almost uncanny ability to score from seemingly impossible situations, especially when his team was staring defeat in the face.

In 1897 he won a game for Auckland when Wellington had led 4-3 with ten minutes to go. He ran around the approaching forwards from his own twenty-five, slicing through the backs to score. For good measure he then repeated it. Smith had the ability to maintain tremendous personal fitness through athletics and could lay off football and return to it with ease. In 1905 he enjoyed a triumphant tour of England with the All Blacks. The try to win the Test against Scotland with four minutes left on the clock began from his own twenty-five and stole the game. By 1907 he had long left behind his days as a jockey, and weighed 12st 2lb. George Smith was both a game breaker, and a match winner

H. R. WRIGHT, Forward.
CAPTAIN.
Petone, 1900   North Wairarapa, 1899
New Zealand in South Africa, 1901-2
Wellington, 1903-4-5-6
Wellington Provincial, 1905-6
New Zealand, 1907

and in him the professional team had a consummate footballer who could play wing or centre with equal flair and ability. The tour offered much as he was at the time a steward for the Auckland Amateur Sports Club, with no long term ties. If offered a professional contract in England he was in a position to accept. At this time he was also considering marriage.

One of the two remaining outside back positions was taken by Edgar Wrigley from the Red Star Club in Masterton. Already an All Black, and a plumber by trade, he was blessed with an ideal physique for a second five-eighths or centre. Standing 5ft 9in and weighing 14 stone, Wrigley was a gifted athlete, with a formidable physical presence. While he could be a hot and cold player, Edgar Wrigley, with his size and speed, was a match-winner and he had the added advantage of being a fine goal kicker.

Joining Wrigley in the centres was Joe Lavery, a mature footballer, 27 years old, who had played for both the Albion Club in Christchurch, and also Temuka in South Canterbury in 1901. He was a clubmate of Turtill's. A Canterbury representative footballer, 1902-04, he had also represented South Island in 1903. Lavery worked for the railways.

H. H. MESSENGER,
Three-Quarter.

Eastern Suburbs, Sydney, 1906-7
New South Wales, 1906   Australia, 1907
New Zealand, 190⁻

The inside backs were an all Auckland combination possessed of great footballing ability. John Richard (Dick) Wynyard and William Thomas (Billy) Wynyard came from a family of great rugby players. Their uncles, George, Henry (Pie) and WT (Tabby) Wynyard were in the New Zealand Native Team that toured England in 1888. Both the nephews were civil service clerks, carrying on a family tradition in public administration. But it was on the football field that they excelled. Playing for the old established North Shore Rugby Club because they lived in Devonport, they represented Auckland when Auckland was the strongest rugby province. Dick had won selection as a youngster aged 20 and played in the Auckland side that lifted the Ranfurly Shield from Wellington in 1905. Billy, the older brother, won provincial honours later, but by 1907 was forging a fine reputation playing for the blue and whites.

Lance Todd, a tailor, completed the inside back combination. Speed and elusiveness were among his greatest attributes, coupled with a keen brain capable of exploiting any weaknesses in the opposition. A member of the Parnell Club, but originally from Otahuhu, and only weighing 10 stone, Todd had special qualities which had been recognised by Auckland, for whom he was the

G. W. SMITH, Three-Quarter.
VICE-CAPTAIN.
City, 1894   Auckland, 1895-6-7-9-1901-6
N'th Island, 1897-1905   N. Zealand, 1897-1902
Toured Great Britain, 1905-6 (Amateur)
New Zealand, 1907
English Champion 120 yards Hurdles 1902

regular five-eighths for Ranfurly Shield games, yet he had not been promoted to All Black or even inter-island level. This was almost certainly due to an abundance of talent in those positions throughout New Zealand at that time. With an eye for a gap, and being only 5ft 7in tall, Lance Todd could cut through the strongest of defences. He was also a cash sprinter in Auckland. This gave him enormous speed off the mark, and was just the sort of acceleration that might take him through the tight defences in rugby league in England. Todd had maestro qualities. He could read the game and dictate the play, and for these reasons alone was ideally suited to the new rules.

In the half-back positions, the selectors had chosen four men. Firstly, Edward (Hone) Tyne, a railway employee, who represented Canterbury and South Island in 1906, and at the time of his selection was playing for the Petone Club in Wellington. Tyne was unusually large for the position at 5ft 10in and weighing 12 and a half stone, but went as a utility; he could be expected to fill most positions - a useful asset in a touring team. The other two scrum halves were Arthur Kelly, also of Petone, and William (Bill) Tyler from the City Club in Auckland. At 13 and a half stone Tyler, a boilermaker, was even larger than

E. WRIGLEY, Three-Quarter.

Masterton Club, 1902
Wairarapa, 1903-4-5-6-7   New Zealand, 1905
Wellington Province, 1905-7
New Zealand, 1907-8

Tyne - he held a regular place in the Auckland provincial team as their wing-forward. Aged 25 when selected, he had won provincial honours in 1905 playing in the Ranfurly Shield match against Wellington won by Auckland. In that game, Tyler scored the winning try that began the long shield reign by Auckland.

Kelly was one of the Wellington provincial team's most promising young talents, renowned for his tackling. He was not playing in 1907, and how this came about, Arthur Kelly was to tell later. An apprentice in the Petone railway workshops, he had some old friends in Nelson where there was an exceptional player. Late one evening, some Nelsonites, extolling their player's talents in the pub, said he could not be caught. Kelly's friends, knowing better, wagered the Nelsonites five pounds on it. Leave arranged, Kelly duly took the field in Nelson as an unknown. The deed was done and Kelly got liberal expenses. At the end of the game the Nelson selectors even offered the stranger a place in their Seddon Shield representative side, but both Kelly's leave and luck had run out and the full story got around. A charge of professionalism could not be proved, but the Rugby Union got their man on a technicality - he was disqualified for three years for playing under an assumed name, but went on to forge a

H. S. TURTILL, Full-Back.

Christchurch Club
Canterbury Rep., 1902-3-5-7
South Island, 1903-7   New Zealand, 1905-7

magnificent football career playing a different code.

Jim Gleeson from the Hawkes Bay took the remaining half-back spot, but his major role was not as a player. He had managerial functions and duties, and helped Baskiville with day-to-day tour arrangements. If there was a weakness to be found in team selection it looked to be in the crucial scrum half position where there seemed to be an absence of straight-out class.

Overall the backs possessed experience and genuine pace. They were chosen as an attractive attacking unit at a time when the All Blacks were noted for this aspect of their game. But could they tackle? No one doubted their courage, but what of meeting the heavy demands of front-on tackling under the Northern Union's rules? Only with practice and experience could they hope to find the answer. They had chosen tough men in the forwards to measure up to the task.

Tom Cross at 29 years of age, and an All Black, worked as a labourer. Originally from Dunedin he played first for the Kaikorai Club in 1896. For the times, they considered Cross a man of large physique. At 6ft and 14 1/2 stone there were few players as big. He first gained South Island honours in 1902, previously representing Otago in 1898-09-1900 and then Canterbury in 1901-02. By 1904 he had moved to Wellington playing for the Petone Club and the

HAROLD F. ROWE,
Three-Quarter and Full-Back.

Newton Club   College Old Boys Rep., 1905
Auckland City, 1906-7   New Zealand, 1907

Wellington provincial side. First playing for the All Blacks in 1901, he won selection again in 1904, helping defeat the touring British team in the Test match, 9-3. 1905 and 1906 saw him consistently selected for New Zealand. He excelled in support play, which was surprising for such a big man, but it made him ideally suited to the faster game they expected to play in Britain, and which they also hoped would materialise from their opponents. A contemporary footballer said of Cross: "Of course the appellation 'Angry' was originally merely a play on the surname but it fitted in other ways. Cross was no amiable incompetent in the field. He worked hard, and talked hard. The writer played against him at Christchurch six or seven years ago, and remembers well his hoarse hypernations." [3] Tom Cross was one of the 'hard men' of New Zealand rugby.

In 'Massa' Johnston, the side had another fine product of Otago rugby. Johnston also played a key role in selection and team management. An ironworker, he first played senior football for the Alhambra Club in 1897, at only 15 years of age. At 6ft and 13 and a half stone Johnston had represented Otago from 1903 onwards. He played for South Island in 1904 before being chosen for the All Black tour in 1905 to Great Britain. Unfortunately he suffered ill health on that tour and played in only 13 matches. A throat infection kept him in

A. LILE, Forward.

Goldfields, 1906   Oriental, Wellington, 1907
Wellington, 1907   North Island, 1907
New Zealand, 1907

London at the tour's end for some time, but he toured Australia in 1907 with the All Blacks, playing in both Tests. When selected, Johnston was at the peak of his career. He had all the typically uncompromising attributes and characteristics of a rugged New Zealand forward, but he had earned respect for his clean style of play.

The hooking position featured another All Black. Eric Watkins, a surveyor by profession, played for the Wellington College Old Boys' Club when in that city. He brought extensive inter-provincial experience to the position, playing for Wellington every year from 1900 to 1906, and then for Wanganui in 1907 when working up in Raetihi. Watkins represented North Island in 1904 and 1906 and New Zealand in 1905. Joining him in the front row was Hercules Richard (Bumper) Wright who held the current Petone and Wellington captaincies. He had played originally for North Wairarapa in 1899, before moving to Petone where he worked as a printer. When in South Africa during the Boer War, Wright played for the New Zealand Army Corps team, this side being the first New Zealand team to play there. There is a reference to him having been chosen to represent New Zealand as an All Black, but that he had to withdraw through injury. In common with the other Wellington forwards, 'Bumper' Wright had played Ranfurly Shield Rugby. A contemporary described him in graphic terms

ERIC L. WATKINS, Forward.

Wellington College Old Boys
Wellington Rep., 1900-1-2-3-4-5-6
Wanganui Rep., 1907   North Island, 1904-6
New Zealand, 1905-7

- "He had the forequarters of a horse. It is said he was a mild-mannered man at heart. Most men would rather play with him than against him for a minute." [4] Wright, a disciplinarian, used to check his club teammates in Petone on Friday nights before a match to make sure they weren't in the hotel. The professional team elected him captain, reflecting not only the high regard in which he was held, but also the democratic nature of the team's affairs.

The other forwards, Con Byrne (originally from Nelson), Adam Lile and Dan Gilchrist, who played regularly for Wellington, were all representative players. Adam Lile, a 14 stone soldier, played for the Oriental Club - a teammate of Baskiville's. Lile had just won North Island selection in 1907 and played well in the final trial against South Island when the amateur All Blacks were chosen. Lile was one of the top 30 players in the country. Byrne, a farmer, kept naturally fit. Both he and Dan Gilchrist, another plumber, were rising stars at 23 years of age, with their best football yet in front of them. Gilchrist, from the Melrose Club, had represented Wellington consistently from 1904 to 1907. He was joined by Arthur Callum, an insurance agent and a clubmate at Melrose, who played for Wellington in 1905 and 1907. Charles Pearce from Canterbury added both weight and experience. He and Joe Lavery were teammates at the Albion Club. Pearce was a regular member of the Canterbury forward pack from 1903-06 and

51

J. C. GLEESON, Half-Back.

TREASURER,

Scinde Napier Sydney University
Auckland and Wellington Universities
New Zealand, 1907

played for South Island in 1906.

The selectors drew on the Auckland representative side for their remaining forwards. These included a strapping clerk named William Trevarthen who had played originally for Ohinemuri in 1900, and was a member of the Auckland provincial team from 1904 to 1907. Charlie Dunning, a naturally fit builder, played for Ponsonby in 1900, and then for Gisborne in 1903-04, before returning to Auckland, which he represented from 1905-07. Dunning was a key member of the Auckland Ranfurly Shield team. He also represented North Island in 1906. Auckland also provided another All Black forward in Bill Mackrell. He had toured Great Britain in 1905, but had suffered with injuries, playing few games. A printer by trade, he played for the City Club and Auckland province, 1901-05, as well as North Island in 1905. Dan Fraser and Bert Baskiville completed the selections. Fraser played for Petone, and joined the tour in New South Wales as an assistant manager, who could play if required to. He gave his occupation as 'gentleman'.

The New Zealand Herald commented: "Taken generally, the vanguard players can be classed as a fine lot and may be depended upon to uphold the traditions of the forward game for which New Zealand have become famous. The

D. McGREGOR, Three-Quarter.

Kaipoi, 1899   Petone, 1904   Canterbury,
1900-1-2-3-6   Wellington, 1904-5-6   South
Island, 1902-3-4-6   North Island, 1904
New Zealand, 1903-4-5-6-7
Toured Great Britain, 1905

Wellington contingent alone is a very strong lot." And of the backs: "The trio: Smith, McGregor and Wrigley must be classed as among the country's best three-quarters"... and "Wrigley is the burly Wairarapa representative and is rightly regarded as one of the best back line players in the country." It also said: "there is no knowing how the younger players may shape, but in such a tour, many unexpected developments may take place." Of their overall prospects, the Herald sounded a note of caution, warning of the magnitude of the task facing the team in taking on the professional sides in England, saying: "They will have a very much tougher foe to contend against than did their amateur predecessors." [5]

The team had an emphasis on quick agile players, large enough in the forwards to combat the opposition, but with sufficient mobility to cope with the more continuous play that the Northern Union rules were known to encourage. Later, when aboard ship Baskiville had time to write of the side, he was optimistic about its chances but knew the team had to prove itself as a combination, and said:

"The team, regarded collectively, should do well in England. There are a number of young players included, but in most cases they are tried men. The leaven of old players should soon teach them the finer points of the game and

L. B. TODD, Five-eighths Back.

City, 1905-6   Auckland, 1905
New Zealand, 1907

bring out any dormant football that is in them. Some people may not consider certain players good enough. It is submitted that these might not be quite up to New Zealand representative form now, but they will improve considerably when on tour and when they reap the benefit of the experience that the older hands will impart to them. The material is there at any rate, and it is very promising at that. Again, when the scheme of organising a team was first mooted people had no idea that such a strong combination would be obtained.... Wright (Petone) has been elected captain and Smith (Auckland) vice-captain, and these two and Johnston will form the Selection Committee." [6] *(See Appendix 2 for details on selection policy)*

Harold Rowe, when he was interviewed, said he thought the team "strong in the forwards, and a back team that will do anything," and added: "The experience of the All Blacks was that the younger members lasted the tour better, and that was a determining factor in choosing the present team." [7] While it was hoped that the team would do itself and the country proud, the Rugby Union had been injured. At an after match dinner in the Hawkes Bay, the President of the Auckland Rugby Union expressed those feelings saying: "All who had the

W. JOHNSTON, Forward.

Alhambra, 1897   Otago, 1903-4-5-6-7
South Island, 1904
"All Blacks," toured Great Britain, 1905-6
"All Blacks," toured Australia, 1907 (Am't'r)
New Zealand, 1907

welfare of our national game at heart regretted the appearance of professionalism in this colony. Its evil effects were so well known..." that it had... small chances of obtaining a place amongst the players generally." The Hawkes Bay manager said: "Every union and player should strive to keep clean the national game." [8] Of George Smith's role and the Auckland Rugby Union players the Hawkes Bay manager, oblivious of that gulf said: "But for the support given to the project by a number of prominent Auckland footballers, it would never have been possible to send away from this colony a professional team." [9] The irony of the situation would not have been lost on Billy Wynyard and Charlie Dunning who were at the dinner having played in that game, but who were also to join the team.

Expressing a player's view, probably formed on the basis of his profession as an accountant, Harold Rowe said: "We go on exactly the same basis as the Australian cricket team, with the difference that we pay our expenses Home, and yet the Australians are regarded as amateurs and their status is not affected, though they gain considerably in a financial sense from their tour. I do not reckon I am professional. I am entitled to something in return for the £50 that I

T. W. CROSS, Forward.

Kaikorai, 1896   Petone, 1904
Otago, 1898-9-1900   Canterbury, 1901-2
South Island, 1902   North Island, 1904-6
Wellington, 1903-4-5-6-7
New Zealand, 1901-4-5-6-7

invest and the work I will do. It is a business transaction." [10] In this he crystallised the gulf between the players and the administrators of the game. It was well known that the MCC allowed English professional cricketers visiting Australia £2 per week on shore and 30 shillings per week on board ship for personal expenses, in addition to £300 for their services, and all travelling expenses. Even in 1873-74 when WG Grace first toured Down Under, the professionals received £170.

The full list of names was finally released, only after the team's departure - could it be there was a lingering doubt about the amateur declaration? Whatever the case, final farewells took place, often with the blessing of the rugby clubs of which the players were members. There was a send off at the Empire Hotel, Petone, for the Petone members of the team and for their Manager, HJ Palmer, and also for Duncan McGregor who had been, until recently, a member of that club. The Chairman presented each with a travelling case on behalf of well-wishers." [11] The Wellington players joined Edgar Wrigley from the Wairarapa and the Canterbury players, Pearce, Turtill and Lavery for their departure from the capital.

J. LAVERY, Three-Quarter.

Albion, 1900 South Canterbury
Temuka, 1900-1 Canterbury, 1902-3-4
South Island, 1903 New Zealand, 1907

It had been arranged that they would sail directly to Sydney where they would be joined by the Auckland members of the team. Baskiville had however announced that the team was not by then complete and that one or two additional players would join them in Australia. Two players, WT Wynyard and C Dunning, were like other players, current Auckland representative footballers, and yet, while Smith, Todd, Trevarthen and the others had withdrawn from representative matches, Wynyard and Dunning played for Auckland against Hawkes Bay on 10 August, 1907. Also neither of their names was included in the list of players provided by the organisers to the New Zealand Mail and published on 14 August. That journal also stated that some difficulty was experienced in completing the team. It said: "On Friday the management committee telegraphed to a half back ... offering him a place in the team." If there were last minute adjustments of team personnel, it must have made travel arrangements quite difficult. 'Bumper' Wright, in 1938, many years later, interviewed for the Auckland Rugby League Gazette, told of the selection difficulties that Baskiville encountered being made more difficult by the Rugby Union ordering them off their grounds, and men who were to join the All Golds being brought off one way or another." [12]

A. F. KELLY, Half-Back.

Petone Club, 1906   Wellington, 1906
New Zealand, 1907

By August 10, 1907, the Evening Post was able to report that fifteen of the members of the team had left Wellington on SS Warrimoo en route for England via Australia: "A number of Wairarapa Maoris who were on the wharf farewelled the Masterton player, Wrigley, with characteristic Maori chants, and the pakehas of the team cheered the team individually as well as collectively. The promoter (Baskiville) met with an exceptionally good reception." [13]

Of the departure scene in Wellington, Baskiville wrote: "The Warrimoo was first timed to leave at 4.00pm and long before that time a curious crowd began to gather about the Pier Hotel, where we were staying, and when we finally left for the boat, we had a fairly large following. The interest shown in our undertaking was made manifest when the steamer was leaving the wharf, cheer after cheer being given for the boys, who responded by singing 'Good-bye My Lady Love' and 'Now Is The Hour'." He must have felt an enormous sense of satisfaction, and perhaps relief, as the ship pulled away from the quay, and then slowly gathering speed steamed down through the rocky blue inlets of this beautiful harbour out into the Tasman Sea on the voyage of a lifetime.

Following their departure from Wellington, further members of the team left from Auckland on the SS Victoria three days later. In spite of the rain, a large

D. G. FRASER.

ASSISTANT SECRETARY.

Petone, 1901
New Zealand in South Africa, 1902
New Zealand, 1907

crowd assembled to see the Auckland men off and the men were loudly cheered which gives lie to the idea that they stole out of the country. [14] For George Smith in Auckland, his departure was seemingly delayed while last minute arrangements were made for the inclusion of Billy Wynyard and Dunning - the last two players. Their membership of the team was however to be very important in the years that followed.

The full team was: H S Turtill (Canterbury), J A Lavery (Canterbury), D McGregor (Canterbury), C J Pearce (Canterbury), G W Smith (Auckland), L B Todd (Auckland), J R Wynyard (Auckland), H F Rowe (Auckland), W T Tyler (Auckland), W M Trevarthen (Auckland), W H Mackrell (Auckland), E Wrigley (Wairarapa), A H Baskiville (Wellington), A Callum (Wellington), E Watkins (Wellington), A Lile (Wellington), D Gilchrist (Wellington), T W Cross (Petone), H R Wright (Petone), A F Kelly (Petone), E Tyne (Petone), C E Byrne (Petone), W T Wynyard (Auckland), J C Gleeson (Hawkes Bay), C Dunning (Auckland), W Johnston (Otago), D Fraser (Wellington).

It was to be a very rough winter with crossings of the Tasman an unpleasant experience. Baskiville and Wrigley did not travel well. Several were making their maiden sea trip. They had an eventful crossing. Baskiville wrote: "All hands appeared at the first meal on board, but there was a different tale to tell at breakfast the following morning, only two answering the bugle call." [15] Only two weeks later, the Warrimoo's sister ship, Monowai, went missing, and the Warrimoo ran aground on Farewell Spit in the search.

1   Scrapbook of H.S. Turtill, unsourced newspaper article.
2   Ibid.
3   L Fanning, Players and Slayers, Gordon and Gotch, Wellington, 1910, p.57.
4   Ibid.
5   *New Zealand Herald*, 13 August 1907.
6   Ibid.
7   *New Zealand Herald*, 13 August 1907.
8   Ibid.
9   Ibid.
10   Ibid.
11   *The New Zealand Mail*, 14 August 1907.
12   *Auckland Rugby League Gazette*, 25 June 1938.
13   *Evening Post*, 10 August 1907.
14   *Canterbury Times*, 21 August 1907.
15   *Littleton Times*, 31 August 1907.

6. AUSTRALIAN CONNECTION

It is now clear that, at the same time as organising the rebel tour to England, the New Zealanders had been encouraging a large and representative group of players in Sydney to join them in breaking away from the Rugby Union. The initial spark to begin rugby league in Australia came from Bert Baskiville and George Smith in New Zealand. Acting on the team's behalf, Smith, with the connections he had in Australia, had telegraphed Peter Moir, a prominent Sydney player, asking if a series of games was possible. With a person of Smith's stature taking the lead anything was possible.

There was no professional rugby in Australia. Then the rumours had started: The rebellion that had its origins in New Zealand was also about to be exported across the Tasman, deep into the heartland of Australian rugby union. Baskiville confirmed the reports in early August 1907 - the New Zealand team, instead of going straight to Britain, would stop in Sydney first, and there would play a series of three matches against state teams. Yet all games there were under the control of the respective Rugby Unions in New South Wales and Queensland, and football was, or was meant to be, played on an amateur basis. The obvious question on everyone's mind in Australia was exactly whom the New Zealanders would be playing against.

Ian Heads, writing of those involved, quotes Harry Hamill in the Rugby League News 1940, as saying: "Peter (Moir) a grand footballer and fine fellow, was in the habit of visiting Victor Trumper's sports depot in Market Street, where David Jones is now erected ... Jim Giltinan, Harry Hoyle, Alex Burdon and others also frequented Trumper's, and it was here that Peter set the ball rolling by getting them interested in the cable... and a return cable was sent to George Smith, suggesting that matches could be arranged, and so the foundation stone was laid of Rugby League today." [1] Naturally the Rugby Union tried to defend its, until then, untrammelled domain, and it castigated the players in Sydney reminding them that expulsion from the Union would be the inevitable consequence of any games they played in against the New Zealanders.

The causes of discontent common to both countries were obvious enough: income from matches staying with the Rugby Union, loss of wages, doctors' bills, the rules of the game, social division on occupational lines. The amateur test series just played between New Zealand and Australia in 1907 had seen crowds of 50,000 attending each game. When the Sydney Rugby Union decided to spend £13,000 to convert Epping Racecourse into a football ground, they added to a volatile situation. The profits to be made from a series against an All Black team made the risk of breaking away worth taking. The reasons for change were the same as in New Zealand: footballers on low wages, with no hope of accumulating savings, paying high rents and having no mortgages available to them. Professional rugby was a way to a house and marriage, a means of

THE ALL BLACKS,

THE NEW ZEALAND TEAM FOR ENGLAND,

WILL PLAY

NEW SOUTH WALES—ALL BLUES

ON THE AGRICULTURAL GROUND,

NEXT SATURDAY NEXT.

AT 3.30 P.M.

PRECEDED BY

AUSTRALIAN FOOTBALL, AT 1.30 P.M.

ADMISSION, 1s; GRANDSTAND, 1s EXTRA.   DE GROEN'S VICE-REGAL BAND.

J. J. GILTINAN, Hon. Secretary,
N.S.W. Rugby Football League.

NEW SOUTH WALES RUGBY FOOTBALL LEAGUE.

A PUBLIC RECEPTION AND

SMOKO TO THE ALL BLACKS,

THE NEW ZEALAND TEAM FOR ENGLAND,

1 be held in the TOWN HALL, SYDNEY, on THURSDAY NEXT, 15th inst, at 8 p.m.
ADMISSION, ONE SHILLING.

J. J. GILTINAN, Hon. Secretary.

Advertisement for the first professional rugby union match in Sydney.
Sydney Morning Herald, 14 August 1907

securing a future. It offered players the prospect of forming a new structure, a game they could call their own. Rugby in Australia was also seen by many as being the creature of the English Rugby Union, unable to act independently in respect to issues about compensation or alterations to the rules of the game. Among a certain section of Australians there was little sentiment for 'Mother England'; in fact the English Rugby Union, with its unyielding opposition to any form of compensation in the colonies, and having shed its troublesome northern clubs in 1895, was seen by many as something of an albatross around the Australian Rugby Union's neck.

Yet rugby union for pay was not new in Sydney. One prominent player commented on past practices saying: "Training at 4 o'clock a couple of afternoons a week also produced seven shillings and sixpence each for lost time; but I was also told when receiving that I must not tell any of the others, for they might all want it." [2] When Peter Moir replied confirming the Australians would play against New Zealand, the fuse was lit. Although the revolutionary impulse surfaced first in New Zealand, there can be no doubt that once offered the opportunity of playing a professional All Black team, the Australians grasped the nettle with great fervour and considerable expertise. By the time the New Zealanders were due to embark for Australia, the same complementary pieces of a professional movement were, gradually at first, and then with great vigour, being put in place in Sydney.

New Zealand Team in Sydney 1907
Back Row: W Mackrell, E Wrigley, W Tyler, and J Wynyard. *Second Row:* T Cross, C Pearce,
C Byrne, H R Wright, D Gilchrist, and E Watkins. *Third Row:* Baskiville, E Tyne, D McGregor, H Palmer
(Manager), L Todd, H S Turtill, and W Johnston. *Front Row:* H Rowe, J Gleeson, and A Kelly.
Absent: J Lavery, A Callam, A Lile and W Trevarthen, besides G W Smith, W Wynyard and C Dunning,
who had not by then reached Sydney.

The Australians acted quickly. They arranged meetings in secret, often at Victor Trumper's shop or at a wine shop opposite. The crucial decision to split away was made when players met at Bateman's Crystal Hotel, George Street, Sydney, on 8 August, 1907. Security was tight at the door, a man named Charlie Wilson scrutinising those permitted to enter, about 50 people in all. The eight senior clubs in the Sydney competition were represented and with their decision to form the New South Wales Rugby League, they severed their link with the amateur code in Australia and also in England. These people - the first state funded and mass educated generation - could organise. One of their best, Henry Hoyle, had been, and continued to be, a prominent member of the Australian Labour Party and an MP. He had been elected to the State Legislature as the member for Redfern in 1891. Later he became a Cabinet Minister. James Giltinan, a businessman and cricket umpire, and the son of a coachbuilder, became the New South Wales League's first secretary. Giltinan personally staked the £500 guarantee required of the Australians for the All Blacks' visit. The arrangements were fair - a fifty percent split of the gate. The New South Wales League were also to pay 15 per cent of their takings in ground charges and return 35 per cent to the players. Of all the early Australian administrators, it can be said of Giltinan that he was crucial to the professional game's beginnings.

The Agricultural Ground was booked for the games to be played and advertising for the series was on show when the amateur All Blacks played Australia.

One hundred and sixty players joined the League immediately, and many were offering for selection for the matches planned. By the next Tuesday, twenty players had been chosen to play against the New Zealanders and also had signed the playing agreement. The New South Wales Rugby League elected the Mayor of Sydney, Sir Matthew Harris, a former parliamentarian, as their Patron and the Treasurer's role fell to Victor Trumper. When Dally Messenger, the star of the recent test series, signed with them, the new body's credibility increased enormously. Those negotiations had been undertaken by Victor Trumper and Jim Giltinan with Messenger's mother, Annie Messenger - the cost of the transaction for the shipbuilder being £180, the equivalent of two years' wages. Rugby in Sydney was in turmoil. Feelings ran high between those who had split away and those who remained with rugby union. Stories are told of players in the same club crossing to the opposite side of the street rather than be seen talking to their clubmates who had turned to the new game. Amid all this, there were practices to be arranged and Giltinan reported the New South Wales team would go into quarters and thenceforward would do nothing but prepare for the first match on the 17 August.

The 'Bulletin,' on 15 August, 1907, probably caught the popular mood when it said: "The sudden apparition of 'professional' rugby in Sydney broke up the fountains of Great Platitude and opened the windows of Canting Humbug. All the so-called 'professional' rugbyites propose to do is establish football on the same basis as cricket. The community that rather sympathises with the cricketers, in their struggle against the proposal of the Board to reduce the fee from £25 to £15 per match, is shocked at the proposed extension of a much milder form of remuneration to the Rugby footballer. Could hypocrisy and humbug go further?" [3] Yet much of the newspaper coverage in Sydney, as had been the case in New Zealand, had stridently opposed professionalism. One of the outcomes was the 'All Golds' name itself, a play on their new status as professionals and later much used to differentiate this New Zealand team from other New Zealand sides, but first coined by the Sydney Morning Herald as a headline.

When the first contingent of New Zealanders docked in Sydney on Tuesday, 13 August, 1907, it was to a fine reception. Baskiville wrote: "We were met at the wharf by Mr Hoyle, President of the New South Wales Rugby League, which has been formed with the object of putting representative players and club players as well, on a better footing financially and otherwise, than they enjoyed while playing under the New South Wales Rugby Union. There were also present Messrs Trumper, Boss, Hennessy, Burdon and Giltinan, all members of the executive of the League. We were driven to the Gresham Hotel, which is to be our headquarters in Sydney. It is situated immediately opposite the Town Hall." [4]

Baskiville's description of the team's first days in Australia is evocative of similar memories from later sides: "The weather here ever since we arrived has been delightful," he said ... "though too hot for a strenuous game of football." [5] Yet despite the heat and dust they practised well, acclimatising to the hotter conditions, but also finding the grounds harder than in New Zealand, and less forgiving. Training provided a chance for some to renew old combinations and gave others the opportunity to get to know their teammates' play for the first time, and also to work with their captain.

Both on and off the field, the leadership of any touring side is important. In electing Wright for that task, they had a fine player as well as a man who commanded respect. For a big person he was exceptionally mobile. Wright played the game with enthusiasm, and he relished opportunities to drive the ball hard back at the opposition. He took the training initially and had an able forward lieutenant in 'Massa' Johnston. Duncan McGregor played a similar role coaching the backs. Practices were not greatly different, at least in the time taken, from today's, usually lasting about an hour and a half with a solid work-out, then a cold shower and a good rub down. They tried to form a combination, but with the Aucklanders not having yet arrived, it was difficult. Both on and off the field it was a busy time and they had to refuse numerous invitations. But when in public, Wright spoke well on the team's behalf.

They also managed to get some spare time for seeing the sights. Baskiville notes: "We visited the Glacarium where ice skating is enjoyed by hundreds of people. Our boys, however, were content to watch proceedings. Perhaps they were wise, as a fall on the ice might very easily result in a severe strain, and we do not want anyone to be out of action." [6] Evenings were free time and they enjoyed the variety of entertainment available in the bustling metropolis. Baskiville observed: "There seems to be no end of theatres and music halls in this city, and some very good nights have been spent by the boys." [7]

They visited the Royal Agricultural Ground on Tuesday afternoon.

With the professional All Blacks cornering much of the available football talent, the amateur All Blacks lost 0-14 to New South Wales in 1907.

C. J. PEARCE, Forward.

Albion, 1903   Christchurch
Canterbury, 1903-4-5-6   South Island, 1906
New Zealand, 1907

Typically, the All Blacks wanted to walk over the field they were due to play on. Then they were also shown over the then Sydney Cricket Club's Ground. When practices started in earnest they found out quickly what Australian grounds could be like. Baskiville wrote: "The men all felt very sore after training, as the ground here is very hard, far worse than our grounds in the middle of summer." [8] They had their first injury when Lavery fell, requiring him to be replaced for the first game. To loosen up next morning, they strolled out to the baths at Woolloomooloo Bay before breakfast and "thoroughly enjoyed a swim." By this stage they would have been looking forward to the arrival of the Auckland members on Friday, the day before the first game. Being keen to do well in it, and realising its importance, they had trained the day before in the morning and all "felt fairly fit." The afternoon was taken up with a visit to the zoo.

The New South Wales Rugby League were determined to host this team in the traditional manner accorded other national sides, and had booked the Sydney Town Hall and sold 400 tickets around the city to give the New Zealanders a full welcome on the Thursday evening. Baskiville noted that the New Zealanders filed in looking very shy. He thought Hoyle made a forceful speech explaining the objects of the new league "which was followed by a splendid variety of

D. GILCHRIST, Forward.

Melrose, Wellington, 1904
Wellington County, 1904-5-6-7
New Zealand, 1907

entertainment." [9] Harry Palmer, the New Zealand Manager, told of the New Zealanders' surprise at the progress made in Australia, and he thanked them for the warmth of their welcome. With a clear view of what he wanted to see also happen in New Zealand, he suggested that the Australians send a team to New Zealand in 1908, and said he would personally put up a guarantee of £1000.

Palmer at that time owned Wellington's leading restaurant and catering establishment on Lambton Quay and he also had other business interests. There was no question about his ability to extend that level of financial backing. Through his personal wealth he could reduce the financial risk associated with any venture of the type he was proposing. "Money would not stop him making the new movement a success," he said. Baskiville speaking a little on how the tour got started said light-heartedly that he and some of his friends had wanted to go "Home" for a trip and that it had evolved from there. In recognition of his pivotal role they cheered Jim Giltinan. Friday saw the arrival of the SS Victoria from Auckland at 10pm, bringing the remainder of the All Black contingent, followed later by Smith, Dunning and W Wynyard. The ship docked after a rough passage. Many players were sick. Four had to play the next day keenly

J. R. WYNYARD, Five-Eights.

North Island, 1905 Auckland, 1905-6-7
New Zealand, 1907

aware of the need both to perform well and to win, and the tour depended to some degree on how well they began.

The All Blacks were under immediate pressure as many had only met one another twelve hours before they were due to play. Combinations could not be worked out. If history is used as a guide, New Zealand's record in matches against Australian sides was impressive. During 23 years of football and 14 encounters against New South Wales, New Zealand had won 11 games and New South Wales two, with one being drawn. However the, then just recently completed, 1907 tour by the amateur All Blacks, had been more evenly contested, with the New Zealand side being weakened by the absence of the players who had refused to sign the amateur declaration, and whom the Australians now faced. That team, while defeating New South Wales 13-0 in the first game, had lost 0-14 at Sydney in the second encounter - notably when Messenger starred for the Australians. The professional All Blacks were therefore about to face well-prepared and difficult opponents.

Sydney, with its tightly assembled housing, stretched from the coast and its beautiful beaches at Bondi and Coogee to the inner city and then west to Glebe and Balmain. In the north there was Manly and then the city spread south

W. T. WYNYARD, Five-Eights.

North Island, 1901-7
New Zealand in South Africa, 1902
Auckland, 1907   New Zealand, 1907

towards Rockdale and Botany Bay. It had a tram system capable of carrying large crowds. The Sydney Cricket Ground was not available to the new league and to stage the games they obtained the Royal Agricultural Society's Ground at Moore Park. It was an Australian Rules ground usually and to fit the rugby ground in, the Rules posts were taken out and the ground's aspect was turned through 90 degrees. Of this it was said the re-arrangement was popular with the shilling patrons, and correspondingly unpopular with the reserves - the stands being at the opposite end. Match day arrangements apart, the organisers were also concerned that Sydney might have recently been exposed to too much football having just had the series against the amateur All Blacks played in that city. The public's reaction to the split was also unknown, but the Australian love for the rebel and the battler might work in the organisers' favour. One reporter wrote: "The New Zealand 'Lily-white' amateur footballers are away, and how to beat the All Blacks is past history. The burning question here now, next to the new tariff reform, is the professional football upheaval. "To be paid or not to be," is the query at every street corner and in every cafe or lounge bar..." and... "Here there is a very widespread opinion that the footballer should receive the same treatment as the cricketer, and get his share of the 'plum'." [10] Every pub,

69

A. CALLAM, Forward.

Melrose, 1903   Wellington, 1905-6-7
New Zealand, 1907

and there were many, had its allegiance to a club in a city that had its own social divisions. It was from these inner city clubs that the new league drew its initial players to play against the Professional All Blacks. The two teams chosen to play were:

New Zealand: Fullback, HS Turtill (Canterbury); three-quarters, E Wrigley (Wairarapa), LB Todd and H Rowe (Auckland); five-eighths, J Wynyard (Auckland), D McGregor (Canterbury); halfback, A Kelly (Wellington); wing-forward, E Tyne (Wellington); forwards, D Gilchrist (Wellington), C Pearce (Canterbury), T Cross (Wellington), HR 'Bumper' Wright (Wellington), C Byrne (Wellington), WH Mackrell (Auckland), E Watkins (Wellington).

New South Wales: Fullback, C Hedley (Glebe); three-quarters, J Stunts (Easts), E Fry (Souths), H Messenger (Easts), F Cheadle (Newtown); five-eighths, A Rosenfeld (Easts); halfback, L D'Alpuget (Easts); forwards, R Graves (Balmain), H Brackenregg (Easts), W A Cann (Souths), P Moir (Glebe), S Pearce (Easts), HC Hamill (Newtown), AS Hennessy (Souths), R Mable (Easts). Referee, George Boss; touch judges, George Hay and W Johnston.

W. TYLER, Forward.

City, 1900   Auckland, 1904-5-6-7
New Zealand, 1907

The organisers might be forgiven if they were nervous. No-one really knew to just what extent the public would support the rebels and how many would continue to only go to amateur football, but they need not have worried. The crowds began to stream into the ground well before kick-off by which time the total spectators had reached 20,000. It was a capacity crowd far exceeding everyone's expectations and the ground was packed. If it had been able to be played at the Sydney Cricket Ground there would have been closer to 30,000 admitted. The special correspondent for the Canterbury Times wrote: "Last Saturday here the most sanguine of professional supporters did not anticipate an attendance of more than 12,000. To see a big 20,000 present was quite a revelation to me, as well as to everyone else." Conditions were perfect, fine overhead. He described the scene at the ground as "quite Italian in fact ... a band played music in one corner of the enclosed space. Boys and men raced through the crowd selling peanuts, chocolates and lemonade calling: "All yer new Australian manufacture: her you are." [11] For a grass-roots rugby revolution, it was appropriate that the New South Wales team for the first match was chosen by Burdon and Graves, both players, and that they were being assisted in that task by Dally Messenger.

WM. TREVARTHEN, Forward,

Newton Club Ohinemuri, 1900
Auckland, 1904-5-6-7 New Zealand, 1907

The All Blacks had stayed in their hotel during the morning, doubtless making as thorough a mental preparation as was possible. They would have been right to be nervous, it was their first game together, they had not been able to practise as a full team, they were playing away from home, and the Australians had just come off a fine series against the amateur All Blacks. Yet with the aptly named Mr Boss as referee, the game was to be one of the best witnessed for years.

Baskiville had a copy of the Northern Union rules, but it was agreed that the game be played under rugby union rules, probably because no-one knew precisely how the Northern Union 13 man a-side rules worked. True to tradition, the New Zealanders played in their black jerseys with the silver fern, the New South Welshmen wore jerseys that were a darker shade of light blue than the orthodox light blue of New South Wales and they were emblazoned with a large white kangaroo. They took the field at 3.30pm to deafening roars of approval. After the New Zealanders did their haka, Jim Giltinan took the ceremonial kick-off. New South Wales won the toss and defended the Paddington end. The first half saw a lot of movement between the two 25 yard lines. One report said of the All Blacks that they were "big lumpy men of the kick and rush variety which

W. MACKRELL, Forward.

City, 1900   Auckland, 1903-4-5
North Island, 1905
Toured Great Britain 1905-6
New Zealand, 1907

bore over everything in their way." For New South Wales, Peter Moir went close to scoring, but held onto the ball. Eventually the All Blacks secured the ball from a long throw into the lineout, Wynyard took it to the backs. He then passed for the captain, 'Bumper' Wright, to score. Just prior to half-time, Dick Wynyard again cut through brilliantly and in passed to Lance Todd diligently backing up to score. Half-time saw the score at 6-nil. Shortly after the resumption, Messenger deftly picked up a ball, which Fry dropped, to score. The New Zealanders, stung into action, swept downfield only to go into touch in goal. Messenger's reputation had gone before him and the Blacks marked him very closely. However, despite having his jersey ripped off his back by two forwards, he still managed to have a major impact, getting attacking kicks away and running with pace. With full-time nearing and at 6-3 to New Zealand it was anyone's game. Wrigley broke clear for New Zealand but Messenger's brilliant tackling stopped the possibility of a try. From a kick, Dick Wynyard passed to Wrigley who goaled for New Zealand.

The crowd urged the 'Blues' on. Messenger picked up near the halfway and shot clean through the All Black forwards - he passed to Cann who scored with two opponents on his back. When Messenger converted there was only one point

C. BYRNE, Forward.

Petone, 1906 Wellington, 1906-7
Wellington Provincial 1907
New Zealand, 1907

in it at 9-8 to New Zealand. Just on full time Stuntz dropped a pass and Tom 'Angry' Cross picked up to drive over for New Zealand, making the final score 12-8 to New Zealand.

Overall the honours were shared, with the stars being Wynyard and Messenger. If the game was characterised by one feature it was the disjointed play on both sides - but this was hardly surprising given the way the teams had been brought together. Of 'regrettable' incidents there were none, and the newspaper reports credited both sides with a good exhibition. Baskiville noted of Rowe's play: "He will be a very dangerous man both on attack and defence." And of Wynyard he said: "He is a young, well-knit lad, who showed considerable promise, and played a really fine game from kick-off to no-side." He singled out his captain, Wright, saying: "This fine player was at the top of his form, and although he played lock in the scrum, it was wonderful to see how he shone in the loose." [12] For the 'Blues,' Sydney newspaper reports spoke glowingly of Messenger's 'individual effort', who was said to have played the game of his life. Of the forwards, they singled out Moir, Cann and Hennessy, the captain, for special praise.

Importantly for the participants and administrators the event itself had been

C. DUNNING, Forward.

Ponsonby, 1900   Gisborne, 1903-4
Auckland, 1905-6-7   North Island, 1906
New Zealand, 1907

a success. The public had attended beyond what had been expected, and they approved of what they saw. The Bulletin commented: "The Maorilanders were a fine-looking set of men, much superior in appearance, decency and honesty of play to the amateur All Blacks. There was no elbow work in the lineouts, the scrums were managed with absolute fairness and the offside tactics (wing-forward play) which disgraced the amateurs, were conspicuous by their absence." The play was vigorous but fair and the paying public were well satisfied with 'professional rugby' antipodes style. The Bulletin described the game as "a fair test of Rugby Football, and not a struggle to score points by any and every means whatever. The result was that the professional team made a good impression on spectators and opponents alike." [13] The teams themselves seemed to get on very well, posing unusually for a joint photograph, as well as a separate one for each team. Messenger, the idol, had drawn his own special fans, being both the Gasnier and Meninga of his era in Australia. The match over, the teams dined together at the Gresham Hotel in the evening, the traditional toasts being made by Harry Hoyle in the Chair.

The day after a football match is usually one for reflection, and for the treatment of injuries, but with a first-up win and only a few grazes, the All

Blacks were in good humour, visiting a boxing competition in the morning. And what trip to Sydney is complete without a trip on the sparkling harbour. In the afternoon Baskiville notes: "most of the 'boys' went across to Manly and all thoroughly enjoyed their outing." The burning question on the public's mind was which would endure - the Union or the League; which would prove to be the elephant and which the small boy. As Mr Harry Hoyle had said after the meeting at Bateman's Crystal Hotel, founding the League: "We Australians have a peculiar knack of doing things in our own way." [14]

1   Ian Heads, True Blue, Sydney, 1992, p.20.
2   Ibid, p.18.
3   *The Bulletin*, 15 August, 1907.
4   *Lyttelton Times*, 31 August, 1907.
5   Ibid.
6   Ibid.
7   Ibid.
8   Ibid.
9   Ibid.
10   *Canterbury Times*, 4 September, 1907.
11   Ibid.
12   Ibid.
13   *The Bulletin*, 22 August, 1907.
14   *Daily Telegraph*, 13 August, 1907.

7. MANAGEMENT & MESSENGER

Team meetings are the hub of any tour, with the side for the next game being announced, and jobs being either allocated to non-playing members or volunteered for. Off the field there was a lot to discuss. They now met together as a team for the first time and the co-operative nature of the undertaking meant they all shared in the team's business affairs. Meetings were a frequent and formal part of this team's touring programme - players and managers discussed what lay ahead, organised schedules for each day and made the arrangements necessary for functions and trips.

Quite apart from the routine day-to-day arrangements, this side also undertook the unique task of forming itself into a legal self-governing entity. Unlike the amateur All Blacks, who were accountable directly to the New Zealand Rugby Union, the professional All Blacks had to define their own responsibilities and also their duties to the team, as well as to the wider public. There were no rules by which they could be guided. They had to impose their own. Their basic objective was clearly acknowledged early - they hoped to not only enjoy the tour but also secure their financial, and therefore their personal, futures. For this to happen a detailed framework was needed setting out what each individual, in the widest sense, had to contribute and what they could expect to receive in return.

Eager minds, some of them quite young, were applied to questions of governance, legal entity, obligations and duties. There were also those among them like Smith, Johnston and McGregor who knew from past All Black tours, and especially the recent one to England, how tours were run, or should be run, and what some of the more usual pitfalls were. Take injuries. Almost inevitably players get injured and cannot play. But who would judge how bad the injury was? Would it be the player, doctor, or manager? Who would pay the medical costs - players out of their earnings or the team? There were other matters. What would happen, if someone got involved in serious misconduct, or worse, broke the law of the country he was touring? Would it be the player's responsibility to deal with the problem from his own resources or would it be a management problem? And if a player shirked practice, what would the penalty be? What if a member of the party was unfortunate enough to die? While it was obviously hoped that nothing of this sort would happen, they had to be realistic and therefore set down rules that took a prudent approach to protect their own interests and those of their fellow players.

Then there was the important question of dividing profits, and by association, the liability for any losses? Would everyone who took part be paid the same amount no matter what their on-field or off-field contribution? Would monies be advanced to draw against? And what of the inevitable round of social functions - would all members have to attend, or could some follow other

E. TYNE, Forward.

City, 1900   Hawkes Bay, 1900-1-2-3-4
Christchurch, 1905-6   South Island, 1906
Petone 1907   New Zealand, 1907

interests elsewhere? Who was ultimately responsible and in charge? Would a manager, or an elected committee, be the final arbiter of difficult decisions? These were some of the issues that had to be considered, and eventually decided upon so "the combination" might achieve its aims, and yet still leave room for an enjoyable tour.

The framework was laid down in a legal document - an historic contract to which all members agreed. "The Agreement" is remarkable for its clarity and foresight. They formed themselves into a legal entity, its purpose: "to engage and take part in football matches against professional rugby football teams," or "other teams affiliated to the English Rugby Union..." during a tour through the British Isles, or such other countries as the Management Committee deem fit." Each of "The Combination" or team members agreed to undertake certain obligations in return for which, if there was to be a profit from the tour, they would be rewarded. Full control of the tour rested in a "Management Committee", the composition of which was agreed by the team members. The committee, reflecting all the different personnel - managers, treasurer and players - was comprised of Jim Gleeson, Harry Palmer, Duncan McGregor,

Mr. J. HILTON BROWN,

An Old New Zealand Player, now located in Manchester.

'Massa' Johnston, Lance Todd, 'Bumper' Wright and Bert Baskiville. The committee had responsibility for the "sole and absolute government of the said combination". "The Combination" demanded of itself that each member signatory "devote his exclusive services" to the tour both "on and off the field" and that "each agrees to conduct himself in a respectable and proper manner at all times..." and agrees to uphold the "reputation of the said combination by "sobriety, honesty and uprightness, and by the payment of his just debts." [1]

The Agreement included strong penalties for breaches. If a member was, in the opinion of the Committee, "unworthy, undesirable, or unfit to remain a member," he was liable to expulsion and would forfeit all money payable to him. Clearly this sanction was designed to prevent major breaches, yet even for lesser misdemeanours the Committee had the power to impose fines "not exceeding ten pounds," and the final accounts show they sometimes had occasion to use those powers, albeit sparingly. Significantly, however, it was the players themselves who decided "The Agreement" should leave little room for behaviour that might embarrass the members and decrease their appeal to the public. Each member agreed to attend all practices and meetings unless he could furnish the committee with a relevant medical certificate. The punitive elements of it, especially the agreement to forfeit all monies, shows just how seriously they viewed the matter of team discipline, and how greatly they wished to guard against incidents that might detract from their efforts. However if the tour went smoothly, with exciting games and winning football being played by a well motivated and well conducted team then it stood every chance of being a success. This was their self-imposed challenge. The document is a unique example of what could be done by a touring team who wanted to be self-governing. In many ways the outcome of the tour rested on it.

This was not a rich team, every man going had to pay, through his contribution, for his own clothing and hotel and travelling expenses. They agreed to pay themselves an allowance of £1 per week from the day they arrived in Britain. This was actually less than the 3 shillings the New Zealand Rugby Union had paid the 'amateur' All Blacks as a daily allowance. Money earned by the side was to be placed in a Reserve Fund, with no advances payable until the fund reached the initial amount paid in by the team, and with sufficient to pay for return tickets to New Zealand. Counter-signatures by three of the Management Committee were required for any disbursements. It is difficult to conceive of any tour by the amateur All Blacks, either before or since, which demanded from its players so much in terms of self-reliance and commitment - the very qualities so intrinsic to amateurism.

The fact that the team had been formed in the first place, and the structure adopted by its members, reflected the attitudes of the times. The industrialised world, including Europe, and the British colonies, was being swept by unrest. In New York twelve thousand drivers in the wholesale meal trade were on strike. Players like 'Massa' Johnston and 'Jum' Turtill, when employed, could earn only £2 14shillings for a week's work in New Zealand in a metal fabricating factory. The poverty and discontent in New Zealand, and in Sydney's inner suburbs, which had in part caused the player revolution, was in many ways as bad as in England. Describing a simple cafe in London at the time one newspaper noted: "Men and women come for breakfast which is of the most simple kind ... some buy a slice of bread and butter and a cup of coffee for 2d. Some who have seen better days and still have top-hats and frockcoats come in. Nobody speaks unless spoken to; each is concerned with his or her own troubles. Some are dirty and neglected, while others are bright and clean. Women, some with children on their arms, also enter." This was the poverty that this team, with their decision to turn professional, was endeavouring to avoid.

For the majority of them, given their occupations, the £50 contribution to the Fund may well have represented their life savings. This large sum seems to have deterred several other prominent players from joining the tour; a number turned professional shortly after the tour, but did not join the team. Also to go on the tour, the Wynyard brothers, Billy and Dick, who like Baskiville were government employees, had had to resign from their positions, with no guarantee of re-employment when they returned. While the amateur All Blacks played for pride alone, for this team there was a lot more at stake, and they all knew it. Baskiville, after the first match in Sydney, wrote: "It is fine to see the interest every man is putting into his work, everyone realising what it means if we are defeated here. We must win every match if we possibly can, and I am certain it will not be for want of training or looking after themselves generally that the team will suffer defeat." [2]

Their next game was midweek and with Wednesday being a working day, the crowd was much smaller. The public's natural curiosity about the team and how it compared with previous New Zealand teams was also gone. The morning broke fine, bright and clear, but as can sometimes happen in Sydney in August a cold wind blew from the south. The practical day-to-day tasks, such as who would be responsible for checking admission to the ground, were duly apportioned out. One newspaper commented that this team of New Zealanders took a more than usual interest in the 'gate' arrangements on match days.

The selection committee, as might be expected, for the second game opted to play those who had not played in the first one. The All Blacks fielded an almost entirely new forward pack, which included Arthur Callum, Bill Mackrell, Bill Trevarthen and Adam Lile as inductees. The halves were also changed, for this match being Jim Gleeson and Bill Tyler, but the outside backs remained as they were. They went from their hotel in a brake to the ground, as was customary, and with new selections there was an eagerness to play well in front of the crowd of 3000. The New South Welshmen had also made changes. Gone from the team were most of the forwards from Saturday's match, being replaced by Glanville, Tibbs, Courtney and Pearce. In the backs, Devereux and Brown came in, and Cann went from the forwards to three-quarters. This was indicative of his utility value that was to prove such an asset to Australia in years to come. As kick-off time drew near, the wind's intensity increased, bending over the local trees and causing large intermittent clouds of the city's orangey yellow dust to rise and blow across the ground. Despite the conditions, it was to be New Zealand's day. Dick Wynyard, known for his quick reactions, scored first, gathering up a loose ball at halfway and sprinting to the try-line. Lance Todd soon emulated Wynyard's effort after an incisive run by Harold Rowe. New Zealand struck yet again when Rowe fell on the ball after the opposing fullback miskicked from behind his line. The tries went unconverted, the wind by then having risen to a crescendo. It was 9-0 to New Zealand at half-time.

In the second half, Todd scored again, this time from an intercept. Stung into action by the 12-0 scoreline, the 'Blues' charged downfield, Holloway scoring in Turtill's tackle on the line and Dally Messenger converting. Just before full-time Bill Tyler got the ball for the All Blacks and scored in the corner, and Edgar Wrigley who, when things were going well for him, was capable of almost anything, kicked the conversion from the sideline into the by then howling gale.

The All Blacks had been impressive, the forwards were particularly dominant, which led the Lyttelton Times correspondent to say that: "The forward display given by the All Blacks on Wednesday was one of the finest it has been my pleasure to witness; every man doing his level best. 'Massa' Johnston was in his very best form and it was a treat to match him, with 'Angry' Cross, charging down amongst the Blue backs." [3]

Some players were standing out already - Lance Todd with three tries in two games was proving to be an exceptional talent. And of Dick Wynyard one reporter wrote appreciably saying: "This fine young player will, if I am not mistaken, make a name for himself before he reaches home again." [4] 'Jum' Turtill at fullback was reliable both in his defence and in line kicking. For the sake of the game, and for playing under Northern Union rules when they got to England, the All Blacks did without the always, at that time, controversial wing forward - leaving the halfback free to clear the ball from the base of the scrum.

Two wins out of as many games had got them off to an excellent start. They could afford to relax a little and, instead of training on Thursday, opted for a journey to the sea by tram. No trip to Sydney is complete without a swim in the surf at Bondi; saltwater being a tonic for sore and battered bodies. They waded into the sea and soaked up the sun and then thoroughly refreshed returned to the Gresham, prior to going to Manly on the ferry and also to other points of interest.

The good on-field spirit between the two teams continued; in two matches the All Blacks had had not more than half a dozen penalties awarded against them. As sometimes happens if football relations are cordial, friendships grow once the game is over. Dally Messenger, a boat builder by trade, arranged for some of them to go out on his launch, but unfortunately, the engine broke down. There was however important business being conducted.

Baskiville had already been asked by a reporter on the night of their arrival in Sydney, about "a rumour that Messenger was going with the New Zealanders (to Britain)..." Baskiville at the time responded cautiously and merely asked: "How could he (Messenger) go as a New Zealander?" [5] It is possible that discussions about his inclusion may have been begun prior to the All Blacks departure for Australia, but the New Zealanders would have been unlikely to have offered him a place without first seeing him play. They certainly would have been impressed by his first game against them, and Messenger was also probably motivated by the possibility of inclusion in the side. Whatever the case, by Thursday morning the Sydney Morning Herald told of what was happening, saying: "Negotiations are proceeding with regard to the inclusion of Messenger in the New Zealand Team for England. Inquiry last night elicited the information that Messenger had not quite made up his mind. Having got so far, it is considered his inclusion in the team is a certainty." [6]

Having already cast his lot with the organisers of the professional code in Sydney, it would not have been too big a step for Messenger to join the patricians of the rugby code and don the black jersey. 'Bumper' Wright when interviewed many years later recalled quite vividly what had actually happened.

He said that the amateur All Blacks had been in Sydney just two weeks previously. George (Gillett) was in the team and wanted to be in the professional team, but could not go. Not wanting to be seen as letting the team down by withdrawing late, the organisers asked him to suggest a replacement and he said: "Why, there is a fellow named Messenger and he is the finest footballer I have ever seen." [7] Coming from Gillett, a gifted footballer and a great All Black, this recommendation was a huge accolade.

Herbert Henry 'Dally' Messenger was in his prime at 24 years of age. Not unusually for the times, he was one of eight children, four of them brothers. The son of Anne and Charles Messenger, he was born on 12 April, 1883, in Duke Street, in Sydney's Balmain area. All the Messenger boys were apprenticed to their father in the boat-building industry. Sport ran in the family - his grandfather, James Arthur Messenger, had been a champion sculler for England in 1854 and Dally's father excelled at that sport. Although also a good cricketer, Dally's cleverness as a footballer made him unique. One of the masters of the Double Bay Public School, a Mr Molair, first saw this ability and gave him encouragement and advice. Messenger was 12 years old at the time. For some years he was one of the three-quarters of the Warrigal Club, playing in the city and suburban competition. He joined the Eastern Suburbs Rugby Union Club at Fraser in 1905 and in 1906 was promoted to first grade, representing New South Wales against Queensland. He was the idol of Australian rugby union having played so well against the amateur All Blacks. Coupled with tremendous speed and elusiveness, he could kick exceptionally, both for the line and at goal. For the All Blacks his inclusion would give them a first-rate kicker, and an added dimension to an already fast back-line. Peter Lester, quoting his contemporaries, says of Messenger: "One of his greatest assets was his physical fitness and toughness. Dally was not simply all dazzle and skill. His team-mates considered him to be the toughest and fittest man they knew." [8]

The All Blacks were by now preparing for the third match. It had originally been proposed that they would play three matches in Sydney and one in Melbourne, the latter being an attempt to foster rugby in that city. The Sydney Morning Herald reported on 17 August that: "There is a strong likelihood of a match between New South Wales and New Zealand being played in Melbourne on August 28. The promoters are awaiting a wire from Mr John Wren of Melbourne." It is not known why negotiations fell through. In New South Wales enthusiasm for the new movement spread quickly. Two country towns had also offered to send down teams to play the New Zealanders. Morpeth and Singleton pledged support for the new organisation and noted in a clear reference to Victor Trumper and J Giltinan that they were... "Happy to know who was involved and that its organisation was in clean hands." The League had exploited the poor treatment of players by the Rugby Union to rally support. Also the changes had happened so swiftly the Rugby Union was paralysed; there was little they could do to counteract it. The major clubs had simply voted with their feet in joining the League. As early as 7 August, 1907, one first-grade club official had said his team would go over as a whole and play "in the partial professional manner adopted by leading cricketers" if the movement were placed on a firm basis.

It was now September and the All Blacks were preparing for their final match with the confidence born of success. The day before saw them relaxing, accepting the invitation from Mr Jack Hellings, a former champion swimmer, to visit his baths in Bondi. They had also now been strengthened by the arrival, finally, of George Smith, Charlie Dunning and Billy Wynyard from Auckland, whose ship had been delayed. Those not chosen to play left for Melbourne on the RMS Ortona with Harry Palmer. The selectors chose the strongest team possible, as did the Australians - the sides were:

New South Wales: Fullback - C Hedley; Three-quarters - E Brown, F Cheadle, H Messenger, A Devereux; Halves - L D'Alpuget, A Holloway; Forwards - H Glanville, A Abercrombie, R Mable, H Brackenregg, S Pearce, W Cann, R Graves, H Hamill.

New Zealand: Fullback - H Turtill (Canterbury); Three-quarters – G Smith (Auckland), H Rowe (Auckland), J Lavery (Canterbury); Five-eighths - E Wrigley (Wairarapa), J Wynyard (Auckland); Halves - A Kelly (Wellington), W Tyler (Auckland); Forwards - E Watkins (Wellington), W Mackrell (Auckland), T Cross (Wellington), W Johnston (Otago), H Wright (Wellington), W Trevarthen (Auckland), C Bryne (Wellington). Referee, Mr T O'Farrell.

Messenger was making his debut as a captain in first-class rugby. While the New Zealanders took the field, confident they could repeat the emphatic win achieved three days earlier, this game was more evenly contested. New South Wales got first points on the board in front of a crowd of 8000 people with a Messenger penalty kick. New Zealand scored through Johnston following up an Edgar Wrigley drop-goal attempt that failed and bounced awkwardly between Brown and Messenger. Turtill added the extra points. Late in the match, New South Wales had a chance to take the game when Glanville 'marked' the ball close to the New Zealand line. Cheadle placed the ball for Messenger and the crowd went silent, but the kick failed. When the final whistle blew, it signalled another win to the All Blacks. The Sydney Morning Herald thought it the best game of the three. Baskiville also thought so saying:

"Much credit must be given to the Blue forwards for the determined manner in which they resisted the onslaughts of the formidable pack, which was opposed to them, our forwards, on paper, being a very fine set. Messenger was again the shining star of the New South Wales backs, his running and kicking being of very high quality. Hedley, a fullback, also played a good game, but he does not like stopping forward rushes. Cheadle was a trifle off, judging by his other games. He is a very promising player, having a very confusing swerve. Cann played in his best form, on one occasion running fully forty yards before being brought down by the New Zealand fullback. He had cleverly intercepted a pass in his own twenty-five. D'Alpuget, at half, showed very much improved form, passing out cleanly and getting down to the rushes in good style. It would be unfair of me to particularise any one of the forwards, every man doing his level best. The lead of three points early in the game put an immense amount of heart and vim into their play." [9]

Of the All Blacks he wrote: "In my opinion it was the best game they played here, forwards and backs all doing their share, but they were opposed by a very determined fifteen. Most of the brilliant forward rushes were only stopped just in the nick of time. Johnston and Cross were in the lead all day, and with Watkins gave a first class lesson on following-up. Time after time these men smothered the opposing backs, and it must have been very disheartening to them to take the ball right to the line, only to see the chance lost, when they got there. Mackrell, Trevarthen and Wright were very prominent at times. The ground here tells its tale, most of the men having to patch themselves up after a game. It would be novel sight in New Zealand to see a cloud of dust rise from the playing field; it is a common sight after a scrum here. Kelly, at half, played a first-rate defensive game, but has a lot to learn yet about attack. He is a young player anxious to improve, and I think we shall hear more of him before long. Wrigley was not a great success at five-eighths. He was without his accustomed dash, but he was very solid on defence. Wynyard also was not so prominent as in the two previous games. Rowe in the centre played very soundly throughout. Lavery had very little to do, but did it well. Smith on the other wing, once or twice gave a glimpse of what he can do, but he only arrived on Friday night, and he can be excused of being somewhat out of condition. Turtill played his usual sound game at fullback." [10]

The series finished on a good note with the teams having a formal dinner together and toasting the success of each other's ventures. The All Blacks then quietly walked down George Street to catch their train to Melbourne. It had been publicly announced only that day that Dally Messenger was joining the team. But his many friends and clubmates had been in the know. At a grand farewell in Woollahra the night before he was due to leave, they presented him with two purses of gold sovereigns, one from the residents of Double Bay, and the other from the New South Wales Rugby League. Many of the New Zealanders, as well as prominent local players, had also been present.

Messenger now had a unique opportunity to learn the 13 a-side game together with the All Blacks and could return to Australia, bringing with him the experience he gained. As they walked onto the platform, a large boisterous crowd gathered to bid farewell. Punctually at 7.50pm the train moved off, the New Zealanders being more than a little amused when even some of Messenger's friends started handing articles up to him to autograph.

There was much to consider as the train surged through the unending eucalyptus trees on the way to Melbourne - they had been part of a rugby revolution. They had won all their games, but there was work to do, especially in knitting players new to one another into a cohesive team. The games in

Sydney had netted them £600. The news from home, however, was not good, but it was as expected. All players taking part had been disqualified for life from

rugby union. While the honour of being first to be disqualified lay already with Baskiville, the expulsion from the establishment in both countries was of massive proportions. And what of their crime when playing a game that already rewarded many involved in it, including the secretary of the English Rugby Union? The difference was that, being professional, these All Blacks now accepted their rewards openly, therein breaking the first rule of shamateurism. The game was split, not over payments, but over whether to recognise that fact. The Otago Rugby Union, however, which had traditionally displayed some independence of thought, dealt more sympathetically with one of its favourite sons, and refused to endorse 'Massa' Johnston's disqualification.

Dally Messenger - All Black.

1   The Agreement of the New Zealand All Black Rugby Football Team, 24 August, 1907.
2   *Lyttelton Times*, 7 September, 1907.
3   Ibid.
4   Ibid.
5   *Sydney Morning Herald*, 16 August, 1907.
6   *Sydney Morning Herald*, 22 August, 1907.
7   Official Souvenir Programme, New Zealand Rugby Football League (Inc).
8   Peter Lester, The Story of Australian Rugby League, Sydney, 1988, p.18.
9   *Lyttelton Times*, 17 September, 1907.
10   Ibid.

8. FOOTBALL - CEYLON STYLE

Baskiville now wrote off a series of letters that described the team's trip to Melbourne and voyage to England via Ceylon where a game was played under Rugby Union rules against the tea planters of that city. His letters provide a personal account of the team's journey on the ocean-going ships of the day going via Adelaide, Fremantle and Ceylon and then through the Suez Canal en route to England.

"We were unable to sleep on the train, except to snatch a half-hour now and again, and we were glad to get to Albury, where we breakfasted and had a wash, and stretched our legs, having to change trains. Time soon went, however, and at 1.15 we arrived at Melbourne, glad enough to quit the train. We were met at the station by the rest of the boys, who had had a lovely trip. After lunch in town we broke away in groups, to see the sights of Melbourne."

At Sea, August 28

"Once more we are fairly underway, having left Melbourne at one o'clock yesterday. We had very little time to see the sights of that city, but we made the best use we could of it. Some visited the Exhibition and the Aquarium in the afternoon, and others were busy looking up friends and relations. In the evening most of us paid a visit to Wren's athletic pavilion to witness a boxing competition between a New Zealander, C Griffin, and Meeghan.

On Tuesday morning we were all up early, having slept on the ship, and, taking the train to the city, we wandered about, some shopping, until noon, at which time we had to leave the station for the boat, which was to sail at one o'clock. There was a fair crowd on the wharf, and we lined up on the boat and gave our war-cry. It was a lovely, still morning, and we were looking forward to a lovely trip, but an hour before we sailed it came on to rain, and almost a hurricane blew.

We did not feel the effect so much on Tuesday night, and after dinner, rags were brought out, and we established ourselves on the upper deck, where we had a concert, Mackrell being the conductor. Some very fair singers were unearthed. We were ably assisted by some of the other passengers, amongst whom was a Miss Russell, who is under engagement to Mr H Rickards as a singer and dancer. She sang some very pretty songs, and is now engaged teaching the boys some good choruses.

In the morning it was still rough, and very little training could be indulged in, but some of us were hurdle racing, which was very awkward, for about half an hour. After this performance most of us felt very seedy, though not sick. The rough weather continued throughout the day and several large seas were shipped, and at lunch time away went plates, cups, etc. on the floor. [1]

Professional All Blacks Souvenir - player portraits

Off Fremantle, September 1

My last letter was from Adelaide, where we had time to go ashore. We dropped anchor at Larg's Bay, and as most of us were anxious to get a glimpse of the city, we hurried over breakfast to catch the first launch for the shore, which left at eight o'clock. The others left the ship an hour later. On arriving at the pier, we were told that it was about ten miles into Adelaide by train. It was rather a novel sight to us to see the train travelling down the main streets, just as our trams do. After a ride of about three-quarters of an hour, passing on our way some very pretty cottage homes, with palms and lemon and orange trees in front of them, we arrived in Adelaide itself. The first thing that caught my eye was the splendid station, which is a very fine building indeed.

The town itself is very slow and dreamy-looking after the bustle and business of Melbourne and Sydney, and it reminded me very much of Invercargill. It seems to be laid out somewhat in the same way, but as the time at our disposal was very short, we could do very little more than wander round for half an hour. The last train to connect with our boat left town at 11.48 am so we had no time to visit any place of interest, but we enjoyed our jaunt thoroughly.

There was not a cloud to be seen, and not a ripple was on the water as we steamed out of Larg's Bay on our way to Fremantle, and it was perfectly delightful on deck in the evening. There was a different tale to tell in the morning, however. We were then in the Great Australian Bight, and there was a fairly heavy sea. Only two of our boys are very bad sailors, Wrigley and Byrne, and they are still unable to put in an appearance at meals. Most of the other members were able to do a good morning's training, and it looked as if we meant business when we all trooped on deck in our jerseys, to run, box, skip, or do anything else that is calculated to keep one in form. The men are all looking fit and well, and we are doing our best to study the rules of the Northern Rugby Union, which are somewhat different from those of the English Union, but they tend to make the game more open and attractive to the spectators. Of course, we shall be handicapped for the early matches, but we anticipate no difficulty in making ourselves conversant with the altered conditions.

Yesterday morning we were again busy with our training, but were not quite so eager as we were the previous morning, as the boat would not keep still, and the deck was very far from being as level as a billiard table. Some good work was done, nevertheless, and will be continued throughout the voyage, and, as we expect to be in England a week before our first match, we should be able to take the field feeling very fit.

About three o'clock this afternoon we were all delighted to see land, and at six we sighted the Albany Lighthouse, a very pleasant sight after a few days at sea, especially as we have not had a very pleasant run from Melbourne. Despite the rough seas, all those who were not indisposed were out of bed at 5.30 am, and quickly got to work on deck under the direction of George Smith, who has a thorough knowledge of what should be done in training. After an hour's work we all had a warm bath, followed by a wave bath in sea water, a novel arrangement which found more favour than the ordinary shower. We rounded Cape Leuwin early this morning and should be in Fremantle by six o'clock this evening. The sea being a lot calmer on the west coast, we ought to make good headway, though at present we are a long way behind time.

Everything is going on smoothly, and we are just like one big family. For the benefit of our friends, I would like to say that our address in England will be the Grand Central Hotel, Leeds.

RMS Ortona, September 4

Once again we are at sea, and this time, I am pleased to say, we are having a smooth trip. We were due at Fremantle at midday on Monday, but did not arrive until 8 pm, so were unable to see much of the place, as we were to leave again at midnight. All the boys contented themselves with wandering round the town, except three of us, who took the train to Perth, more to say we had been there, I think, than to see the sights, as we only had an hour there. One thing that struck me there was the excellence of the fruit, but it was far from cheap. The display of apples was about the best I have ever seen in shop windows.

On the following morning we were out of sight of land. For the first time a net was put around the ship, and we were able to practise with the ball. This was

TRAVEL IN LUXURY ::
BETWEEN
ENGLAND & AUSTRALIA
BY
ORIENT LINE.

Palatial 12,000 Ton Steamers. Luxurious Lounges.
Cabines de Luxe. Bedstead State Rooms.

**ROUND THE WORLD TICKETS.
COMBINED SEA & RAIL TOURS.**

GIBRALTAR.	COLOMBO. AUSTRALIA.
MARSEILLES.	TASMANIA.
NAPLES. EGYPT.	NEW ZEALAND.

Head Offices: FENCHURCH AVENUE, LONDON.
Offices in Australia at Fremantle, Adelaide, Melbourne, Sydney and Brisbane.

R.M.S. "ORTONA"
at Sea

Souvenir
STEWARD'S CONCERT,
Saturday, 21st September, '07.

Advertisement typical of the Orient Line by
which the team was travelling to Britain.

A memento of shipboard life,
RMS "Ortona"

greatly appreciated, and it makes the training far more interesting and effective. We have been practising a new formation for the scrum, one of three-two-one, and as we have two teams, we are able to gauge the strength of it. The forwards we have with us are all of a good stamp, with the exception of two, perhaps, and as they are 'second call' men, we should be able to place a strong team in the field for every match. A sun bath usually follows training, and we are all as brown as berries, everyone being well now.

Lile, who is an old Permanent Artillery-man, acts as our instructor in physical drill, and it is an amusing sight seeing twenty-eight men lying flat on their backs on the deck lifting one leg after the other. Yesterday afternoon wickets were brought out, and we had some cricket. A North Island and South Island match was played, six men a side, Messenger making the sixth man for the south. He was born in New Zealand (incorrect: author's note) so we have not gone away from the Dominion for our men. The match resulted in an easy win for the south. McGregor, Messenger, Pearce and Johnston all batting really well, and the first named three retiring unbeaten. Tyler and Callum were the only ones to stand up to the bowling of McGregor and Turtill, and the north lost by an innings and 20 runs.

We are now enjoying beautiful weather and a calm sea, but it is gradually getting better, and summer clothing is the order of the day.

This morning we were again hard at work, but it is enjoyable now, as we are able to practise with the ball.

We were joined at Fremantle by the Canadian lacrosse team, which had a very successful tour of Australia, losing only one game. They are a very decent lot of fellows, and at dinner yesterday their manager made a neat little speech saying that he hoped we would be the best of friends. They gave us their war-cry in a very hearty manner. Our manager responded briefly, and called on us to greet the Canadians with our war-cry, which greatly amused them.

We are getting through a varied programme of sports. The members of our team have been very successful as Pearce and Palmer won the deck quoits, and Messenger played off for first place in the peg quoits. The event that caused the most fun was cock-fighting. An entry of thirty was received for this, and, after some amusing preliminary heats, the final was left for Pearce and Turtill to contest, and after a good tussle the first named managed to get his opponent out of the ring.

A very enjoyable concert was held on deck one night this week, all the first saloon passengers attending. Of the 'All Blacks' Callum gave a fine recitation, and Johnston, Rowe, Watkins and Turtill each contributed a song. The Canadians and New Zealanders were prevailed upon to give their war-cries. The second-class passengers were invited to take part in a cricket match with the first saloon, which resulted in a win by one run for the second-class. Four of our boys played - Johnston, McGregor, Messenger and Turtill, and all justified their selection. A very successful euchre tournament was held last night, and resulted in a win for one of the Canadians. Lavery, going right through without winning a game, had first claim to the booby prize. [2]

September 13

Another stage of our journey has been passed, and a day of days has been spent in 'Sunny Ceylon.' Long will the memory linger in the minds of those who visited its capital. We were early astir yesterday morning, and we were told that land was sighted at 4.30 am, and could be easily seen by those who were early on deck. About eight o'clock we passed a small fleet of fishing smacks, boats equipped with one square sail, and a peculiar outrigger, and shortly afterwards we were able to distinguish objects on land. When we entered the moles, a novel sight was presented to us. Boats crowded with natives were everywhere in evidence, and about a dozen boats, or rather logs of wood lashed together, were paddled alongside, four or five native boys on each, and cries of "Me dive, boss," were heard on every side; and they could dive, too. Three-penny and sixpenny pieces were thrown by the passengers, and in the twinkling of an eye they were brought to the surface, pennies they would not dive for until they found that the silver had been exhausted, and then they would grab anything.

While this was going on we were being moored to a buoy, well out in the harbour, and presently a launch was alongside, in which were representatives of the football authorities of Ceylon, and we were informed that a match had been arranged for us against a team representing the whole island. A correspondent of the 'Times of Ceylon' in Fremantle had cabled to his paper asking it, if possible, to arrange a match. After a very cordial welcome we took our places in the launch, and were soon ashore, and were escorted to the Grand

Professional All Blacks v All Ceylon at Colombo: combined photo of the two teams on the day of the match, September 12, 1907. About 3000 people assembled on the racecourse to watch the game, which resulted in a win for the "All Blacks" by 33 points to 8.

Oriental Hotel, which was selected for our headquarters for the day.

Great interest was taken in the match by both white and black people, and excursions were run from all over the island, and the town was packed with prosperous-looking planters and their wives, and others who had availed themselves of the opportunity of seeing a match against the New Zealanders.

Most of us had a run around Colombo in rickshaws, visiting the Museum, the Cinnamon Gardens and a Buddhist temple. We were the guests of the football authorities at lunch and spent a most enjoyable time with them. The match was timed to begin at 5pm, the heat making football impossible earlier in the day, and soon after four we left for the racecourse, half an hour's journey from the hotel.

We took the field shortly after five o'clock. Three hearty cheers greeted us, and we responded in our best colonial style. We were informed beforehand that we were to give our war-cry. It gave great amusement to the people and one lady was heard to remark: "Poor fellows; I wonder if they can speak English at all." Others, we were informed, fully expected to see a lot of blacks when they heard that we were called All Blacks.

We lost the toss, and kicked off against the wind. About three minutes after the start, Messenger dodged through and scored a few yards from the line, and, taking the kick himself, he placed a fine goal. This roused our opponents, and shortly afterwards they also scored a try, our backs being out of their places. No goal resulted. The home team kept up the pressure for a time, but the Blacks soon

reversed the position, and Messenger again got over from a passing rush. He converted again and the score at half-time was: New Zealand 10, Ceylon 8. On changing ends, the Black forwards soon asserted themselves, and Dunning, after a fine dribble, scored near the posts, Messenger converting. Then Cross broke away, and beat the fullback badly, scoring behind the posts. Messenger again converting. The home team, securing the ball, Skrimshire ran up to Turtill, who upset him, but Norman, who followed up fast, snatched the ball and, beating Smith badly, scored at the corner. The kick at goal failed. This was the Ceylon's team only rally in the second half. Tries were scored subsequently for the Blacks by Kelly, Wrigley, and Tyne, two being converted by Messenger; in fact, this player only missed one out of seven attempts, and scored 18 points out of the 33 that were registered. The final score was 33 points to 8 in favour of New Zealand.

The game over we had to hurry back to our hotel, and we had to make our way to the Ortona as soon as we had dressed.

The Ceylon team, with three exceptions, was composed of men over 5ft 10in in height, and it certainly looked as though we would have a hard nut to crack, and we were very hard pressed in the first spell, but all were in fine fettle, and in the second half we were hardly ever out of the home team's quarters. Lockman, as fullback for Ceylon, fielded and kicked well, but his tackling could easily have been improved. Norman was the best of the three-quarter line, and is fit for any representative team. MacWilliam, who scored Ceylon's first try, and Clarke, were also in very good form, while West showed that he was a very good captain as well as a hard-working forward.

Messenger was the best back on the ground and his record speaks for itself. The other backs all did what is asked of them, with the exception of Smith and Wynyard who were far from their best form. Of the forwards, Cross, Dunning, Johnston and Byrne showed first-class form, but the others were little, if any, behind them.

We were given a hearty send-off at the wharf, and everyone regretted that we were unable to stay to a banquet that was prepared for us at the Grand Oriental Hotel. During our brief stay we were treated magnificently, our hosts being untiring in making our day enjoyable.

We recently played a cricket match against the officers and first saloon passengers, and were badly beaten by an innings, but at the finish of the game, our opponents were persuaded to have another innings, and we had the satisfaction of disposing of them for two runs. McGregor was in great bowling form and took seven wickets, and Messenger took two." [3]

After the pleasant time in Ceylon as guests of the tea planters, the physical demands of training going through the tropics and the Suez Canal area would undoubtedly have been felt. The 'Ortona' docked in Marseilles in the south of France, which gave rise to a story that Dan Gilchrist later told. It will be remembered that most, but not all of these players were tradesmen. Jim Gleeson, being a lawyer as well as a player, had been invited to tour on the basis that he would shoulder most of after-dinner speeches and also attend to protocol. They stayed overnight in their hotel, but at breakfast the players, not being familiar with French, asked Jim to give their orders to the waiter. Jim tried valiantly in broken French but without success. Eventually the waiter said to him: "If garcon would speak English, I can get the men what they want." True to their colonial instincts, to the other players Jim was 'garcon' for the rest of the tour.

The playing of a game in Paris had been proposed, but arrangements fell through. That was not too great a concern, however, as their itinerary was already set in place. Of more concern would have been the news from home.

The week following the professional All Blacks departure, the New Zealand Rugby Union involved the New Zealand Amateur Athletic Association and other sporting organisations in talks to get Parliament to pass a law to make professional sport illegal. The Rugby Union canvassed forming an organisation, the Federation of Sport, to promote the legislation at a conference of all sports bodies to be held in Wellington "so that members of Parliament" could attend. New Zealand, with the Liberal Party in government, had entered a phase of major legislative reform. In labour relations the Arbitration Court decided disputes. Government regulatory agencies in housing, land and old age pensions were put in place to enforce the new laws. Much of this reform was welcomed and indeed probably needed. The passing of laws to enhance security and expel the 'evils' that beset the country's citizens was attractive. If a law could be obtained that prevented professionalism in sport, the Rugby Union's dominance would be assured and could, if necessary, be enforced by the Police or some other agency.

They moved swiftly. The football season was over for the year and if Rugby was to be protected by law the statute must be in place before the 1908 season opened. They hoped Parliament would act on their wishes during the current parliamentary session. On September 14 and 15, 1907, when the professional All Blacks were on the high seas, the New Zealand Sports Foundation was formed at a meeting in Wellington. Representatives of many governing sports bodies attended: NZ Amateur Athletic Association, NZ Swimming Association, Hockey, Boxing, League of NZ Wheelmen (Cycling), NZ Lawn Tennis, NZ Football Association (Soccer) and the NZ Rugby Union. Mr George Dixon, the manager of the All Black Team to England in 1905-06 and President of the New Zealand Rugby Union, was appointed Chairman. Mr JE Green of the NZ Amateur Athletics Association was Secretary. Mr Green explained that the chief object of the Federation was: "to obtain legislation for the protection and security of all existing sports organisations, both from external and internal disintegration." There was no promoter involved in the professional tour, but the conference leaders said, "private speculators had encroached on sports such as football, athletics and boxing." [4]

If the Federation of Sport's founders had their way, no mercy would be shown to those persons who broke any new law. They enunciated further precepts to be kept saying: "Another great principle which should be affirmed by the conference is the mutual recognition and enforcement of all disqualifications. An offender in one sport should be made an offender in all." They stated that, "with proper organisation, and thorough organisation, the newly formed Federation can be a law unto itself." To impose these restrictions there was to be a Board of Advice - a kind of sporting Star Chamber "to adjudicate on all questions involving general disqualifications." Of the professional All Blacks, one delegate said: "The Rugby Team which recently went to the Old Country was nothing more than a joint stock company, and the sports bodies of this country should protect themselves." [5]

The Federation had been brought into being by the Rugby Union because of Baskiville's team, yet when its members met subsequently they could not get agreement on how they would act. The New Zealand Cricket Council, with powerful arguments, opposed legislation, knowing its own sport was professional. The Federation did, however, become the self-appointed guardian of sporting morality, each sport agreeing to disqualify from their sport those who were professionals in a different sport. They did seek legislation to prevent betting on sports grounds - and obtained it. The Gaming Act 1908 remained on the statute books until major changes were made by the New Zealand Parliament in this area in 1995.

The Rugby Union, during 1907-08, was not satisfied with the outcome and sought agreement from the Federation to have the 'professionals' disqualified from their respective sports: "disqualifications imposed prior to the formation of the Federation." In other words the Federation should have a retrospective facility to disqualify. This measure was aimed specifically at Baskiville's All Blacks. The Cricket Council Chairman the Hon ECJ Stevens said it seemed to him: "a most unproper thing that, because a man was disqualified by say the Rugby Union, he should also be prevented from playing cricket." Another of the Council noted ironically that: "It means if Webb (referring to the World Champion Professional New Zealand Sculler) were to also come down here, he would be prevented from playing cricket." [6]

When retrospective disqualifications were not obtained, the Rugby Union seceded from the Federation. Bereft of its founder, and with the Rugby Union's plans for it thwarted, the Federation met seldom and by 1909 ceased to exist, but not before having disqualified several athletes. These included a 16 year old Invercargill girl who took part in the locally run Caledonian Games on New Year's Day at which prize money had been an accepted practice since the 1880s.

For the moment, however, the All Blacks had more pressing concerns than their future in other sports. As they approached England, their thoughts turned to the daunting prospect that lay ahead - they were to play combinations who made their livelihood from football in games, the finer points of which would be new to them. It was generally accepted that the real strength of the Rugby Union game had been in the north of England in Yorkshire and Lancashire before the historic split in 1895, and also in Wales. But in recent times, the best Welsh players had also 'gone north.' All these factors combined to present a formidable obstacle; the question was not so much whether they would complete their tour undefeated playing the new game, but rather how they would fare against such well-organised and experienced opposition.

1   *Lyttelton Times*, 19 September, 1907.
2   *Lyttelton Times*, 21 September, 1907.
3   *Lyttelton Times*, 2 November, 1907.
4   *Canterbury Times*, 18 September, 1907.
5   Ibid.
6   *The Press*, 12 June, 1908.

9. PHANTOMS REVEALED

The previous All Black tour to Britain in 1905 had created enormous interest in rugby; their vigorous, open style of football investing a special aura in the All Black name. Reports were received that the present All Blacks had beaten "all Australia in three matches," that they were now on the high seas, and that before too long ardent followers of the game in Lancashire and Yorkshire would be seeing them play against their beloved professional clubs. There was an almost insatiable appetite for news about this controversial team; the footballers who had defied their parent body and been banned for life were now about to visit. Right up till the time they arrived in England only two men, both officials from the Northern Union, knew the names of those in the side. They kept their secret well. This sense of intrigue may well have been orchestrated; with the telegraph then in everyday use it would have been relatively straight-forward for someone to get the names of those who played in Australia from Sydney. Whatever the case, sheer curiosity led to a tremendous sense of anticipation and excitement in the north.

Initial doubts that the All Blacks would come at all had been aroused in January. Shortly after the clubs received the circulars from Baskiville, a cablegram from New Zealand reached England saying the news of a tour was not correct. Baskiville had however moved quickly to counter this, sending a cablegram a few hours later which stated emphatically that, "a side - and a powerful one, would tour." [1] The reputable 'Athletic News' carried background articles on the developments in New Zealand and of the actions taken against the players that made even more intriguing reading. It told of players being dropped for not signing the amateur declaration and of the difficulties the New Zealanders had encountered, saying: "Men like D McGregor, who may captain the coming team, and GW Smith, whose skill was so admitted on the trip of the All Blacks, were deliberately overlooked when it became necessary to choose a

The All Blacks arriving in Leeds.

Officials of the Northern Union
Back row: Mr J B Cooke(League President), Mr J H Houghton (NU President), Mr W D Lyon (Northern League), Mr J Lewthwaite (NU Hon. Treasurer)
Front row: Mr J Platt (NU Hon. Sec.), Mr J Clifford (Northern League), Mr J W Wood (Hon. Sec. Yorkshire County Union)

side to visit Australia in July." [2] The news also included how Baskiville had been warned off any, and all, grounds where rugby was played. With the reasons for the split in England still within recent memory, people in the north identified with what was happening. It had a familiar ring to it and it struck a sympathetic chord. The reports spoke of the tour being "cleverly, nay audaciously performed," [3] and, "they will not be a holiday-making party any more than were their immediate predecessors." [4] Adding to the excitement, reports indicated that the example of the New Zealanders in forming a professional side was being copied in Australia, "whence we may in short time have a team to do battle against the Northern Union." [5] All this speculation and conjecture added to the public's sense of anticipation.

RMS Ortona finally berthed in Marseille after a long hot voyage via Bombay, and then through the Suez Canal into the Mediterranean. From there, the All Blacks went across France by train to Boulogne and boarded the 'Empress'. They finally reached England on Monday, 30 September, 1907, disembarking early that afternoon at Folkestone. There was an excited scene on the dockside and a real sense of anticipation among the players lining up along the side of the ship. Then it was down the ramp and onto the wharf to a fine welcome from their hosts, the men from the Northern Union - Messrs H Ashcroft - President, J Platt - Secretary, JB Cooke - President, Yorkshire, JH Smith, Past-President and WD Lyon of Hull. The 'phantom team' was no longer.

They might be forgiven if they felt relieved as they finally stepped ashore. Baskiville, especially, had had an arduous and demanding nine months since he first circularised the Northern Union clubs. Those involved, or even thought to be, had been publicly criticised by the press in their own country for what they were doing. To have got a team together at all was a triumph on its own, but with the strength of the professional sides they were to play against being unknown, they must have been wondering what the future held. However, for the moment, arrangements had been made for them to stay overnight in London. The Northern Union officials were delighted to be able to introduce their All Blacks to the gentlemen of the press, even more so with London being a stronghold of the English Rugby Union. The whole tour had been so surrounded by conjecture and secrecy; everyone wanted to know who the mystery players were and what they looked like.

First impressions were favourable, especially those formed by the northern papers. The Yorkshire Post writing of them said: "The New Zealanders proved to be a fine body of young men." [6] The Athletic News wrote: "The men of mystery, 'the imaginary team', the 'phantom side', the 'bare thirteen' are with us and the most sceptical critic is silenced." [7] The Daily Mail described the team as: "one of the finest built set of men who could form an invading team." [8] There was also negative comment, notably in The Times, which took issue with the fact that only four of the 1905-06 team were in the party. It neglected to say the side contained nine All Blacks in all, and Messenger, and that it included six other players who had been nominated for the North Island v South Island All Black trial but who refused to sign the amateur declaration. The New Zealand Rugby Union's actions against the players and the fact that the players, unlike other teams, were paying their own touring expenses were not mentioned.

The management was quickly called upon to discuss the team and its prospects, while the players themselves could look forward to two weeks of preparation before the first game. George Smith spoke optimistically about their chances saying: "They are every bit as good in every way as the (amateur) All Blacks, more especially in the forward division" and: "there are plenty of young and lusty players in the team who would go a long way." [9] Earlier reports had spoken of 18 New Zealand Internationals being in the party. Baskiville clarified this quickly. He pointed to the fact that 14 original All Blacks had made written application for a place and four more had made personal requests to him for inclusion. It was clear from this that the obstacles to success placed in the team's path, later confirmed by 'Bumper' Wright, had taken their toll. Baskiville did however state, with some justification that this side was as strong as could be brought together in the circumstances that had prevailed in New Zealand. He had in fact supplied the Northern Union with the names of those coming shortly after the final selections had been made.

They had a short, but enjoyable, stay in London as guests of the Northern Union, joining them at the Tivoli Theatre that evening. The next day, Tuesday, 1 October, 1907, saw them catching the train for Leeds, travelling in a special saloon carriage of their own next to the engine. While they probably enjoyed the journey north through the gently rolling countryside, they were fast approaching cities that were quite different to any in New Zealand. In Yorkshire lay some of England's most important industries, coal, iron and steel and textiles. Hedgerows of workers' houses clustered around mill and mine. This was industrialisation on a scale which many of them would not have seen before. Some of the players had relatives in this part of England and the Bradford wool market and the mills in Manningham were in part being supplied by New Zealand wool, but links with New Zealand were tenuous. With the exception of Turtill, they had all been born in New Zealand, and although New Zealand, the British colony, was still then only sixty-seven years old, they had their own national traits, they spoke distinctively and their general manner was different; they came from a country which at that time, at least outwardly, placed a strong emphasis on equality.

They were due into Leeds' Midland Station just before eight o'clock in the evening. When the shunter told them the train had to stop a little way out so their carriage could be shunted alone to a separate platform, they might have got an idea something special was happening. The surrounding railway yards were in darkness, but as they reached the platform the scene under lights was chaotic. A huge crowd had been gathering after work. For those who lived in these industrial areas, it was a great thrill to at last have an All Black team in their city. There were 6000 people on or near the platform alone, all wanting to see the famous football team. As the train slowly approached the station, the Wellington players immediately saw that Alf Ramsden, the ex-Petone and Wellington representative halfback, was also there to greet them.

The All Blacks in London.

The official welcoming party comprised representatives from most of the major clubs, as well as the committee members from the local Hunslet and Leeds Clubs. Baskiville described the noise and action once they got onto the platform, saying: "A shout of welcome arose. This swelled to a roar as we emerged from the station. It was with the utmost difficulty that we pushed our way through the cheering crowd." [10] When the All Blacks performed their haka the noise erupted again.

The Hunslet Club's officials had arranged for them to travel to the hotel in a decorated char-a-banc, or high open carriage, bearing the emblem 'Hunslet Welcomes the New Zealand Team'. They finally managed to reach their coach and, with the Hunslet officials moving ahead in their carriage, the vehicles slowly made their way down Leeds' main street. Briggate, flanked on either side by its impressive Edwardian buildings, was so crowded, all traffic, including the trams, temporarily ground to a halt. But the interest in the All Blacks and the sheer enthusiasm of the people in Leeds did not end there.

Starved of any international football since its break with the south in 1895, the Northern Rugby Union had eagerly seized the opportunity to publicise the tour Baskiville had offered them. News of a possible tour had been published throughout the country the very day the circulars sent from New Zealand in January arrived. The visit of the Native Team in 1888 to the north, too, was remembered by older people - their open style of football had been immensely popular. All these things had helped create interest and once they got to the Grand Central Hotel, another crowd pressed in to get a closer look at these All Blacks, enthralled by the fact that they had defied their Union and travelled 12,000 miles to play against local teams. The All Blacks who were on the 1905 tour said the welcome they got in the north far exceeded anything on the earlier tour to southern England. [11]

When they eventually got to their hotel, they found a banquet had been laid on by the Northern Union Committee. It was a formal black tie occasion and included the after-dinner speeches that are part of such events. Their hosts told of how the doubts of the tour taking place, encouraged by the New Zealand Rugby Union's representative in London, Mr C Wray Palliser, through his interviews with newspapers like The Times, had been thoroughly dispelled. Cooke, the Wakefield Secretary proposed the toast to "the phantoms" saying "they look pretty substantial." 'Bumper' Wright, Baskiville and Palmer replied on the team's behalf, and it remained for Jim Gleeson to propose the toast to the Northern Union. With the insight expected of a lawyer, he showed a clear understanding of the significance of what they were doing, and the reasons for the tour now taking place; he attacked what he saw as the hypocrisy in New Zealand rugby, saying of those who had joined the team that: "it was better for them to come into the limelight and show they were professionals than remain pseudo-amateurs, who received their bonuses and obtained what they call in New Zealand 'billets' in which they obtained recompense for their football services. Referring to Smith, McGregor, Johnston and Mackrell, who had been on the 1905 tour, he said in showing they were professional they: "were only doing what any honest man should do." Baskiville noted Gleeson: "surprised all by his stirring and able speech." [12]

New Zealand had officially merged its future with professional rugby. It was an historic night with yet more in store. To everyone's surprise and delight, when the formal speeches were over, Joe Platt announced the All Blacks had brought a letter with them from the New South Wales Rugby League, dated 27 August, 1907, which they had given to him the previous night. In it, he said, the New South Wales Rugby League officially advised the Northern Union of the details of their organisation and asked whether England would host an Australian team. It was becoming clear that this particular tour by the New Zealanders was not to be an end in itself. It looked instead to be the beginning of a new era, one that involved international recognition of England's newest football code. The evening then gradually drifted to an end as such evenings do. For all involved, it ended a busy and momentous few days. As they retired for the night there was a lot to look forward to, and certainly already a great deal on which to reflect and remember.

Next morning, the New Zealand Management Committee - Wright, Palmer, Todd, McGregor, Johnston, Gleeson and Baskiville - sat down to business with their English colleagues. The conditions for a successful and harmonious tour were put in place with an eye for detail born of experience. It had already been agreed with the English that the team would be guaranteed £50 for Wednesday matches and £100 for Saturday games. It was also agreed that the New Zealand Manager and Secretary would check gate receipts, and the New Zealanders would be entitled to 70 per cent of gross receipts with the host club paying all the match expenses out of the remaining 30 per cent. To prevent any delay in the payment of gate takings, the secretary of the home club had to provide a statement for Joe Platt, countersigned by Baskiville, showing the amount of the gate within three days of the match, together with a cheque for the amount owed to the New Zealanders. The Northern Union was required to pay the New Zealanders their share of the gates every two weeks by cheque and no complimentary tickets would be issued. They set a minimum entrance charge of one shilling; transport to and from each club to the nearest railway station was to be provided by the host club. To keep matches fair, clubs could not 'borrow' other players, and were also barred from approaching any New Zealand player to obtain his services prior to the completion of the tour." [13]

While important, the gates, like any tour, depended very much on how well the side performed. If they could get good combinations going, play attractive football and win games, the numbers going through the turnstiles would not be a problem. They had studied the new rules thoroughly on board ship, but to play any game straight from the rule book is an impossibility, and so the business of learning the new game began. They were down to training early, mastering the new rules, organising practice matches and working on combinations. There was a lot to be learned, things they had done for their entire football careers had to be forgotten. Some were immediately obvious. When tackled, they now had to hold onto the ball instead of letting it go. Kicks for touch had to be bounced out. With no lineouts, good scrummaging was essential, or they would be spending long afternoons without the ball and be continuously having to tackle their opponents. They were used to having fifteen players, now there would be thirteen and there would be little prospect of cover defence by loose forwards if a break happened to be made through their backline. Accuracy and concentration would be required in man-on-man marking. The odds were really against immediate success no matter how good they were. Also the quality of the opposition looked ominous. Baskiville, writing for The Canterbury Times from Leeds said:

"We have put in a solid week's training, and the whole team is now in fine fettle, with the exception of Watkins, who is still in bed with his injured knee. He is progressing favourably now, however, and is in hope of being about on Saturday. Our training has been carried out on the Headingley ground, but it is very rough, and no doubt this was the cause of Watkins's accident. The training quarters are, however, entirely up-to date, and there is no lack of willing hands to rub us down. On Saturday afternoon, we saw for the first time a match under Northern Union rules. It was between two of the teams we have to meet later on, Leeds and Hunslet, and resulted in a win for the latter by ten points to five. It was a very hard game from start to finish, and gave us an idea of what we will

---

NORTHERN UNION TEAM INVITED TO AUSTRALIA

Dear Sir, - I am indeed very pleased to inform you that we have formed a New South Wales Rugby Football League, to be carried on on similar lines to your Union, only in our country we have not sufficient population to pay men as you do - that is payment solely for playing football... We have some splendid talent in our country, and under the new system must improve "out of sight. " We will be able to train our men to play the game as it should be played. Will you kindly forward per first post about fifty of your rule books and instructions on your game, for it is the intention of our League to adopt it in Australia. Perhaps it is premature to ask you to invite our League to play your Union in a series of matches in the season 1908-9. Should your Union see its way clear to agree to such an invitation, it would help our League considerably, and we feel confident we could hold our own in representative games, having the material to make the best of players. Should you consider this proposal we shall be pleased to receive a cable at the earliest possible date. Terms could be similar to those laid down for the New Zealand team, and we would like a Northern Union team to return to Australia with our team and play a series of matches in Australia and New Zealand. You might inform us what guarantee you will require to send a team to Australia. An Australian team coming to England would be the first of its kind that had ever left our shores, and should be a great boon. I will write to you later giving you further particulars of our movement -

Yours faithfully,
J. J. Giltinan, Secretary, New South Wales Rugby Football League.

J C Gleeson, J H Smith, H H Messenger, H R Wright & G W Smith.

have to face, and I predict that we will have a very hard programme to get through." [14]

Off the field the local hospitality continued to overwhelm them. Baskiville commented on it, and on the scale of the shows and entertainment that were theirs to see for no charge.

"The officials of the Union, and the citizens of Leeds vie with each other to make our stay enjoyable, and we are invited to everything that takes place in the city, theatres and music-halls are thrown open to us, and the various managers have invited us to go whenever we please. We have already been to the Theatre Royal, and the Grand Theatre, but the best entertainment we have had the pleasure of hearing was the final rehearsal for the Leeds Festival, which we attended last evening, and it was a musical treat indeed. There is a chorus of four hundred and sixty, and an orchestra of more than half that number, and the sight alone was worth going to see. Miss Ada Crossley and Mr Plunkett Greene were the principal soloists, and their duet at the close of the performance was a revelation. Tickets for the Festival cannot be obtained for love or money, and the lowest charge for any seat is eight shillings. It is being held in the Town Hall, a very handsome building both inside and out. As the New Zealand team filed in last night, the whole assemblage (chorus and all) rose and cheered to the echo, greatly to the embarrassment of our boys." [15]

The entertainment was, however, only light relief. Training had begun in earnest.

"Yesterday we had a practice on the Barley Mow ground, the one on which we are to meet Bramley on Wednesday, and it is a far better playing field than the one at Headingley, but the training quarters are nowhere near the same standard. This morning the selected team were allowed a spell, but the remaining members were given a good morning's work. Everyone is anxious to keep his best form, as our opponents are trained to the minute." [16]

They were not, however, the only footballers who were quickly having to adapt to the new code. Clubs in Wales were starting to join the Northern Union. It has generally been considered that the game in the north had been experiencing a drop in popularity - soccer had made great inroads in the region since the split. The prospect of a New Zealand visit had begun to stimulate flagging interest. Wales until then had been regarded as a stronghold of the 15 a-side game. The Principality had produced many fine players from its valleys and collieries and, as the benefits of playing on a professional basis in the north gained circulation, many had joined the Northern Union. In May 1907, at the end of the football season, news of developments in Wales were carried in English newspapers and also in New Zealand ones twelve thousand miles from the battlefield. 'The Weekly Press' in Christchurch reported that a Welsh Rugby Union Club had decided to go in for the professional game. That club was Aberdare, and its officials had been summoned to explain their actions to the Welsh Rugby Union. The Northern Union had also assisted the process by guaranteeing the club £15 a match for expenses towards travel incurred in playing every other game in the North. More clubs were soon to follow Aberdare's example.

It was also generally recognised by even the most ardent rugby union people, that the rule changes adopted by the Northern Union had improved the game, both for the players and as a spectacle for the public. Baskiville was already painting an optimistic picture regarding its prospects. Speaking of the future professional rugby held in the Southern Hemisphere he said: "In Australia it has already taken firm root," and he predicted that "in a couple of seasons amateurs will be wiped clean out." [17]

But with their first game only two weeks away, the New Zealanders had to adapt quickly and this was not a time for predictions. The new game was faster; there were fewer stoppages in play, and fewer chances for players to catch their breaths. It was not only the adaptations that would be hard. In Yorkshire and Lancashire ground conditions were heavy, the weather wet and cold. The chances of playing open rugby would be severely hampered. The Native Team, the only other New Zealand rugby side to play there had lost half of their games when in the north, falling victim to Hull, Wakefield Trinity, Halifax, Bradford, Castleford, Oldham, Leigh and Swinton. And of course the 1905 All Blacks played none of these clubs. Together with their tradition of rugby, the northern clubs had vast population centres on which to draw. Being professional clubs, they were well organised and they played twice weekly; their players had forged well understood partnerships. It had been said before the New Zealanders left home that it would be a difficult tour; just how difficult it would be they could not have known. Only with the benefit of historical hindsight can this be fully appreciated.

It was a full itinerary; they would be playing non-stop for five months. There were thirty-five games in total. The first twenty-five were against clubs, and then there were three against the county sides, Yorkshire, Lancashire and Cumberland. In between were two games against Wales and an English XIII, and after these there would eventually be three Tests played against Great Britain. They also had their own individual pride to uphold as players, as well as high expectations to be met at home. When it had become obvious the tour was going ahead, New Zealanders started to cast aside earlier prejudices. The side's victories, and early good form and discipline in Australia, also helped immensely. Newspapers in New Zealand posed the question as to whether these All Blacks could defeat the teams the 1905 team had not played.

For the players, there was much to consider. They knew the side had potential; it contained a set of forwards hardened by fiercely contested inter-provincial and Ranfurly Shield rugby. In the backs they had talented players, backs who had great speed and personal skill. But would they be a match for the well-drilled professionals on their home grounds? It was important they begin well and then go on to establish a reputation of which they could be proud.

There were two practice games at Headingley. JH Smith of the Northern Union Sub-committee acted both as their coach and as an interpreter of the strange rules. By 9 October they were ready for their first scheduled match against Bramley. They had come such a long way, and their organisation had been so attentive to detail, that to lose the first match was unthinkable. Bramley had finished second to bottom of the league in 1906 but in the current 1907 season they had won three of their four matches. The New Zealanders, aware they were playing against a winning side, and wanting to start their tour on a winning note, saw the danger and selected a top team for the first encounter played on 9 October, 1907, at McLaren Field.

1   *The Athletic News*, 9 September, 1907.
2   Ibid.
3   Ibid.
4   Ibid.
5   Ibid.
6   *The Yorkshire Post*, 1 October, 1907.
7   *The Athletic News*, 7 October, 1907.
8   *The Daily Mail*, 1 October, 1907.
9   *The Yorkshire Post*, 1 October, 1907.
10   *The Press*, 13 November, 1907.
11   Ibid.
12   Ibid.
13   Minutes of Northern Union, 2 October, 1907.
14   *Canterbury Times*, 27 November, 1907.
15   Ibid.
16   Ibid.
17   *The Yorkshire Post*, 1 October, 1907.

10. FIRST GAMES

Bramley proved a far harder side than the New Zealanders had been led to believe, and were difficult opponents when playing on a perfectly groomed, though slightly sloping, ground in front of six thousand parochial supporters. One commentator wrote: "The Yorkshire Club never played so well or pluckily." When the All Blacks tried the rugby union tactic of screwing the scrum, Bramley merely fell on the ball before the All Blacks could dribble it away downfield. The All Blacks also played five forwards against six, Tyler acting in the wing-forward role. This saw them getting pushed off the ball and Tyler, compounding the problems when he came around the scrum, was penalised for being offside. The manner of the All Blacks play was to be expected; they were after all a rugby union team playing rugby league for the first time.

Bramley's backs ran well, especially Sedgwick, and the All Blacks took a long time to get into the game. When they did they impressed, especially George Smith and also Wynyard, with clever running from scrum-half. Tries eventually came in the second half. Tyler scored twice, and Wrigley, Smith and Rowe, got one each. Messenger goaled some of these, and with one kick hit the top of the uprights from halfway. A perceptive commentator said: "in a close match his ability to bring off these long shots may prove a winning advantage to his side." The final result saw New Zealand beating Bramley 25-6. They had played well, and in a way had served notice on the other clubs that, despite being new to the rules, there was plenty of talent in this team. This had been shown by the fact that although they had had trouble getting enough ball, and had also kicked away far too much good possession, they had still managed to win, and win well. They were early days, but the omens looked promising.

The All Blacks also liked the new rules, and Baskiville, having seen Leeds and Hunslet play their local derby, wrote: "There was more crammed into the first half of it than one would see in three New Zealand inter-club matches. It was a revelation to us," and, "football played under Northern Union rules would suit New Zealand spectators right down to the ground except that it seems very much faster than the amateur game." The quick passing also impressed him. Of this he said it replaced: "the tiresome monotonous kick into touch and the subsequent lineout." [1]

Off the field, Leeds had a lot to offer. A thriving city, it boasted some of the grandest architecture of the period, and during October the team could stroll in its avenues and parks bathed in autumn colours. Being invited to an endless variety of shows and entertainment helped fill in the evenings; they were even asked to judge a beauty show.

The next game was against Huddersfield, an improving club in the middle of the league table. Huddersfield drew strongly on tradition, its George Hotel having hosted the meeting in 1895 at which the Northern Union was formed.

The opening match of the New Zealand Professional Football Team in England.

9

Also, not being far from Leeds, the people there were taking a close interest in the tour. At this stage of the tour the All Blacks wanted everyone to have a game, and for this match selected most of the players who had not played against Bramley. On the day of the match it was blowing a howling gale but that didn't stop 10,000 enthusiastic Huddersfield fans going to the game.

Duncan McGregor at first five-eighths was injured early in the game and Lance Todd replaced him. He was finding his feet quickly, the new game suited him. The sides were fairly evenly matched and the All Blacks took time to find combinations in the backs. Huddersfield had the lead at half-time, 8 to 3, Todd scoring. After the break New Zealand improved and Wright scored from a forward push over the line. Later, Harold Rowe also scored when the All Blacks passed skilfully. Now ahead, and with only ten minutes left, Con Byrne and Lance Todd scored brilliant tries, and the final score was a win, 19 to 8.

Lance Todd won special mention; one report said of him: "As regards physique, he is the smallest player in the Combination, but on Saturday, he was the man of brains and brilliance, who turned a possible hard looking defeat into a glorious victory." [2] Messenger's goal kicking had been affected by the shape of the ball, it had been difficult to kick and Baskiville described it as being as round as an orange. [3] But even if the ball had blunted Messenger as a scoring force, if the other teams played as well as Huddersfield the tour was going to be demanding. Baskiville recognised this and took a sanguine view, saying: "These Northern Union clubs play grand football. They are all preparing and laying for us, and in a professional club you know what that means. No stone is being left unturned to bring about own downfall." [4] Wright, interviewed after the match, spoke of scrummaging differences between the two codes saying how hard the New Zealanders were finding it, but for pace and cleverness he thought the professionals superior to the amateurs. [5] Thus far clubs in Yorkshire had been tough, and the crowds partisan. There would be no easy games.

Yet despite the quality of the opposition there were encouraging signs - the backs had exceptional pace, Wynyard, an elusive half-back, could slice through, and Todd was showing signs of being a good tactician; he seemed able to read the game well. Outside him, Smith had shown what a fine tackler he was, and Rowe was a good finisher. Turtill not only caught the kicks that had gone his way at fullback, but as a last line of defence had also tackled well. The forwards' speed to the ball was also paying dividends and they were becoming a crowd pleasing, if slightly unpredictable, team. They had played on dry grounds so far allowing their brilliant backs free rein. What might happen as autumn turned to winter, and as grounds became quagmires, lay in the future.

The New Zealand Executive met the Northern Union Sub-Committee after the Huddersfield game. The New Zealanders wanted to prevent a repetition of the 'round ball' incident and the Northern Union accepted a suggestion they made that a new ball be used for each match, and that it be presented to the New Zealand captain at the end of the game. Also the agreement about payment of gate monies now took effect, with the New Zealanders being paid their share from the Bramley and Huddersfield fixtures in the form of a cheque for £448.15/6.

They now left the open spaces of Yorkshire and crossed the Pennines to play Widnes, one of the large industrial cities of Lancashire, and a centre for the manufacture of chemicals. To win scrum ball was vital and they hatched plans in their Leeds hotel. The rule book revealed there was nothing to prevent them adding a further player - a seventh, to the scrum. It would leave them one back short, but if they didn't get the ball the backs could not be effective anyway. They may also have thought that with their speed the back line could still operate one player short on defence.

Widnes, a club ranked near the middle of the league table, had a proud history, but with it being a working day, many could not see the match. The full-house crowd at Naughton Park of 8000 had been swelled by people who had travelled by special trains from Liverpool and Manchester. With it being their first game in Lancashire, the All Blacks were treated to a rousing reception. The New Zealanders rested some of their back-line stars, Smith, Messenger and Todd, but players like Arthur Kelly in the halves had an opportunity to impress. In fact shortly after the kick-off, Kelly dodged through the Widnes defence cleverly and Wrigley scored off this. With Messenger not playing, the goal-kicking responsibilities fell to Edgar Wrigley, and although he failed to convert his own try, he kicked a penalty shortly after, and later from a difficult position converted a try scored by Harold Rowe.

Sketch of H S Turtill,
New Zealand's outstanding fullback.

Widnes held their own in the first half, Barber and Taylor being prominent, but the game swung New Zealand's way dramatically when Wynyard scored two tries, one from a long run down the touch line. The experiment with seven forwards was giving them more possession and Wright also scored, running clear through his opponents. In the end the All Blacks won convincingly, scoring six tries. The Daily Mail, echoing other reports, paid them tribute saying: "The New Zealanders played a great game, always interesting, and at times absolutely enthralling." [6]

By now the question everyone in the north of England had been asking, that is, whether a team comprised solely of rugby union players could adapt successfully to rugby league, in such a competitive atmosphere and at this level, was starting to be answered. However, the overall quality of the sides in the north of England was high, and although they had played well in their first three games, their victories had not been totally convincing. Neither Bramley, Huddersfield nor Widnes were regularly in the top six places of the league. It was thought the next game would provide a better test.

The Broughton Rangers Rugby League Club no longer exists, yet in the first fifteen years of the Northern Union, this club was a real force. Drawing, as it did, on the vast population of Manchester, Broughton was usually to be found in the top six of the table. Manchester, the Lancashire capital of northern England, was often ahead of London in its vision and enterprise. There is an old saying: "What Manchester does today, London thinks tomorrow." The illustrious Broughton Rangers had won the Challenge Cup in 1901-02 with a decisive 25-0 victory over Salford. They were also to repeat their success ten years later, beating Wigan 4-0 at Salford. In the same season as the New Zealanders' visit they played the Lancashire Cup final against Oldham. Some idea of the support for the game there, at that time, is found in the fact that Broughton's Wheater's Field ground was the venue for five Lancashire Cup finals from 1905 to 1913.

Writing before the game Baskiville said it was to be the New Zealanders' "first big test". They had been training well at Headingley under the coaching of JH Smith, a former player, and also an influential administrator on the Northern Union committee. Smith, in The Athletic News, said he was optimistic and confident the side would acquit itself well, saying they would surprise those who had not seen them. But in preparation for the match Broughton had also been undergoing special training.

On the Saturday morning the All Blacks left Leeds for Manchester by train and as usual got a great welcome at the station. They were given their preferred pre-game lunch, sandwiches and a cup of tea, and when the game started Wheater's Field was at bursting point with a crowd of 24,000. Of the 19 Challenge Cup finals played between 1897 and 1915 only one attracted a larger crowd. Such was the drawing power of these two teams. Both had reputations for playing open football or, as it was called, 'the passing game'. The New Zealanders fielded their top side: Turtill, fullback; wings, Billy Wynyard and George Smith; outside-centre, Edgar Wrigley; inside-centre, Dally Messenger; stand-off half, Lance Todd; half-back, Dick Wynyard. The forwards comprised Bill Trevarthen, Dan Gilchrist, Wright (captain), Con Byrne, Tom Cross and 'Massa' Johnston.

As it turned out, Billy Wynyard scored for the All Blacks after only two minutes, and Messenger converted. Broughton responded, playing their characteristically open exciting football and twice scored. But then dazzling passing by the All Blacks saw Dick Wynyard scoring two tries, the second initiated by Todd after a fine run. Just before half-time, Todd again cut through,

111

New Zealand team in Leeds.

The New Zealanders are Picking up the Game.

The New Zealanders surprised the English Northern Clubs with their early successes.

'Massa' Johnston backed up, and this magnificent forward scored a fine try. The game had turned into a remarkable spectacle.

The second half had Messenger kicking a penalty and Rangers replying with two. For the first time on the tour, the All Black forwards showed they could play as a cohesive unit, their short inter-passing and backing-up causing problems for Broughton. The retirement of one of the Broughton players through injury saw the New Zealanders take off Johnston to keep the numbers even. As the game drew to a close, reports told of play being almost impossible because of semi-darkness in the last quarter during a torrential downpour. The final score had New Zealand 20 - Broughton 14, but it did it not really reflect the dominance the All Blacks achieved, one correspondent noting: "The clever Rangers were always bettered for speed ... and at times the Rangers were bewildered by the rapidity of their opponents' methods... The ball never seemed to be settled, for if one man was brought down he somehow or other managed to make his transfer." At the after match dinner there was time for officials to enliven the occasion with wit and humour. Bert Baskiville and Jim Gleeson shared these duties with Harry Palmer.

They next faced Wakefield Trinity. After the free-running football style of Broughton, this game represented a return to Yorkshire forward play of a hard kind. Trinity, playing at Belle Vue in front of a fiercely partisan crowd drawn from a close-knit town, were to serve them a warning. The All Blacks experimented in team selection, resting star players. Joe Lavery from Christchurch replaced Wrigley at centre. Dick Wynyard went to stand-off in place of Lance Todd, and Jim Gleeson took on the half-back duties. It was a makeshift back line that had not played together previously. The forwards also saw changes with Dunning, Tyler and Charlie Pearce being played. Baskiville later said: "We badly underestimated our opponents." On the day rain fell steadily all morning and a blanketing fog hung over the town and its tenements. The ground conditions were as might be found in Dunedin or Invercargill on a cold winter's day.

A smallish crowd of 5000 saw the Wakefield forwards dominate and the All Blacks made a tactical mistake, frequently kicking to the opposition fullback Metcalfe. This seasoned professional took every kick that came his way. The fight for possession saw the All Blacks get a thorough lesson, Northern Union style, with Wakefield having their feet well up in the scrums. It ended as a 5-all draw, with a try and a penalty to each side, the game only saved for the All Blacks in the second half, with Rowe being the scorer. They had in fact taken a mixed side into a game against fast-improving opponents. Wakefield went on to win the Challenge Cup the next season defeating Hull 17-0, and in 1909-10 won the Yorkshire Challenge Cup beating Huddersfield 8-2.

The now wary New Zealanders chose their best line-up to play Leeds - a club ranked alongside Wakefield. It was largely the same team as had taken the field against Broughton, except Billy Wynyard moved to inside centre from the wing and Messenger went into the three-quarter line. Leeds, a pleasant city, had hosted the team, and Wright said the All Blacks felt as if they were playing in front of their home crowd at Headingley. Leeds however had a reputation of being hard to beat there.

Under a warm October sun, and notwithstanding a counter attraction at Elland Road, a crowd of 12,000 saw a fine game. Despite winning only one out of every five scrums, New Zealand went on to post an 8-2 victory. One newspaper, describing them as: "The late King Dick's Darlings" (a reference to long-standing New Zealand Prime Minister Richard Seddon who had died in office the year before), thought Dick Wynyard ran too often but that Turtill, at fullback, played with distinction. Todd got special praise for scoring a fine try down the touch-line. Their forwards played well, with Trevarthen scoring, but Cross was lucky to stay on the field receiving only a warning from the referee for reckless use of the boot. Referring to what had been a hard game another reporter said: "The Colonials could no doubt keep their end up in a Yorkshire cup-tie." But it was the total commitment to tackling by the All Black backs that had eventually won the day.

They rested on Sunday and on Monday the Management Committee went to Manchester for a meeting with the Northern Union Subcommittee. There they gave Baskiville a cheque for £1,036.10/8, being the New Zealand share of the gates at Widnes, Broughton and Wakefield. It was by then clear the tour was heading towards a healthy profit. Just why Baskiville publicised the financial details, he did not say, but it had a two-fold effect; it showed the tour was not going to be the financial failure forecast by the New Zealand Rugby Union, and it also showed the arrangements were open to public scrutiny.

They had several issues they wanted to raise, among them the possibility of playing a series of three Test matches rather than one. With the international being set down for Headingley, they pointed to the fact that free admission of season ticket holders to the ground and stand, for the Test, would materially affect gate receipts. It was too late by that stage to change the venue and the New Zealanders, confident, and as yet unbeaten, suggested two additional tests be played - one in London and the other in the Midlands. The prospect of large attendances obviously formed part of their reasoning. Games prior to the Test scheduled to be played against England at Headingley on 25 January included matches against five other representative sides - Yorkshire, Wales, Cumberland, and an England XIII at Wigan and Lancashire. While this would place them in an awkward position the All Blacks had traditionally played test series against Australia, and in New Zealand wins over national sides carried far more status than victory over provincial teams. As sweetening, they proposed that the gate be split 60 per cent to them and 40 per cent to England instead of the usual 70/30 split.

The English agreed, and tests were set down for playing on the 8 and 15 February 1908, three months away. For the Northern Union, it offered the prospect of taking their game to the capital for the first time and the Secretary, Joe Platt, was to make enquiries with respect to suitable grounds. The English Rugby Union's grounds were, of course, not available and Platt made enquiries first with the Crystal Palace Football Club. When their ground was also not available, he negotiated the use of the Chelsea Football Club's facility, and also obtained the same ground at Cheltenham that the amateur All Blacks had played on.

They returned from the Manchester meeting satisfied and looking forward to the next stage of the tour. It included matches against St Helens and the then recently formed Welsh club, Merthyr Tydfil. With an increasingly long and worrying list of injured players, and with mineral waters considered useful to the healing process, they now moved from the Grand Central Hotel in Leeds, to Ilkley, a spa town on the edge of the Yorkshire dales and there stayed at the Hydro.

The trip to St Helens offered a pleasant change. They arrived at the London and North Western Station to an enthusiastic reception. Then they were driven around the town in a coach before going to The Raven and The Fleece hotels, the party being split because of the size of the accommodation. That evening saw them attending the Hippodrome Theatre at the manager's invitation. Apart from being a very friendly town, St Helens also held special interest for them as the birthplace of Richard Seddon, and they visited Eccleston Hill, his birthplace.

Remarking on the size of the house, Jim Gleeson observed dryly how strange it was that such a large and important man had been brought up in such small quarters. Then there was time for a light lunch, as guests of the Conservative Club - Norman Pilkington of Pilkington Glassworks, a key employer in the town, welcoming them.

Knowsley Road was well packed for the kick-off at 3.30pm. Joe Lavery displaced Edgar Wrigley in the centres, based on an excellent performance at Wakefield. The game against St Helens turned into another fine spectacle, Pearce playing particularly well and Lavery fulfilling the confidence placed in him. The score see-sawed with first St Helens and then New Zealand, through George Smith, scoring. Messenger showed the star quality somewhat lacking up to this point of his tour, when he took the ball in his own half, dodged two opponents and then hurdled over a third to score. Baskiville remarked: "This match saw the colonials very nearly at their best," and that was probably reflected in the final score of New Zealand 24 - St Helens 5. The press lauded the All Blacks - the South Islanders, Turtill and Lavery, receiving special praise.

The side was riding on a wave of popularity created by their attractive free-running style of play and by still being unbeaten. Nowhere was this to be more evident than when they visited Wales. From St Helens they travelled to Liverpool and there boarded the South Wales Express. At stations en route people peered into their carriage just to get a glimpse of the as yet unbeaten New Zealanders. From Glamorgan Baskiville wrote: "Not for many years has there been so much excitement in Merthyr as has been provoked by the New Zealand footballers. On the platform it was almost impossible to move about, and every vantage point was occupied. People stood on boxes, hung onto the railings, mounted trolleys, some fell off, and that didn't matter. The New Zealanders endeavoured to make their way down the platform, but it was well nigh impossible to budge an inch ... In the great rush and crush several ladies were injured, hats and caps were lost. The All Blacks finally managed to get to the Castle Hotel in a special tram." [7]

Interest in the new code was running high. That same week in Wales the Penygraig Club had joined the Northern Union. With Merthyr being famous for its deep coalmines several of the team visited these. The papers also interviewed 'Bumper' Wright, Baskiville and Dally Messenger asking about the new game. The captain had nothing but praise for the new rules, saying: "It beats the Rugby game out of sight," and, on the no kicks into touch rule, "We are highly pleased that this rule should have been introduced. It suits our men. It allows no delay." [8] Later during a discussion with some Welshmen at the Castle Hotel, Dally Messenger queried claims that rugby was amateur in Wales, and is reported to have asked: "What about money in boots?" [9] On the wider implications of the tour and what they planned for the future, Baskiville signalled his intentions, saying: "We are delighted with it and so will the people at home be when they see it played. We expect we shall be professionalised when we get home." [10]

In the age before films or television, sketches were used to illustrate newspaper reports of games.

Baskiville's references to the rugby league "Play the Ball" rule also reveal how, even by then, the game was quite different to rugby union. He wrote: "When tackled the player gets up quickly on their feet, the latter still with the ball in his possession. He then drops it to the ground between himself and the opponent's goal line, and then either side may play it with their feet. If other combatants arrived on the scene while this was being done they gathered around and practically formed an impromptu scrum, far safer and more attractive than the "scraps" you see on these occasions in New Zealand," where "it is a common sight to see his opponents gather around him and hustle or grab him along with them. Nothing like this occurs on Northern Union fields." [11] Baskiville had found the game he wanted and wrote, "The amendments have done exactly what

"WHO WOULD BE THE HAPPY WARRIOR"?

The " All Blacks " finding that Leeds life with its festivals, dinners, and other odd things, is not conducive to good play, are retiring to an Ilkley hydro where they will undergo treatment and live the simple life.

The Tyke (acting as Turkish Bath-man) " It's er tiring job is this ere fer yer can nivver tell when ye've gotten 'em clean."

A depiction of life for the All Blacks in Ilkley, a spa town.

the Northern Unionists desired they do - this is, they have made Rugby a game of skill." [12]

The traditions of Welsh Rugby were legend in New Zealand; the common element being that the game in both countries crosses all social boundaries. A game between Wales and New Zealand was, and still is, played as the best of one people against another. The Merthyr side prepared splendidly, undergoing special training. Special trains ran from Llanelli and other parts of Wales on the morning of the match contributing to the large crowd. The Cyfarthfa Band entertained the crowd prior to the start and College Field was packed with the largest attendance ever at a football match in Merthyr. The finances of the Merthyr Club were in a healthy state, Merthyr had recently strengthened their side signing Paddum, their captain, from Suffolk.

The game lived up to its pre-match billing, with the Merthyr forwards holding their own. On the New Zealand side, Dan Gilchrist sustained a knee injury, leaving them with twelve men. Not until Messenger broke through and passed to Todd, who scored, did New Zealand get some ascendancy. Just prior to half-time Rowe also scored, as did Reed for Merthyr. The Welsh side was still well in the game, being encouraged at half-time by the crowd singing the Welsh national anthem, leading Baskiville to write: "To say that the chorus sounded uncanny would be putting it mildly." [13]

The second half brought further tries to New Zealand, the ebullient Lance Todd scoring three. Merthyr also crossed again and the game finished at 27-9 to New Zealand. In the end it was the All Blacks' extra pace in the backs, coupled with the opportunism of Todd and Messenger that told heavily on Merthyr. The organisers could only be pleased, the match being a fine showpiece for the Northern Union code in Wales.

The All Blacks returned to Ilkley and the compressed itinerary now began to be felt. They were due to play Keighley, then ranked in the top five in the league, on Tuesday, Guy Fawkes Day. The number of injured made selection difficult, Smith, Messenger, Billy Wynyard, Tom Cross and Dan Gilchrist all being unavailable. It was also an understood thing in Northern Union circles that the team capable of beating Keighley on their home ground was good enough for anything. They were now to grapple with some of the hard men of Yorkshire football and to do so with a much re-arranged team. 'Hone' Tyne, Adam Lile, Bill Tyler and Trevarthen took forward positions, Wrigley filled a wing spot and Harold Rowe joined Joe Lavery in the centres with Todd as five-eighths.

Despite it being a working day, eight thousand Keighley supporters were out in force, encouraged by sunny conditions. The gate of £350 far exceeded Keighley's previous best of £256; mute testimony to the drawing power of these All Blacks. The general feeling was that Keighley would now do what the other teams had not yet done, beat the All Blacks. It was thought their home ground advantage, coupled with the Lawkholme Lane ground being uneven, and also short and narrow, would disadvantage the New Zealanders' expansive back play; but to the contrary Baskiville noted: "it favoured us because of our inclination to cut in and run straight. " [14] Keighley was ahead at half-time and then the All Blacks clawed back in the second half with two unconverted tries to Dick Wynyard and Lance Todd, the colonials winning a close contest 9-7. With sparkling wins against sides like Broughton, St Helens and Keighley, and with the team still unbeaten after a month of football, this side had silenced some of its early critics.

1   *Canterbury Times*, 27 November, 1907.
2   *The Athletic News*, 14 October, 1907.
3   *Canterbury Times*, 27 November, 1907.
4   *Otago Daily Times*, 28 November, 1907.
5   *The Press*, 28 November, 1907.
6   *The Auckland Weekly News*, 28 November, 1907.
7   *The Express*, 2 November, 1907.
8   Ibid.
9   Ibid.
10   Ibid.
11   *The Auckland Weekly News*, 28 November, 1907.
12   *Canterbury Times*, 27 November, 1907.
13   *The Press*, 21 December, 1907.
14   Ibid.

11. HARD GRAFT

The All Blacks were now due to play the Wigan Club. Formed in 1872, it went on to be one of the great founding clubs of the Northern Union. Wigan, the town, renowned for its manufacturing in the Middle Ages had become an important textile centre with a large population, during the expansionary years of the industrial revolution. As far as professional football was concerned, Wigan's credentials were impeccable. In 1894, a year before formally severing its connection with the English Rugby Union, it was, like many other rugby union clubs, already paying players. Its committee members argued vociferously for the legitimisation of broken-time player payments and later for permitting players to be full-time professionals. Many footballers owe their livelihoods to the principles upheld by Wigan and the other breakaway clubs about open financial dealing. Wigan also surpassed other clubs in winning the Lancashire League Championship five times between the turn of the century and the outbreak of World War I. From the rows of neatly formed terrace houses came loyal support for a football team built on a reservoir of local players enhanced by the regular inclusion of the cream of Welsh rugby union players. On the day of the All Black game, 30,000 spectators passed through the turnstiles into Central Park, breaking the ground record. As the crowd swelled beneath a dull sky there was even some pre-match entertainment courtesy of the Wigan Old Borough Band and an acrobat.

For this important match the All Blacks wanted to field their best team, but because of injuries, could not. George Smith took the injured Billy Wynyard's place at five-eighths - a position with which he was not fully familiar. Messenger played at centre and Harold Rowe and Edgar Wrigley were the wings, Turtill was fullback. Adam Lile, Charlie Pearce, Cross, Wright, Byrne, and the utility player, Tyler, went into the forwards. Johnston and Dan Gilchrist were also on the injured list. For Wigan great names abounded, Sharrock, James Leytham, with his explosive pace, and the Welshmen, Jenkins and Thomas.

Just three minutes after the kick-off Jenkins burst through for Wigan, passed to his captain, Leytham, and this mercurial footballer chip-kicked over Turtill and regathered to score; New Zealand never recovered the initiative. It was one of Leytham's greatest personal performances as he went on to score three tries. For the All Blacks, Wrigley scored in the corner and was unluckily forced out over the touch-line close to the corner on another occasion. Dick Wynyard also went close to scoring only to be held up near the try-line. Compounding the All Blacks misfortune, neither Messenger nor Wrigley could land a goal between them from numerous penalty attempts. Not all the action was on the pitch. The crowd was so large and enthusiastic, a barricade gave way at one point pinning Harold Rowe underneath, and as the spectators poured onto the field, he was temporarily injured.

In the second half Adam Lile scored and the remainder of the game saw the All Blacks desperately attacking trying to get a try, but Wigan held on to win 12-8. Notwithstanding their losing the game the All Blacks had actually played well, and it showed just how hard fought these games were. Newspaper reports described it as "a titanic struggle" and "the most exciting game ever contested at Central Park". Baskiville caught the Wiganers' sense of euphoria saying in an article for The Press "thirty thousand people of Wigan are in high glee because their representatives defeated the All Blacks," [1] and: "Central Park is a place noted for the number of reputations that have been lost there. To defeat the wearers of the cherry and white "at home" requires super-human energy." [2] Many later teams were to echo these sentiments. He also commented that the experiment with George Smith at five-eighths was not a success, and that Edgar Wrigley's tackling was disappointing.

In many ways it had been a match of contrasts. Wigan, with robust scrummaging, securing far more possession, and having nippy halfback moves, got the ball to a three-quarter line which could do nothing wrong on the day. On the other side, the All Blacks, although starved of ball, ran well, zig-zagging and changing the angles of attack with short hand to hand passing and brilliant work in the loose. It was Wigan's day though and The Athletic News said, in superior tone, "Needless to say, the approved English methods were successful." [3] Both teams were treated to a champagne banquet at which messages from the King were read out. Wigan, recognising their players' efforts in a tangible way, paid them a 30 shillings bonus on top of winning money.

For a touring team defeat brings its own problems, often unconnected to the events that led to the loss. Despite losing by only four points it appears they could just as easily have won, but the spell had been broken. Newspaper comment became harsher, the honeymoon period was over. One columnist rebuked them saying: "This defeat may only be wiped out if the New Zealanders are as serious off the field as they are on it." [4] It is difficult to know if the comment was justified. Baskiville emphasised just how strong the sides were that they were playing, and that injuries meant they were playing players out of position. Later Baskiville also had to react strongly to an article in similar vein that appeared in The Times, and he pointed out how hard it would be to indulge themselves when only receiving £1 per week.

Defeat at Wigan made the rest of the tour more difficult. There was the disappointment to cope with, and it would be surprising if their morale was unaffected. Games would become harder as teams tried to emulate Wigan's feat. The tour now took a turn for the worse with games ahead being against Barrow, Hull and Leigh; Barrow was still unbeaten.

The New Zealanders had not been competitive in scrummaging; during the Wigan game they had won only one scrum to every five won by Wigan. Scrums, as practised in the Northern Union, were in the New Zealanders' view a shambles. It was obviously frustrating, and what they could not fix on the field they tried to correct in the boardroom, with the Northern Union Committee, in the days immediately following the Wigan game. They asked that something be done so each team had a fair chance at hooking the ball in the scrum, that it not be put under the hooker's feet, and that there be a definite ruling as to which side would have their man closest to the man putting the ball into the scrum - that is, who would have the loose head.

The outcome was the Committee "did not think it wise to lay down any hard and fast definition as to the exact formation of a scrummage", but it did decide a properly formed scrummage must "provide a clear opening or 'tunnel' into which to insert the ball." They also resolved that "the defending side may in all cases claim to be allowed to pack the 'loosehead' on the side of the referee." It was hoped the changes would mean orderly scrums, a clear tunnel, and a defined 'loosehead' before the scrum was fed. The new regulation came into effect immediately, a copy of the rulings being sent to each club in the Union. [5]

It was also at this meeting that the Union voted unanimously to accept the proposed tour by the Australians in either 1908-09 or 1909-10. For the most recent games, Leeds, St Helens, Merthyr Tydfil and Keighley, an amount of £965.7/10 was on this occasion paid to the New Zealanders - in four games alone they had netted one sixth of the total costs for the tour. Financial and fixture affairs dominated these discussions at Manchester, with the Chelsea Football Club having responded positively to the concept of renting their ground in London as a Test venue. There was greater difficulty though in staging a Test match in the Midlands. The Leicester Rugby Union had refused their ground, as had Leicester Fosse, and it was decided to approach Aston Villa Football Club instead. For the match against Wales, the New Zealanders thought the Merthyr ground unsuitable, probably because of its limited capacity. Merthyr themselves suggested Pendydamen Park as an alternative. The minutes point to a high degree of co-operation and goodwill existing between the parties.

Despite everyone's best efforts, some games seem fated before they begin; arrangements go astray, morale can be low, bad weather can tip the balance. In their first match in the far north west, against Barrow at Craven Park, New Zealand experienced all three. The team arrived late, the train being delayed, and the game was dogged by rain. After joining the Union in 1900 Barrow had won the Second Division in 1904-05 and had been promoted. Unbeaten in the current season they drew players from vast shipbuilding and iron works in the region, like Vickers and Main. Barrow were physical and determined opponents.

Spectators had travelled by excursion trains from all over Cumberland and North Lancashire. A crowd of more than 7,000 stretched the limits of the enclosure and would undoubtedly have been greater if the shipyards had closed, as was their original intention. Playing 'Hone' Tyne, Arthur Callum and McGregor, the team was certainly a weaker one and had a Wednesday look, with Wrigley deputising at fullback for 'Jum' Turtill. Blinding rain not only made open play difficult, it also ruined the match as a spectacle. It was generally agreed Barrow played above even their usual high standard and they shut the All

UNEASY LIES THE HEAD THAT HEARS A CLOG.

"The New Zealanders have gained many impressions since they arrived on the shores of Old England. One of those impressions, that of the "clang of the wooden shoon," will long remain. The "All Blacks" simply couldn't rest in the early hours of the morn when the thousands of Wigan's mill girls were proceeding to their work.

An unsourced Northern newspaper's pithy view of the All Blacks' reasons for their form lapse in Wigan.

Blacks out of the game, winning 6-3. Significantly, this was the first match the New Zealanders had played in the rain, and they could not get the ball to their dangerous back line. Barrow asked the Northern Union for a Saturday match later in the tour, knowing the crowd and the shipbuilders at work had been disappointed, but the itinerary had by then already been extended by a month, with two extra Tests and by the addition of games against Ebbw Vale and a second one against St Helens.

They were now to play Hull, on the east coast, which involved more railway travel and these two narrow, but successive losses, gave cause for reflection. The dictum was that the 'seaporters' were a difficult proposition for any side, at The Boulevard, their home ground. Travelling on the day of the match at Barrow had been a fiasco and they decided to go to Hull the day before. If anything, their defeats at Wigan and Barrow had heightened interest, with Hull's supporters eagerly awaiting an opportunity to repeat them. The Daily Mail included full details of the course their entourage would take, and the streets of Hull were lined with townsfolk eager for a glimpse of the All Blacks. Their arrival at the Paragon Station preceded a crowded journey to the Imperial Hotel. In the afternoon they visited Wilberforce House and Earle's Shipbuilding Works, and in the evening there were complimentary circle seats at The Palace. The morning of the match saw them being driven to the Hull Brewery Company's premises for a tour. There Major Glendow, on the company's behalf, presented Bert Baskiville with an intricately worked commemorative beer tankard that is still in existence, having been recently passed by Baskiville's niece to the New Zealand Rugby Football League for safekeeping.

This time the weather gods were smiling on the All Blacks, and despite the higher price of 1/- replacing the price for admission to the sixpenny stand, twelve thousand spectators filled the ground under a bright sunny sky. Being a Saturday match they chose a top side. McGregor earned a place in the team at inside-centre, following a sound display at Barrow, being the first time this famous All Black from the 1905-06 tour had been able to get into the top side. Dan Gilchrist had now recovered from his injury in the Merthyr game and joined Adam Lile, Cross, Wright, Johnston and Pearce in the forwards. The New Zealanders knew they would have to play at the top of their form if they were to win, and did so. One newspaper reported: "Few finer exhibitions of pluck and good football have been seen." Another, "If such games as the New Zealand and Hull match, on the Boulevard ground, were the rule rather than the exception there would be no fear of Northern Union football losing its hold on the affections of the Yorkshire public." [6]

The New Zealanders had the lead, 13-5, at the break, having got three tries and they then stemmed a fierce fightback by the proud Hull side, winning 18-13. The try of the day was started by George Smith and finished by Lance Todd. One report said of Smith "....the famous hurdler, who played a splendid game throughout, made this try in perfect fashion. Getting away from his own half, he beat several men and doubled towards the centre to get past another couple. Todd had flashed up on the left, and at the right moment Smith sent the ball out to his colleague, who went around Holder and Taylor and scored a magnificent try. Such an effort as this deserved to win the match. It showed the Colonials have real quality." [7]

Another commentator noted how the All Blacks were starting to get more familiar with the vast differences in the two codes, "They have realised, at last that kicking, under Northern Union rules, is only advisable as a last extremity and as a consequence, they gave a very attractive display and scored some delightful tries." Although he also noted: "In the later stages they were as helpless in the scrummages as ever." [8] Hull had used a forward in the backs and had still won the scrums through what the All Blacks knew as 'feeding'. Baskiville wrote, "Smith and Todd were at the top of their form. Wrigley showed that he still can defend well if required. McGregor's coolness and football knowledge were of great service to our side. He is well adapted for the Northern Union halfback game. Among the forwards, Lile was noticeable and Cross followed up like a racehorse." [9]

The mere fact that they were playing in Hull, together with the circumstances under which the tour had been arranged, earned them their hosts'

Salford Football Club Co., Ltd.

The Directors

request the pleasure of the Company of

Mr. H. H. Messenger

to Dinner, at the Corn Exchange Hotel,
Fennel Street, Manchester, on the occasion of
the match, New Zealand v. Salford, at the
Willows, Weaste, on Saturday, Dec. 28th, 1907.
Conveyances leave Ground for Hotel, 5-30.
Dinner, 6-15.

MORNING DRESS.   **R.S.V.P.**

---

gratitude; the Club's Chairman at the post match dinner said he "admired the All Blacks for tackling what to them was practically a new game, and playing under different conditions to the old 'All Black' team, because they were meeting trained professionals." [10]

Having played twelve games in England, for nine wins, one draw, and two narrow losses, a pattern was starting to emerge; the footballing standards were very close, and if the weather conditions were fine, and if the New Zealanders fielded near to their top team they could beat the best professional sides in Britain. Their strength lay in brilliant improvised back play, and sharp interpassing in the forwards; their weakness was that the reserve players if called upon to play were not of quite the same standard, and if the ground was wet the balance could quickly swing in favour of the professional sides. Mistakes came from a slippery ball; this meant more scrums and in such conditions the traditional strength of the English forward game came to the fore. This was borne out in their next Wednesday game.

Leigh, the Lancashire club, had strengthened its side for the match with two famous players. Todd, who was by then a recognised star performer, was injured, and the New Zealanders suffered defeat in the rain, being beaten 15-9. Baskiville wrote: "The New Zealand forwards could not get the ball from the scrum. I don't think it was their fault as the Leigh half-back took great liberties in putting the ball in the scrum, but the referee thought otherwise. On the other hand a newspaper critic stated later that we put the ball in too fairly, and he gave us a veiled hint to sail closer to the wind in the future." [11]

The Saturday players now had to play Oldham. This city, the centre of the Lancashire cotton industry is set high up on the side of the Pennine hills, overlooking Manchester. In 1888 it had 265 mills and a population of 130,000. Baskiville wrote: "The New Zealanders invaded 'The Gibraltar of the Northern Union' on Saturday, November 23, and by the narrowest of margins were defeated again." [12] Oldham, together with Hunslet, were among the top four clubs in the league. The men in red and white hooped jerseys had forged an impressive record since they had split from the English Rugby Union, winning every championship trophy on offer - the Challenge Cup, Lancashire Cup and the Championship.

Drenching rain fell all day on Friday at the Watersheddings Ground, one of the highest in the Northern Union; being 850 ft above sea level it was subject to variations in the weather. Heavy snow fell that night when the players were at the theatre and then it sleeted. Yet 15,000 undaunted spectators watched the game next day. Had the weather been fine the ground would have held twice that number. The All Blacks were beset with injuries, the list: Byrne, Lile, Todd, R Wynyard, McGregor, W Wynyard and Eric Watkins. Arthur Kelly, the Wellington and Petone player was substituting for Dick Wynyard at scrum-half. Possibly feeling at home on the wet ground he featured in the early exchanges. Wrigley played at stand-off half forming a new combination. Tyler was pressed into playing in the three-quarters. Oldham fielded their best side including the star players Oldershaw, Benyon and Thomas.

A blinding snowstorm, a new experience for the All Blacks, plagued the second half of the game, yet the football remained of a high standard. Oldham scored twice, New Zealand once - that try being set up by Smith and finished off by Joe Lavery. New Zealand attacked Oldham hard for most of the second half but their defence held. Smith almost won the game when he broke free in the last minute, much as he had done against Scotland eighteen months earlier on the Rugby Union tour, but Oldham grabbed him just short of the try-line. This time it was Oldham who were fortunate to win, and the one point margin with the final result going to Oldham 8-7, was indicative of the high standard the New Zealanders were now playing to.

Amongst all this there were some positive signs; middle ranked players were starting to seize their chances and press for more regular games, these included Kelly, Lavery and Tyler. The Athletic News noted them as: "a trio of players whose abilities are certainly above a periodical place in the team." [13] Charlie Pearce had already established his reputation and was now in the first-team selections. For their next game against Runcorn, in Cheshire, New Zealand fielded a similar team; it rained in torrents and the Runcorn forwards, before a small Wednesday crowd of 5,000 controlled both the game and the outcome which ended in their favour, 9-0. The New Zealanders' form was described as 'poor'; the Daily Mail stating that misfortune seems to dog the footsteps on the All Blacks in their midweek matches.

A string of defeats can test the character of the any football side, whether they be a touring team or just a junior side playing in the local competition. Morale can drop, practices can become burdensome and internal bickering may cause division. It takes a good side to set their face to the wind, learn from defeats and make changes. It helps if the team is basically a happy one. Management also has a role to play - not dwelling on what cannot be mended. The same bad weather that had caused them so much difficulty now changed to snow. Many players from the North Island had never been in snow before and Baskiville wrote: "We had rare fun in it. But the members of the team are not taking kindly to the climate on the moors. The majority of them have had colds and cannot go outdoors. It has been decided to move further south on Monday." [14] At this stage of their tour it would have been easy to let morale slip, yet that did not happen. The Management Committee decision to move the team away from Ilkley - leaving the memories of their defeats where they lay, was the right one in the circumstances. They caught the train to Manchester staying at the Grosvenor Hotel and practising on the Salford Club's ground. They had now been playing continuously for two months and needed some relief. A game of hockey was arranged with the local team, Messenger, a natural sportsman, shone and the proceeds were donated to charity.

They were now at a half-way point in the tour; much had been achieved; the organisation of the tour itself taking place as it did within the conservative social climate in New Zealand was momentous. They had also thrown the amateur game open in Australia, and it looked as if they intended to do the same in New Zealand when they returned home. The game, especially in Australia, had stampeded towards compensation for players. In November 1907, the New South Wales Rugby League adopted a code permitting payments to players of 10/- per day for loss of salary, medical expenses and £2 per week while injured. [15]

In addition to being an integral part of the revolution in Australia, they had won their three games against that country before moving to England to challenge the professionals under their own rules - rules which, while known in an academic sense to the New Zealanders, were really quite foreign. The confidence to undertake the trip undoubtedly had sprung initially from the success the All Blacks had met on their tour to southern England, eighteen months earlier. But even more fundamental to the success they had had in England was the confidence the New Zealand All Blacks always try to exude - never letting the opposition believe they can win, keeping a tight control of the football. Also few teams could boast the blinding pace of an Olympic athlete like Smith, and the Wynyard brothers combined speed with youthful inventiveness. In Dally Messenger they had one of the greatest individual footballers of all times - a man who could beat players with pace, swerve and sidestep. Together with this was the erratic genius of Edgar Wrigley who, weighing close to 15 stone and playing in the centres, made a great impression with power running. Lance Todd at stand-off half had made an enormous impression on the English. He was ideally suited to the game, and being small and quick, he could dance his way past opposition markers. Around these players other members of the team were playing well, some with distinction; Harold Rowe being a fine finisher at wing or centre, and 'Jum' Turtill was a courageous fullback.

In the forwards Johnston, Wright, Tom Cross, Dan Gilchrist, Bill Trevarthen and Charlie Pearce carted the ball up field, and indulged in the subtleties of forward play that only those who have played there know of. They had shown mobility and speed. In the forwards it had been problematic that their opponents could form up their scrum very quickly and be pushing over the ball as the half-back fed the scrum. Wright was diplomatic about this, but nevertheless criticised the practice, meaning as it did that the New Zealanders were losing scrum possession and were starving their talented backs, as well as giving them more tackling to do. The All Blacks were taking too long setting their scrum and adjusting their positions before competing for the ball. The solid but sometimes dangerous set scrum used in rugby union had evolved into the Northern Union's fast-working confrontation which, because it was more loosely formed and looked untidy, infuriated rugby union purists for many years to come. In this phase of play, the professional All Blacks were proving uncompetitive and no match for opposition sides.

It was not the perfect team, and there were some obvious weaknesses at this stage - which Baskiville in writing home readily conceded. Their tackling was not as good as the Northern Union teams. They were having trouble adjusting to that because as rugby union players they had not been asked previously to make so many front-on tackles. This weakness could prove fatal if players of the same or greater pace as the All Blacks broke through. Yet Smith on occasions could pick them up from behind, tackling one player after another - a feat unsuited to his 35 years, but illustrative of his tremendous speed and competitiveness.

But the limitations were not only of an operational kind - structurally the team, although containing nine previously amateur All Blacks, and the cream of Wellington and Auckland provincial players, could not of its very nature be the most powerful side New Zealand as a rugby playing nation could field. The side had been limited in its choice by the fact that any player wanting to be considered for selection had had to pay the equivalent of half a year's wages in today's earnings. Not every player was willing to take that kind of risk, when it was obvious that membership of the side would bring a life sentence - disqualification from the amateur game.

Selection policies also played an influential role - the team was chosen for speed so an entertaining game that attracted large crowds could be played, and the expenses could accordingly be paid. The passing game was reliant on good ground conditions and good weather. Add to these factors the unknown qualities of the Northern Rugby Union and it meant the All Blacks were forging a pioneering path in uncertain territory. In the meantime the team could count many positives; they had established themselves as a highly credible combination having defeated two of the top six clubs in the league emphatically. Their management had been astute. Baskiville had led them diplomatically through a tough media focus, and Harry Palmer, or 'The Boss' as he was called by the men was a disciplinarian, each player having to submit details to him of where they were going and what they would be doing.

Relationships with their hosts had been constructive and Baskiville attended all meetings. The cheques were handed to him and the minutes show he accepted them in the presence of his fellow committee members - usually Jim Gleeson, the Treasurer, and Wright, Johnston, or Lance Todd. At the age of just 25, he had fully earned the respect of the English administrators, who were successful businessmen in their own right. He took on an enormous workload having the overall responsibility for arrangements, and was ably assisted with the public speaking engagements, by Harry Palmer, Wright and Gleeson, who could always be relied on to entertain. Gleeson, in particular, was a great enthusiast for the new code and its development. Writing to an Auckland Rugby Union official early in the tour he said: "Professionalism is extending all through Wales; I think Swansea and Cardiff will be playing professional football next year. In nine matches played so far, we have far exceeded the takings of the last team. We expect tremendous games against Wigan, Oldham, and Hunslet ... I honestly think this tour will realise £10,000 profit." [16] Events were to prove his views entirely correct.

1   *The Press*, 27 December, 1907.
2   Ibid.
3   *The Athletic News*, 1 November, 1907.
4   Undated newspaper article, HS Turtill Scrapbook.
5   Minutes of Northern Rugby Football Union, 12 November, 1907.
6   Newspaper Article, 18 November, 1907, HS Turtill Scrapbook.
7   Ibid.
8   Ibid.
9   *The Press*, 1 January, 1908.
10   Ibid.
11   Ibid.
12   *Otago Daily Times*, 8 January, 1908.
13   *The Athletic News*, 25 November, 1907.
14   *Otago Daily Times*, 8 January, 1908.
15   *Otago Daily Times*, 2 November, 1907.
16   *The Weekly News*, 24 December, 1907.

12. MUD & WATER POLO

With the injury list being worryingly long the team's capacity to field a good side for every match became a problem. Physiotherapy was decades away, and seven players were still out, including Eric Watkins, who had not played at all since being injured in the first week. Without antibiotics, colds and influenza could lead to pneumonia. Months living in hotels away from their usual work meant it was easy to get jaded and listless. And then there were the social engagements and dinners. Menus signed by the players point to endless helpings of roast beef, Yorkshire pudding, roast goose and apple sauce, followed by plum pudding, apple tart, jellies and cream. It must have been a delight to their young appetites, but could it all be trained off?

Yet there were advantages in being a touring side. There was time to work on problems and combinations and to get good match fitness; this often had them winning games in the second half. And there was the camaraderie and pride in being a national team. Also there were some mudlarks among them, Johnston, Pearce, Kelly and Turtill excelled in the wet. As weather conditions deteriorated these players started to play better football, 'Jum' Turtill catching the greasy ball to perfection. Johnston's handling skills, learnt in the harsh conditions of Otago, made him a front-line selection. He, and other forwards like Cross and Pearce, had obviously adapted well. In fact by the tour's mid-point, ten or eleven players, barring injuries, commanded regular top-team places, - Turtill, Smith, Messenger, Wrigley, Todd, Dick and Billy Wynyard, and in the forwards: Cross, Johnston, Gilchrist, Wright and Charlie Pearce. A further group were playing well enough to be sometimes picked for matches against top sides, but they were played more regularly in Wednesday fixtures; they included Bill Tyler, Con Byrne, Adam Lile, Bill Trevarthen and Joe Lavery. Then there was a group who were being selected only rarely: McGregor, Charlie Dunning, Bill Mackrell, Arthur Kelly, 'Hone' Tyne, Jim Gleeson and Arthur Callum.

They won their next game 18-8 under fine conditions against a combined side from the Dewsbury and Batley clubs. Batley were in the top six and Dewsbury were not far behind. Dick Wynyard, back to top form, scored, as did Messenger and Smith, and also Pearce, after a break from Smith. Typically tries were being made by the backs, but important lessons had been learned - for the first time they got plenty of possession from the scrums. Baskiville commented: "It was predicted that we should be overwhelmed, but the New Zealanders rose to the occasion and showed form which had been lacking for a fortnight." [1] They kept the same form against Swinton. Of their prospects for this match the Daily Telegraph said: "The heavy turf and greasy ball have been particularly severe on the New Zealanders in their several recent engagements. They had to oppose Swinton under conditions very damaging to their prospects." [2] This time the All Blacks shone in the mud, improving their scrummaging to the point where they got possession at a rate of 2 to 1. Conditions were frightful and at one point players scurried for shelter covering their faces and heads from the stinging sleet and hail, and stopped the game for five minutes. New Zealand outplayed the good Swinton side comprehensively, Kelly had learnt from the Runcorn game not to kick, and gave a fine display at scrum-half in the mud. Messenger kicked four fine goals, three from the sideline and when he was injured, the versatile Pearce substituted for him at centre.

The good form continued, and against Rochdale Hornets, New Zealand won 19-0. They had studied the rules again before their previous two matches and had found there was nothing to stop them having four men in the front-row of the scrum. Gilchrist, Lile, Cross and Pearce, took up these positions and for the first time on the tour the All Blacks had a good supply of ball. Despite heavy ground conditions, this meant their backs could get moving more often and passed and ran well, Kelly from half-back showing touches of class. For Wrigley it was a special day at Rochdale. His father came from there and relatives still lived there. Baskiville wrote: "This seemed to inspire him. His strong 'healthy' dashes were a feature of the game." [3] An unusual incident occurred during the game. Against all the practices of the day, Dick Wynyard, from a penalty tap-kicked the ball to himself and scored, but the try was disallowed. Play was instead taken back to the mark and New Zealand were given the shot at goal - which Messenger duly missed.

Baskiville had nothing but praise for George Smith, saying: "He takes upon himself half the defence of our backs as, with his giant pace, he can drive two men before having to tackle a third, and he does this successfully in almost every match." [4] It was not all serious however, and in an amusing episode at the dinner in Rochdale various players who were palming themselves off as Wrigley were told they looked like his father. [5] Their spirits had lifted and Baskiville wrote: "We are beginning to believe that our move from Ilkley was a step in the right direction as we have won every match since departing from the Hydro and I must say it is far more interesting to be in a large city." [6] The Management Committee's lighter touches, and the change from the Yorkshire moors had helped. There was more to do in Manchester, and the training facilities at Salford's ground were better. After training they could swim in the pool, and there was the theatre in the evenings. Popular shows like 'The Bandsman' were seen at the invitation of the Grand Theatre. Day trips added interest and they were shown over the vast Manchester Cotton Exchange by Mr Cheetham, a prominent member of the Oldham Club.

They now faced two difficult games, one on the Tuesday, against Bradford, and then a Saturday match against another top six club, Halifax. Bradford, situated in a bowl of hills, and with a population of 300,000, epitomised prosperous Victorian northern England. Its grand buildings housed the vast wool trade and drew on the best in local architecture. Wool prices on the Bradford Exchange were of particular interest to farmers and were regularly quoted in New Zealand newspapers.

Invitation to Match Banquet.

OLDHAM FOOTBALL CLUB

Oldham v. New Zealand

AT OLDHAM

SATURDAY, NOVEMBER 23rd, 1907.

DINNER

AT THE TOWN HALL

President:

HIS WORSHIP THE MAYOR

TOAST LIST.

THE KING, QUEEN, AND ROYAL FAMILY.

+ + +

THE NEW ZEALAND TEAM.

+ + +

THE OLDHAM FOOTBALL CLUB.

+ + +

Bradford was an early member of the Union, Championship winners in 1903-04, runners up in 1904-05, and Yorkshire Cup winners in 1905-06. With that recent history they were likely to form strong opposition. It is not immediately clear whether the All Black selectors knew just how hard Bradford would be, and whether they underestimated them; perhaps they just had to rest certain players. Whatever the case, the selection committee chose a side that did not contain many stars, and the usual price was paid for doing that. George Smith who had played nine consecutive games was rested, Gleeson, really only a manager, and who had played only one game, deputising for him on the wing. Dally Messenger was also rested. With Todd and Billy Wynyard still injured "it left our rear division in a very weak state." [7] Smith's devastating tackling was sorely missed. Sadly, too, the weather turned the Bradford Club's new Greenfield ground into a quagmire. Headlines posed the question, 'MUD OR WATER POLO?' and told readers the conditions up in Bradford were the vilest possible with gale force winds and driving rain. With there being no covered stands 4,000 brave spectators huddled together, and saw a win to Bradford. Baskiville wrote: "It was difficult for players to maintain a foothold, or even walk, let alone run, pass or kick. Under the circumstances the game practically developed into a farce." [8] Bradford outmuscled the All Blacks 7-2, becoming the first Yorkshire side to beat them. That evening they dined and visited the Empire Theatre afterwards.

Baskiville's match reports to New Zealand kept the team's public profile high and knowledgeable commentators conceded that the teams they were opposing were of a far different kind than those faced by the amateur All Blacks. Back in New Zealand the push to ban professionalism in all sport gave rise to a public lecture entitled 'Clean Sport' in the Christchurch Town Hall. JE Green, an administrator, said if professionalism were to invade football in New Zealand it would in every way be advisable that the New Zealand Rugby Union should take control of it. He said if that was to happen "it could keep the game clean, even when professionals were concerned, but out of its hands professionalism would run riot." [9] The 'Truth' emerged as the only newspaper in New Zealand that consistently supported the team and the reasons for its formation. Taking an opposite viewpoint to the others it drew attention to the fact that the New Zealand Rugby Union had paid the amateur All Blacks three shillings a day over and above expenses on their tour of Britain in 1905. Pointing to the Rugby Union's decision to disqualify all the present team's members, the 'Truth' exclaimed - "There is nothing in the Ten Commandments against professional football. What is the difference between a professional rugby player and an amateur? THREE SHILLINGS. How so? The average wage of the English labouring classes is about 21s per week. In the case of the young men who play football, frequently their earnings are as low as 15s and 12s per week. With such scanty earnings a player can ill-afford to lose a day's pay ...Now ask yourselves who receives the fruits of the footballers' labours - certainly not the labourers (players). No, the persons who derive the greatest rewards from the players' efforts correspond with the capitalistic class in the daily walks of life." [10] Amidst this public debate, the Rugby Union was moving to put in place its creation, the Federation of Sports, which would police all sports, keeping them 'clean', and keeping rugby amateur. But others were not so sure. Legal minds asked how anyone who was a professional in one sport, say a jockey like George Smith, could possibly be disqualified for life from playing amateur sport such as hockey? Might not the administrators be bound for an appearance in Court instead of the players?

The Rugby Union, however, were clearly going to try to resume control if at all possible - governance would not be in the hands of those who played the game. New Zealand Rugby was at a turning point in 1908. Would players desert the traditional game on the return of the professional All Blacks and set up a new code, or would the New Zealand Rugby Union gradually absorb the criticism of its rules being too slow and change the rules? Would the players' demands for compensation be somehow met with the amateur regulations in place? The members of the present side must have wondered what the future held for them, having been disqualified already for life. Would their next few years see them playing in England, or perhaps Australia, or would they need, on their return, to spearhead a new game in New Zealand?

There was much to occupy their minds as they turned out to play every three days and were facing their next hurdle, Halifax. Little wonder that Baskiville wrote in his report after they lost this game that the team was in another "Slough of Despond". Halifax had won the League Championship. They were quite properly regarded as "one of the severest ordeals which we would have to encounter during the tour." [11] Rain had fallen the night previously leaving the Thrum Hall ground in wretched condition. In an attempt to make footing possible they added straw to it. With the rain continuing, what should have been a large crowd only reached 11,000. Despite their best attempts at passing, the All Blacks couldn't score. Baskiville wrote despondently: "Try to imagine running over six inches of mud covered with a thick layer of straw. Todd's efforts to do so were at times laughable." [12] The Halifax players adapted in far superior fashion with sustained dribbling rushes. Their 6-4 lead at half-time came from two tries, to two Messenger penalty kicks. Halifax, through Eccles, scored again in the second half. The forwards had played well despite the conditions - it was the backs this time who let the opposition go past them - Dick Wynyard playing out of position did not perform up to his usual standard. Eccles and Thomas were the stars for Halifax. Summarising the game, The Athletic News said of the All Blacks: "Smith was the best, he ran well and tackled and saved soundly. He has not much to learn in what I shall term obstructive techniques. Messenger does not seem to improve. Wrigley found Eccles just a little too fast and clever for him. In the forwards, Johnston, Lile and Trevarthen played splendidly and deserved better support." [13]

It was not the rehearsal they wanted prior to their first county match against Yorkshire at Wakefield. That county had proud rugby traditions to uphold; it was to be a showpiece encounter. The All Blacks chose their best team and the dry ground suited them. At no stage did the game go well for Yorkshire; the All Blacks took the initiative right from the moment when Taylor, the county fullback, fumbled the ball from Wright's kick-off. First points came from a potted goal to Messenger. The All Blacks scrummaging had improved greatly; they were getting possession at almost every scrum. Adam Lile then scored in a race for the ball with Smith who had chipped over the unfortunate Taylor. Wright and Tom Cross took command in the forwards and then Dick Wynyard scored from scrum-half completely fooling the Yorkshire defence. Messenger struck some good form sending a penalty back well over the cross-bar from halfway, but when Smith was the recipient of a heavy tackle he left the field with suspected broken ribs and a doctor in attendance. As he was not permitted to return, they played the remainder of the game down to 12 men. But showing the magic touch, the ball was sent from sideline to sideline, the All Blacks backs running and passing fluently, and with style. Rowe scored under the bar and finding exceptional form set up play for Turtill to score, only to see the fullback drop the pass. It made no difference - Johnston scoring after dribbling the ball from halfway.

For a proud county side like Yorkshire, it was a forgettable day's football; their backs had little understanding of each other's play. Of the individual players, Baskiville wrote, "Dicky Wynyard was a shining light all game, and he certainly has a better headpiece than Kelly. He made the Yorkshire backs look very sheepish when he scored his try.".…"Rowe played a nice game, and showed a marked improvement on some of his more recent displays. Smith was a tower of strength to his side, and it was very unfortunate that he was disabled so early in the second half. Wright who came out of the pack when Smith was injured, filled his new position with credit, and was very unfortunate in not crossing the line on one occasion. Both five-eighths I have seen in a better mood. Todd was certainly the better man of the two." [14]

The English newspapers were scathing of Yorkshire's performance especially as they had beaten Lancashire earlier. They lambasted the players and selectors - "The forwards were apparently chosen when the committee men were in queer mood" and "With some players carrying a super abundance of weight, they were unlikely to stay out such a fast game as that with New Zealand gave promise of being." They praised the New Zealanders display, saying: "They seemed to enjoy the fine afternoon and comparatively good going and fairly dry ball. Their team seemed to have laid themselves out to give of their best" and "Sometimes they demoralised Yorkshire" but "things have come to a pretty pass when five New Zealanders can smother six Yorkshire forwards." It had been a commanding All Black performance, with Yorkshire not scoring tries and the final score being 23-4. But it came with a price; a medical examination found that Smith's rib was fractured.

Match card: New Zealand vs. Warrington.

This setback did not however dull the post-game banquet, Baskiville noting: "A goodly number of the other sex were present. A most enjoyable evening was spent. We retuned to our headquarters the same night. Today the majority of the team have journeyed to Oldham, where they are to be shown over a large cotton mill an in the evening will be guests of the officials of the Oldham Football Club at a theatre party with a smoke concert afterwards." [15]

With their opening representative fixture a success, they prepared confidently for the tough games that lay ahead. There were matches against Warrington, their last match before Christmas, and Hunslet, two of the top four clubs in the league, followed by county games against Cumberland and Lancashire, and internationals against Wales at Aberdare on New Year's Day and then an England XIII at Wigan. In between these fixtures there were also four further club games. This itinerary would take them up to the Test series; the arrangements for these had now been settled, with Cheltenham being the venue for the third test.

Warrington went into this match with impressive credentials; they held the Challenge Cup having beaten Oldham 17-3 in the final in 1906-07. The New Zealanders were conveyed in carriages to a civic welcome from the Mayor and Sir Gilbert and Lady Greenall. The fervour of the welcome matched the strength of Warrington's team, but unfortunately the weather ruined the prospects for a good match.

Wilderspool, Warrington's ground, was struck by slanting rain, but 10,000 spectators still filled the stands and enclosures. The 'Pro-Blacks' as they were sometimes called, fielded, as best they could, their top side, Tyler replacing the injured Smith, and Trevarthen and Byrne gaining forward positions. Fish, a famous Northern Union winger scored first, going at speed around Tyler. The All Blacks then replied with a fine try to Messenger after most of the backs handled. With kicks New Zealand led 7-5 at half-time. Messenger was playing exceptionally well and was unlucky in having penalty kicks hit the cross-bar twice. Playing with the wind, Warrington hammered at the New Zealand line for most of the second half scoring only minutes before full-time. In the final minute New

George Smith, an extraordinary sportsman: a cup winning jockey, a champion sprinter and hurdler, a prodigious tryscorer as an All Black wing and a Rugby League 'All Gold'.

Zealand turned thirty minutes of defence into attack and rushed downfield. Warrington were penalised and, we are told a deadly hush fell over the ground when Messenger lined up the kick. But he missed this one and Warrington had won a bruising encounter.

Baskiville commented on just how good Warrington were and why they

were worthy Challenge Cup holders; he wrote: "We think Warrington well deserved the title - the Gibraltar of the Northern Union. For once the All Black forwards were opposed by a pack of forwards who were their equals in every way, weight included. It was a magnificent battle - at times the referee had to administer cautions or advice, whichever way the players liked to take it." [16] Baskiville's team made a genuine effort in their after-match speeches. Invariably they tried to find at least some connection, however tenuous, between their hosts and New Zealand. To everyone's amusement at the dinner in Warrington, Gleeson told them it was the wire from Warrington that kept the rabbits out of the farms in New Zealand. Also, in a time when international tensions were rising, the close links between the 'Mother Country' and 'The Empire' were often spoken of. Looking to the future, and what it might hold for Rugby in New Zealand, Gleeson in an elegant speech said they wished they could have taken back the ashes of victory: "so they could fan to the flame the cause of Northern Union rules from one end of the Australasian colonies to the other." [17]

Despite their narrow 7-8 loss they had thoroughly enjoyed their trip, and the Warrington Rugby League Club generously invited them to stay in Warrington as guests of the club till Monday, arranging entertainment and visits for them. These can take the tension out of touring, providing an opportunity for players to mix and talk with local people. They can see, and be seen, and can walk off stiffness. In hotels minds can easily become dulled. On Sunday they were driven by motor car to Knutsford in the heart of the Cheshire countryside visiting one of the oldest solid oak churches in the area, built in 1296. Monday saw them being shown around the then famous Crosfields soap works.

For Christmas Day they were back in Manchester enjoying the festivities, but also preparing for one of the hardest club matches of the tour, against Hunslet, scheduled especially for Boxing Day at that club's Parkside Ground in Leeds. Hunslet had few peers in the Northern Union. One of the founding clubs, they had been Yorkshire Cup winners in 1897-98 and 1905-06. In 1907-08 they went on to be Championship winners and won both the Challenge and Yorkshire Cups, the Challenge Cup going to them in a replay against Oldham. Their star player, Albert Goldthorpe, was widely thought the most complete kicker of the football in Britain at the time.

New Zealand scored first, when Wynyard made a remarkable run to send Wrigley away. A Messenger conversion and penalty goal saw New Zealand leading the best club in Britain 7-0. Messenger had struck great form, and increased this to 9-0 by half-time with a sensational goal from halfway. Goldthorpe dropkicked two goals after half-time keeping Hunslet in touch. The game then became a contest between Messenger and Goldthorpe who then kicked two more, to Messenger's one from his own side of halfway into the wind. This seemed to settle the issue with New Zealand leading 11-8. Hunslet had a player ordered off, the first during the tour, and then, in the last minutes when they kicked the ball to the normally reliable Turtill, it bounced away from the fullback into the arms of one of their players, who scored. A conversion on the bell, as had happened at Warrington, would have brought defeat, but Goldthorpe's kick hit the posts and rebounded back into play. The final score was an 11-11 draw.

Since landing at Folkestone three months previously, the All Blacks had played twenty-six club games in England, and the best county team, Yorkshire, for 17 wins, 2 draws and 8 losses. They had had to adapt to new rules, which made games into what is now recognised as a totally different sport from Rugby Union. Players like Billy and Dick Wynyard, Dan Gilchrist and Lance Todd, who had been injured, were working their way back into playing. Playing combinations had been forged where none had existed previously, the most notable and dangerous being between Dick Wynyard at scrum-half and Lance Todd at five-eighths. Messenger and George Smith had plotted tactics with remarkable success.

The forwards had largely overcome their problems; they were now getting possession from the scrum, and their mobility showed to advantage when the ground and weather conditions permitted. Messenger's goal kicking had also been a potent force; during the game against Leeds, he had given a goal kicking exhibition at half-time, kicking ten out of eleven from all angles. The All Blacks' attractive style of back play which was their trademark drew in the spectators, the crowds easily breaking records at most venues, sometimes despite the worst weather England could put on for the occasion. For all these reasons the public interest had never tailed off.

Nowhere was this more in evidence than for their game against Salford where, in spite of the wintry weather, 12,000 people paid admission. In the first half, Messenger wove some magic as he backed up breaks by Todd and Wynyard in the midfield, scoring twice. Strangely the conversion attempts were astray as well as a drop goal. 'Jum' Turtill also made several fine runs from fullback; he was now starting to seize the possibilities inherent in attacking from that position in the 13 a-side code.

The second half saw another Wynyard break, this time leading to a try to Wrigley. At one point the match seemed to sour, or as Baskiville wrote, became "strenuous", and: "the referee had to call the players around him once and give them a lecture on socialism or brotherly love. Both sides offended in this respect so all sides were satisfied." [18] The reporter for the Athletic News spoke of the hardness of the game making it the most disappointing of the tour so far with the referee having to read the 'riot act'." [19] He also lamented the fact that defence dominated the game in the second half saying: "We saw few of those pleasing back movements which have gained the team their admirers." [20] In Baskiville's view, Turtill was the best player on the ground, fielding the ball without error in a veering wind, and kicking for the line with expert judgement. Salford were another top eight side and with the final score being 9-2 to New Zealand, it increased their victories to 18. It had however been won at some cost, Todd having to leave the field in the second spell with injury. This placed him in doubt along with Smith for what was known would be a titanic struggle against Wales at Aberdare.

1   *Otago Daily Times*, 16 January, 1908.
2   *The Press*, 10 January, 1908.
3   *Otago Daily Times*, 23 January, 1908.
4   *Lyttelton Times*, 2 January, 1908.
5   Ibid.
6   Ibid.
7   *Lyttelton Times*, 2 January, 1908.
8   *Otago Daily Times*, 23 January, 1908.
9   *Otago Daily Times*, 6 February, 1908.
10 *Truth*, 3 August, 1907.
11 *Otago Daily Times*, 30 January, 1908.
12 Ibid.
13 *Lyttelton Times*, 1 February, 1908.
14 Ibid.
15 Ibid.
16 *Otago Daily Times*, 6 February, 1908.
17 Undated Newspaper Article, HS Turtill Scrapbook.
18 *Otago Daily Times*, 13 February, 1908.
19 *The Athletic News*, 30 December, 1908.
20 Ibid.

13. VINDICATION

Nowhere, other than perhaps in South Africa, is rugby union played with such passion as it is in New Zealand and Wales, yet these two nations share the honour of having played the first ever rugby league international. The amateur All Blacks had forged such a magnificent reputation, and the rugby union game had such complete dominance in New Zealand that a brief explanation of the events that led to the playing of an international match under Northern Union rules between the professional All Blacks and Wales may be appropriate.

The fact that an All Black team was again in Britain, and that it was playing the Northern Union clubs had excited interest in the northern rugby code. But even prior to this, rugby union in Wales found that players were moving north in increasing numbers. Robert Gate, in 'Gone North', tells of how the movement of Welsh players to the Northern Union clubs in the 1890s gathered further momentum after the turn of the century. Going hand-in-hand with the exodus to the openly professional code was a concern of rugby administrators that clubs in Wales were paying players. 'Boot' money was widely rumoured. Several instances drew down the wrath of administrators.

The Aberavon Club had been censured in 1901, and then expelled for inducing Mountain Ash players to the club with cash. The Aberdare Club was refused grants from the Union on suspicion of making payments to players. The great Dai Jones was suspended for receiving payments, yet many were in favour of football becoming openly professional - that is having money paid above the table rather than under it, and professional rugby took root. First Ebbw Vale joined the Northern Union in 1907, and then Merthyr Tydfil, which had been strengthened by the seven players disqualified for life from Aberdare. The prospect of playing the All Blacks gave added impetus to the movement and after the tour they were joined by other clubs, Treherbert, Barry, Aberdare and Mid-Rhondda. By the time the professional All Blacks were due to play, it seemed not to greatly concern the average Welshman that these All Blacks were professionals; they wore the same black jersey as those that had gone before them, with the same silver fern, that alone was sufficient.

For the New Zealanders, it was a first step to establishing an international reputation and also an opportunity to avenge the defeat of the amateur All Blacks. The New Zealand management and the English subcommittee chose Aberdare as the venue for the match, with its large capacity and it being just over the mountain from Merthyr, at the time one of the largest cities in Wales. One newspaper wrote: "and it was appropriate too, seeing that it was from Aberdare, that the bombshell was thrown into the Welsh Rugby Union camp alleging that payments were being made to amateurs." [1]

Curiosity and interest in the new code saw 12,000 patriotic Welshmen pack

Prominent Northern Union Players
Back row: W Little, Halifax & Cumberland. R Wilson, Broughton Rangers & Lancashire. Gifford, Barrow & Lancashire.
Front row: J Leytham, Wigan & Lancashire. J Fish, Warrington & Lancashire. J Lomas, Salford & Cumberland. J Jolley, Runcorn & Lancashire. A Goldthorpe, Hunslet & Yorkshire.

---

the Aberdare Athletic Ground. From colliery and chapel they came. Whether conversion to the new code would result, and whether the Welsh would win, no-one knew, but the prospects looked good. Wales was talented, they had fast backs and most of the players had long experience in the professional code. In the All Black camp, both Smith and Todd were still out injured and they fielded a reshuffled backline; Arthur Kelly a half-back, playing at inside-centre, and Billy Wynyard taking Lance Todd's stand-off half position. The full teams were:

Wales: Fullback, Chick Jenkins (Ebbw Vale); three-quarter backs, Dai Thomas (Aberdare and Halifax), S Llewellyn (Treherbert and Oldham), B Jenkins (Mountain Ash and Wigan), Llew Treharne (Penygraig and Wigan); half-backs, D Beynon (Pontypool and Oldham) and J Thomas (Maesteg and Wigan); forwards, 'Dai' Jones (Welsh amateur International and Merthyr), DP Davies (Merthyr), O Burgham (Forest of Dean and Ebbw Vale), J Thomas (Pontnewydd, Newport and Warrington), D Rees (Penygraig and Salford), D Franks (Aberavon, Pontypridd, and Bradford).

New Zealand: Fullback, H Turtill; three-quarter backs, H Messenger, H Rowe, A Kelly; five-eighths, W Wynyard and E Wrigley; half-back, R Wynyard; forwards, W Johnston, W Mackrell, D Gilchrist, C Pearce, T Cross, and H Wright.

With Britain gripped by a penetrating cold, playing on the frozen Aberdare Athletic Ground was a new and not very pleasant experience for the New Zealanders, yet they struck first when Kelly scored after gathering a clever cross-kick from Rowe. Messenger's conversion attempt failed. The Welsh responded quickly, their Halifax and Aberdare player, Dai Thomas, beating Messenger and scoring. The All Blacks, though, were playing exceptional football and continued to do so for the rest of the first half, Billy Wynyard scoring and Messenger converting. New Zealand led Wales 8-3 at half-time.

Then Wales turned with the wind behind them; Johnny Thomas the Wigan player started to shine at outside-half and one reporter wrote that the Welshmen exhibited "rare dash". The pressure on the All Blacks continued right through till the game's end and Wales received their reward just minutes before full-time, Dai Jones scoring the try that put them a point in front. Seconds before the final whistle, the New Zealanders could have taken the game, but Dick Wynyard, somewhat uncharacteristically, dropped a pass in front of the try-line and Wales won 9-8.

Punctuated throughout by strong defence and expansive back play the game had all the elements of a typically uncompromising New Zealand-Wales encounter. Yet despite that, or possibly because of it, the New Zealanders admired the way the Welsh had moved the ball, which was more akin to the All Blacks' own open style of play. Baskiville, said that "although the result was disappointing the game was not". It had in fact, apart from everything else, also been a fine advertisement for the northern code. The Aberdare Leader noted: "The spectators were greatly impressed with the new game, especially as the ball was always kept in play by virtue of the quickness in breaking up the scrummages with the abolition of the lineout. In truth it is a faster game than the old-fashioned amateur methods." [2]

For the Welsh once again their team had defeated the All Blacks, Aberdare was catapulted into the Northern Union and before too long there was a separate league in Wales playing rugby under Northern Union rules. Ironically it had been an Aberdare man, Teddy Morgan, who had scored for Wales in their famous victory over the amateur All Blacks just eighteen months earlier.

The All Blacks left Wales the next day on their 12-hour train journey back to Manchester and then over to Hull, for their second visit, this time to play Hull Kingston Rovers. There, despite a bitter wind blowing off the Humber, an excellent crowd of 10,000 saw another tightly fought game. Many of the players were still swathed in bandages from the frozen ground in Aberdare. Tyne scored first for New Zealand and Hull Kingston Rovers replied. Snow began to fall. Baskiville commented that Turtill "played magnificently, and was the means of frequently getting his side out of difficulties with clever line kicking. A player of rare ability, his value to the side cannot be underestimated." [3] In the second half, fine passing saw Messenger scoring next to the corner flag. In front, 6-3, the New Zealanders now had the difficult job of defending their lead till the end.

Baskiville wrote: "The home team was by no means playing a gentle game, and had to be reminded of this fact by the referee once or twice ... play hovered near the New Zealand line. It was the scene of many warm scrums, but despite the pressure, our defence was too stubborn, so the game ended with New Zealand 6 points, Hull Kingston Rovers - 3 points. Turtill was the soundest back on the field." [4]

They now faced a difficult match programme. During the next month they were to play two county matches against Cumberland and Lancashire, four more club games, an International against an England XIII, and finally three Test matches against Great Britain. They now went up to Carlisle to play Cumberland and being close to the Scottish border some of the team visited Edinburgh. Britain remained in the grip of a storm-filled winter and the journey brought the All Blacks to the northern extremities of where the game is played. Cumberland, the top county side, had beaten both Yorkshire and Lancashire that season. All these county sides were chosen on an 'origin' basis and the clubs in Cumberland had been a nursery for many of the Northern Union's finest footballers. Against this background when it came to playing against the All Blacks they fielded a magnificent forward pack and an experienced back-line.

The itinerary now placed them in something of a dilemma. They knew Cumberland would be strong, the earlier game against Barrow had been testimony to that. In three days there was the International against an England XIII to be played at Wigan and they had to decide whether to risk their top side against the county champions, or whether to rest some of them. In the end they settled on a mixed team, and paid the, by then, almost inevitable price. The Cumbrians took a 15-point lead in the first half against a brittle All Black defence, assisted by what was described as a "perfect gale" blowing down the field. At the changeover, the All Blacks still had a faint chance if they could play equally as well with the wind as had the Cumberland side, but that did not eventuate. Cumberland, befitting a county champion, continued their fine form and won 21-9, the great Jimmy Lomas being the outstanding player.

Their next game was much more evenly contested. A crowd of 12,000 at Central Park, Wigan, witnessed England and New Zealand contribute to one of the best matches of the tour. The ground although frozen had had a thick layer of straw laid over it for several days prior to the match and that helped take some of the sting out of it. Conditions favoured an open game, and with the return of Lance Todd and George Smith the All Black back-line began to show its former flair. One reporter wrote: "Some of their passing was frequently brilliant, and evoked loud applause from the crowd." [5] The All Blacks were trying innovations, including using the skip passes more usually associated with modern football. "There was much to be learned from their long passes out to the wings," wrote one correspondent. And another said: "Messenger, Smith, Wynyard and Todd were the pride, and the defensive play of the old hurdles champion was exceedingly fine." [6]

By half-time the score was 11-all. Of the New Zealanders, Baskiville said

A dispute among the forwards.

that they were "putting in some fine work and deserved more points - once when Todd cut right through the defence and stumbled after beating the last defensive unit, and again when Messenger failed to put over a free kick awarded us in front of the home crowd." He added "luck went with the home team ... the ball rolled towards the New Zealand goal-line and Wrigley had ample time to touch down under ordinary circumstances, but the ball hit a goalpost and bounced to one side. Lomas, their nemesis from the Cumberland match, was handy, and was simply presented with a try which he converted himself." [7] England won 18-16. The Daily Despatch reiterating Baskiville's comments said: "The vast majority of those who saw the match came away pleased that England had won, but convinced that the real honours of the game lay with the colonials." [8] Dick Wynyard's sheer elusiveness and anticipation had made him the outstanding player with two tries, and Smith had shone with fine tackling; he and Messenger combined effectively again on attack. In the forwards, Cross, Johnston and Pearce, who, with Wright, had been the heart of the New Zealand pack for months, more than matched their English professional opponents for whom Padbury and Ferguson starred.

The match had been of a high standard, and was such an even contest, it served notice that not too much could be read into the New Zealanders' recent losses. The Times however used the opportunity of the two-point defeat to lambast the All Black management. It had carried reports before the team even set foot in England deprecating the concept as unworkable, unfinancial, and a figment of rabid northern imaginations. The defeat by England gave that journal an opportunity to attack them. "The team had," it said, "been demoralised by financial success." It continued that this was the cause of the defeats by England and Wales. This drew a response from Baskiville in his role as secretary of the team. To the newspapers he put the team's viewpoint and his own. He said of the 'demoralised by financial success' charge: "It is a most unjust and untrue thing to say... It gave our friends in New Zealand the idea that having made money here by football we had taken to drink and dissipation, and therefore that our players, as well as our morals, must be going to pieces... What does our financial success mean to us personally? Why nothing at all? All the money is banked, not spent by us. All we get while on tour is an allowance of £1 a week each. There is surely not much margin there on which to spend heavily on drink, even were we inclined to do so, which as a matter of fact we are not." And further, "I myself am next door to a total abstinence. I never take much even at the numerous public banquets at which we have been so hospitably entertained." And on the football successes: "We have won a substantial majority of games. Had we even gained a base majority it would have been good in the circumstances... England only beat us by two points and Wales by only one. The fact is that this New Zealand team and the English professional teams are very closely matched. We have suffered through those who made our arrangements keeping back our chief matches until too late. The consequence has been that we have become thoroughly stale and tired - almost deadbeat - so that the name of football is quite loathsome to us." [9]

Throughout the tour they had wanted to accept as many invitations as were extended, and in doing so were trying to imbue interest in matters other than football to allay the almost inevitable day-to-day tedium of practices associated with playing so many games. A special moment came when they were invited to take lunch with the Duke of Portland on whose property the famous galloper 'Carbine' was stabled. The visit to Welbeck started with them being shown over the famous abbey; the underground passages providing an insight into the history associated with it. A visit to the riding school followed; George Smith with his racing background was especially interested. Others in the party also followed racing closely and they were all intrigued to see 'Carbine', the horse that just about every New Zealander considered to be the best ever foaled. "On being permitted to go to his box, the men saluted the stallion by raising their hats; whilst the old groom, who had come with him from New Zealand, had his arm almost shaken off. Each player left with a trophy of Carbine in the shape of a small hand of hair taken from his tail and presented to them by the groom." [10]

They now moved their headquarters to Blackpool, traditionally used by Association Football teams preparing for Cup ties; five teams had been there the week before the All Blacks arrived. Now, just prior to the first Test they suffered defeat, 20 points to 4, at the hands of Lancashire. However the tour was starting to have important effects with the trailbreaking international between Wales and New Zealand having been followed by an international match between Wales and England. To the Northern Union's delight, a further three Welsh clubs notified their intention to join the new code.

The first Test was now due to be played; there was as yet no yardstick from other tours against which they could measure themselves, but if a series win was gained against the best that Britain could offer in professional rugby, they would undoubtedly secure a unique place for themselves in sporting history. Urging them on perhaps, quite apart from their own individual pride, and the pride in the black jersey, was the thought that the New Zealand football public demand nothing less than test victories from their national sides. The Northern Union selected a powerful Great Britain side: fullback, H Taylor (Hull); threequarters, A Hogg (Broughton), T Llewellyn (Oldham), B Jenkins and J Leytham (Wigan); halves, J Jolley (Runcorn) and J Thomas (Wigan); forwards: J Ruddick (Broughton), D Jones (Merthyr), A Robinson (Halifax), A Smith (Oldham), H Wilson (Hunslet) and T Warwick (Salford). The All Blacks were represented by Turtill, Rowe, Smith, Wrigley, Todd, R Wynyard, Kelly, Cross, Gilchrist, Pearce, Wright, Johnston and Trevarthen. Messenger, McGregor and Con Byrne, all being down with influenza were unavailable and were left behind in Blackpool. Wrigley had the same affliction but pronounced himself fit to play.

The advantage, if any existed, appeared to lie with the British - they knew the rules instinctively, having played under them since the break twelve years earlier, with on-field decisions being made in a split second that could be important. And Great Britain did not lack combination - both Wales and England having already played the All Blacks and also each other. Also each player knew the individual strengths of those around him from club football. They were confident of victory; both England and Wales having beaten New Zealand in the lead-up matches. And then there were the home crowd and ground advantages.

After six months of non-stop football and travel the All Blacks were tired. They had made the adaptations necessary to the new rules but could they be expected to make correct decisions in the intense pressure of a Test match. Could they

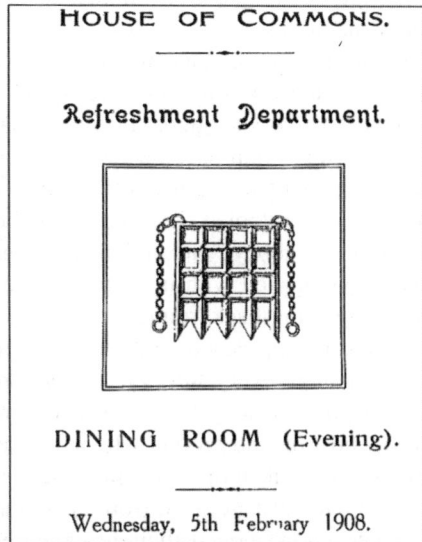

HOUSE OF COMMONS.

Refreshment Department.

DINING ROOM (Evening).

Wednesday, 5th February 1908.

In London the New Zealand team was invited to dine in the House of Commons.

even win enough scrum ball? Could they tackle well enough? They had speed in the backs but it was countered by the pace of Leytham, Llewellyn and Jenkins in the Northern Union's team. And with Messenger not playing, it would reduce the goalkicking advantage the All Blacks had. What, too, of their recent form? They had suffered heavily against Cumberland and Lancashire. What could be read into that? Quite a lot it seemed, for although a crowd of 16,000 was predicted it only reached half that. Baskiville was inclined to blame it on: "A record week's fog," that, "though it dispersed in the morning, kept people at a distance away, and also had a marked effect on local enthusiasts." [11] Others were more realistic; of the New Zealanders' recent matches they said. "Folk interest had been diminished by reason of the moderate form of the New Zealanders."

As it turned out, they need not have worried; the game was a good one, very even and full of exciting football. Great Britain won the toss and, playing with a strong wind it took them thirty minutes to break the deadlock, with a fine drop goal from Jolley. New Zealand tackled their hearts out and Todd made several fine runs. The British forwards however gradually gained ascendancy and the exceptionally fast winger Leytham scored in the corner. Just before half-time, they scored again through Robinson; Johnston, rather unusually, missing a vital tackle. Great Britain led 8-0 at half-time.

Now playing with the wind, and with new energy, New Zealand improved. Cross took the ball to halfway, and with the short interpassing that was their trademark style, 'Jum' Turtill scored his first try on tour, and the first by a New Zealander in a rugby league Test. Wrigley failed to convert. Dick Wynyard

147

providing a golden opportunity to level the scores, took an intercept at halfway. Being a sprinter he quickly reached the fullback Taylor, but lacked support from his team-mates, and the opportunity to keep in touch with the British was lost. When Robinson scored again they were virtually unassailable, and notwithstanding a late try to Wynyard; the final score was a win to Great Britain, 14-6.

Tom Cross had had an exceptional game, showing how experience at international level counted. In the forwards he was assisted by Gilchrist and Pearce. "Smith also played well up to his reputation," Baskiville wrote. "The crowd gave him a good hearing, loudly acclaiming his fine work on different occasions." [12]

With the second Test only two weeks away the All Blacks were kept up to the mark with matches against York, and Ebbw Vale where a big crowd of 10,000 saw them have another victory. Then it was off to London and Chelsea for the crucial middle game of the Test series. The *Athletic News* highlighted the importance of the match, and venue,

The First Test. The New Zealand Captain, 'Bumper' Wright, and Harry Taylor lead their sides onto Headingley, 25 January, 1908.

saying: "Saturday, February 9, in the Northern Union calendar was to be a day of history. The responsible officials had long recognised that if progress was to be made, an extension of area was necessary. Further, it was considered advisable that opportunities should be given of witnessing the game to rugby football supporters other than those of Lancashire and Yorkshire. London held out possibilities, and some time ago negotiations were opened with the Chelsea Club officials." [13] What the newspapers did not know, and what the Northern Union minutes show, is that initiative for the three match series had come from the New Zealanders. Arising from that, at Stamford Bridge, a professional rugby match, and a Test to boot, was played for the first time in London.

The All Black selection committee made several positional changes, most

MONDAY, JANUARY 27, 1908.

New Zealand Lose the First Test

Jolley opened the score with a dropped goal.

Turfill obtained the first try from a pass from Wrigley.

Smith proved too fast for Hogg.

A determined effort to stop Wrigley.

Leytham outpaced Todd.

Taylor's outfit suffered from Johnston's attack

Bumpered.

notably to the forwards. Whether illness or injury, or previous form played a role can only be speculated on. Charlie Dunning came in for Wright, and Messenger joined the back-line to which Bill Tyler at centre was also added. The game would have a crucial effect on the series' outcome and Great Britain's side was changed little. A fine crowd of 12,500 from the nation's capital, and a bowling green pitch, coupled with fine weather, seemed to both inspire the New Zealanders and unnerve the cream of the Northern Union's talent. The game began as it finished, in total contrast to the first Test, with New Zealand taking the early initiative. The pendulum had begun to swing.

The key to the game lay with forward dominance gained early. Pearce, Cross, Gilchrist and Johnston laid the platform for the backs to work from, creating gaps and getting their opponents moving backwards. Bill Tyler also

New Zealand and Great Britain.
3rd Test, Cheltenham.

fitted in well at inside-centre - a wonderful find late in the tour, as he splendidly ran Smith and Messenger into space. Wrigley, with his big tackling, was deadly in killing off British attacks. Freed from this role that he so often played, Smith's attacking game prospered on the wing, the position in which he had always seemed to excel. Following a series of scrum wins by the forwards, George Smith set the scene perfectly, opening the scoring ten minutes after the start. He got the ball from Wynyard somewhere near halfway and sensing the possibility of attacking himself, drew the defence in the form of both Llewellyn and Eccles across towards Messenger before suddenly swerving infield at high speed. The British fullback, Taylor, a magnificent defensive player, could not match Smith for swerve and pace and the great player beat him on the outside scoring close to the uprights. Also the fullback, Turtill, caught every ball on the full kicked his way, added to some good tackling. The All Blacks typically lifted the pace further, playing inspired attacking football, coupled with punishing defence.

Just prior to half-time, Great Britain went close to scoring, the exceptional Leytham being dragged down close to the line after a good run by Jenkins. After half-time in the battle for supremacy, and for the game, Great Britain cracked first; Messenger dashed away, passed to Wynyard who then passed the ball to Johnston. The big forward scored in the corner with what was described as "a great crash, which fairly roused the Chelsea crowd." The decisive moment in the game then came; Smith got the ball from Wynyard and dodged his way through the opposition before passing to Todd at halfway. There was still a lot for Todd

to do, but he beat Taylor, and then with Llewellyn, Jenkins and Leytham, three of the fastest players in the Great Britain team in hot pursuit, he ran half the length of the field and scored under the posts. The game was gone, and then Wynyard scored, once again near the posts. Great Britain's only points came in the last five minutes, making the final score 18-6 to New Zealand.

New Zealand had completely outplayed the British in what the press described as a crushing victory. Both sides were now chasing the deciding final Test due to be played on 15 February, 1908, at Cheltenham, Gloucestershire. It was to be a climactic clash. Set in the midst of the Cotswold Hills, this city with its elegant Georgian architecture has much to offer. At its fine hot mineral pools the well-to-do 'took the waters' to relieve aching limbs. They also had time to attend whatever other attractions might be on show at the time. It was an ideal choice in several ways, providing a platform for the rugby league game in what is still a stronghold of rugby union. It was to this rather cultured and leisured setting that the All Blacks and Great Britain teams came to play out their final act in the series. As it was to turn out, Cheltenham had not seen the likes of it either before, nor probably has since. The stakes were high, New Zealand emerging Lazarus-like from their form slump just prior to the series, and bracing themselves for a fierce response from the British seeking to avenge their humiliation in the second Test in the nation's capital. New Zealand, to finish their tour on the highest possible note, was chasing a win and glory at home. Thrown into this explosive mix, was the individual pride that each of the twenty-six players had in their football ability.

The London Test had been played on a firm ground in ideal conditions. The organisers hoped similar conditions would prevail in Cheltenham, and right up till the morning of the match it seemed their hopes would be fulfilled. But during the morning, a fortnight's fine weather broke and a deluge ensued. While it may have dampened the enthusiasm of some spectators, it was noted that "the ardour of the players appeared to rise above their unfavourable surroundings." [14]

Defeat had forced changes to the Great Britain team, and for the first time in an international, Billy Batten, a name to be heard on many football occasions, was included. They also made several changes to the forward pack. The New Zealanders, in the tradition of All Black teams left their winning side unchanged. The full teams were:

Northern Union: H Taylor (Hull), W Batten (Hunslet), B Jenkins (Wigan), P Thomas (Leeds), G Tyson (Oldham), T White (Oldham), J Jolley (Runcorn), A Smith (Oldham), H Wilson (Hunslet), JL Clampitt (Broughton Rangers), J W Birch (Leeds), J Spencer (Salford) and W Holder (Hull).

New Zealand: H S Turtill, H H Messenger, G W Smith, L B Todd, W Tyler, E Wrigley, J R Wynyard, W Johnston, T Cross, C J Pearce, D Gilchrist, W Trevarthen and C Dunning.

Great Britain attacked from the start and New Zealand was all defence. Batten claimed the ball twice on the wing, making fine runs on each occasion before finally being grounded, first by Messenger and then by Turtill. Rain fell in torrents and flew in the faces of the New Zealanders who were playing into it. Britain eased out to a 2-0 lead with a penalty from White. In contrast to the cavalier-like backline exchanges of the London Test, this match developed, mainly because of the conditions, into a battle for yards, it was trench warfare. Smith had to leave the field for medical attention. The rain and mud made passing suicidal. Just prior to half-time the British moved near the All Black line and, when a scrum broke up their half-back, Jolley pushed his way through, forcing his way across the line. This took the home side out to a 5-0 lead.

With the rules at the time not permitting any replacements, Smith's continued absence may have been a telling blow; but this fine sportsman returned heavily bandaged. He inspired the New Zealand side with strong defence and then, when the second half commenced, just as crucially he attacked. Going with the wind and rain, the game started to swing towards the New Zealanders. An early try seemed likely when Bill Trevarthen dived over the home line only to have Dai Thomas hold him up and prevent him grounding the ball. When the British rallied to the All Blacks goal line, Turtill sent them back with several fine line kicks that bounced into touch at halfway.

Gradually, however, New Zealand gained forward supremacy, despite being

0-5 down. With just seven minutes to go, the British finally cracked. Bill Tyler, as the utility player, or 'rover', as he was called, took the ball and passed accurately to Messenger. He had little room in which to move down the sideline, but, evading all tacklers, touched down in the corner. From the sideline, and with the rain still streaming down, and with the ball heavy with mud, a conversion seemed unlikely. It was thrown to Wrigley, and to the astonishment of everyone present, including the players, he kicked it from the sideline straight between the uprights, levelling the scores at 5-all.

The forward struggle now reached epic proportions, and Tom Cross was sent from the field. Stung by the referee's action, the All Black forwards pushed hard in the scrum near the line, and Johnston, taking the ball out of the scrum, surged across the line to the unrestrained delight of the players and team management, clinching the game in the final moments. With the series won, the professional All Blacks had imbued the 'All Golds' name, which the Australian press had coined, with a new, quite literal meaning.

1   Undated newspaper article, HS Turtill Scrapbook.
2   David James, Code 13, p22.
3   *Otago Daily Times*, 21 February, 1908.
4   Ibid.
5   Undated newspaper article, HS Turtill Scrapbook.
6   Ibid.
7   *Otago Daily Times*, 25 February, 1908.
8   Ibid.
9   *The Weekly News*, 1 April, 1908.
10   *The Athletic News*, 27 January, 1908.
11   *Otago Daily Times*, 12 March, 1908.
12   Ibid.
13   *The Athletic News*, 10 February, 1908.
14   Undated newspaper article, HS Turtill Scrapbook.

14. AUSTRALIAN TRAGEDY

Australia had still not yet seen any matches played under Northern Union rules. Who better to introduce the game to Australia than the All Blacks with their test victories over Britain, backed by five months of playing the 'New Rugby'? The New South Wales Rugby League now invited the All Blacks to tour Australia on their way home from Britain.

But first the New Zealanders returned to rugby league's heartland in the north of England for the closing match against St Helens. Baskiville had kept training with the team throughout the tour and with his main secretarial and managerial duties discharged, he now played for the first time. He fitted straight into the playing thirteen. Freed from the pressures of the tour, and coming off their series win, they drew down the curtain on the tour quite brilliantly. Baskiville was personally rewarded with a try, Tyne scored three times, Wynyard twice and Tyler once. Messenger kicked three goals and New Zealand won 23-10.

The playing side of the tour now came to an end and the offers of professional contracts made to a number of players had to be taken into account. The legal agreement, established in Sydney by mutual consent, could be changed by the same process. The Management Committee and players discussed what to do at a meeting held on 27 January, 1908. Every member had previously agreed to the condition that the tour would officially end in Wellington on the team's return. For the legally minded, it might be said that this legal 'ending' had to take place before a division of the profits could be made. This was a restraining factor and being self-governing they decided to alter the agreement. In this way those who wanted take up professional contracts in England could stay on; it also meant the Australians' offer could be accepted.

Both Smith and Todd accepted professional contracts. George Smith's daughter relates the circumstances and how clubs obtained their signatures as quickly as possible after the final game was played, saying: "My dad and Lance Todd signed for English clubs on the same day - my dad signed first - when he was in the bath and Lance Todd signed in the dressing room." [1] Smith joined Oldham, receiving £150 for eleven matches, the equivalent of two years wages. It was the opportunity he had been wanting. He had enjoyed the tour and the offer from Oldham together with his share of the tour profits meant that he could marry. His fiancée was invited over from Auckland once he had signed for Oldham.

Wigan's offer to Lance Todd, carrying as it did a £400 sign-on fee, as well as the captaincy, was even more impressive. [2] Wigan gave him the opportunity to play and also study for his tailoring diploma in London. Joe Lavery and Duncan McGregor, too, remained in England, Duncan McGregor starting a sports shop business in Gloucestershire and Lavery playing professional football. Jim Gleeson stayed on, completing his final legal examinations at the Inns of Court. He had kept the accounts meticulously; it was not intended at the time that the full balance sheet of the tour up till they left England would become public, but it found its way into print (see: Appendix 3).

Their departure from England with five remaining behind was an occasion for handshakes and good humour; the colonial character prevented a show of emotion. The main body was now bound for Australia, to play ten matches including a three test series. Farewelled by their hosts, they sailed on the P&O liner, Moldavia, via the Suez route, leaving England on 29 February, 1908. Before leaving they discussed a reciprocal tour by Great Britain to New Zealand in 1910. Their own tour now had an unusual and totally unexpected impact in one quarter. The New Zealand Rugby Union had invited the amateur Home Unions to send a Great Britain team to tour New Zealand. The Scots and the Irish believed tours encouraged professionalism; they were tantamount, in their view, to breaking the amateur regulations. They refused to take part and were very critical of the decision by England and Wales to send the Anglo-Welsh team. The irony was that the New Zealand Rugby Union had invited the Home Unions to bolster the game and combat the spread of Northern Union rules to the antipodes.

The All Blacks kept training on the ship but when they landed in Australia they lacked match fitness. With five players in England and Dally Messenger joining his New South Wales and Australian team-mates, cover was needed. To meet that contingency, J Barber, one of several standby players, and the Wellington representative scrum-half who could play any backline position, now joined the side in Australia. Bert Baskiville also began to play on a regular basis.

The season in Sydney had not yet got underway - the traditional starting date being 1 May. The All Blacks arrived on 9 April, 1908. This gave them a clear two-week break before the first games against Newcastle and Northern Districts at Newcastle. The Australians wanted to hear about the new rules. In

New Zealand salute New South Wales with their War-Cry.

fact the All Blacks had developed an almost reformist zeal for the new code; the purpose of their visit to Australia was twofold - first to play football, and to do so on a professional basis, but also to act as catalysts and as proponents of the new game. The Sydney Mail commented on the New Zealanders' infatuation with the Northern game. [3]

At a reception arranged by the New South Wales Rugby League to mark the visit and welcome the side back, Wright spoke of how he saw the game, saying: "They had learned many lessons on the tour, one being that the old amateur game was not the only game in the world. He felt sure the public would flock to see the new League game." As the Northern Union did not officially change its name until the 1920s to Rugby League, Wright's reference to the game of 'League' is noteworthy. Also, Wright, nothing if not a diplomat, deservedly praised his Australian team-mate saying he thought: "There was not a single player in England who could kick goals like Messenger". Johnston was interviewed later and commented that he "Never saw or played football till he played the Northern Union game. It was largely built on giving spectacular displays all the time." And of the problems adapting to the new rugby he said: "The greatest difficulty the New Zealanders experienced was not in learning the new but in forgetting the old rules. Games were exceedingly fast." [4]

The New Zealanders were out helping Sydney club sides with the new rules and tactics before the first games took place. Dick Wynyard was telling the local players that to kick the ball away, giving possession to the opposition, as happened in rugby union, was to court trouble. On Easter Monday, 20 April, 1908, the League played the first round of club matches played under Northern Union rules in Sydney. Sydney at Easter had a lot to offer: the Royal Easter Show, the Sydney Cup, polo at Kensington for the Burdekin Cup, cycling and motor racing, together with an international lawn bowls clash between New Zealand and St George at the Rockdale greens. Competing with these events there were races at Ascot and New South Wales playing Victoria at lawn tennis.

Kelly has taken a pass close to the NSW goal. Cheadle (threequarter) is the tackler.
The players behind Cheadle are Rosenfeld and Hennessy.

Australia is nothing if not a sporting nation, and, in addition to the rugby union being played, there were strong Australian Rules and Soccer clubs in Sydney. With the New Zealand side being due to play their first representative match under Northern Union rules, on May 2 in Sydney against New South Wales, there were lots of counter-attractions and still many unanswered questions. Were the new rules an improvement on rugby union? Was it more attractive to watch? The All Blacks had just defeated Newcastle and Northern Districts by wide margins - the first game under Rugby Union rules, the second under Northern Union rules. Would the New Zealanders, fresh from a test series against Britain, prove too strong for the local players? Would defeat by the All Blacks spell doom for the fledgling code?

The day was unseasonably warm for May in Sydney, the leafy avenues of Paddington, and beyond, playing host to thousands of inner city people walking, riding or catching a tram to the lushly carpeted stadium. The All Blacks had traditionally always drawn a good crowd in Sydney and eighteen thousand spectators packed the Royal Agricultural Ground, in anticipation of seeing what the new game was like. The pace of it surprised everyone, including the players, their only experience of Northern Rules previously being on the softer grounds in England. The hard Australian grounds suited the frantic passing. With no stoppages for lineouts the score at half-time was 14-7 to New South Wales, and ended with a win to the home side, 18-10. Being Australian means being a confident sportsman, and despite having only played two club games, the Blues had played exceptional football in the historic first encounter. The newspapers were ecstatic. The Sun- "The first half of the All Blacks versus All Blue match under Northern Union rules was one of the finest football spectacles I have ever witnessed. I shall hope to see the return match, and shall be careless as to which side proves victorious, providing the game is as good as the first." [5] The more conservative Sydney Morning Herald pronounced: "It was a great game ... there was some uncertainty as to how the public would view it. Many went out to the ground out of curiosity - they remained to applaud." [6] Without doubt the future of the game in Australia was established by this match. The date - 2 May, 1908.

The return match was also to prove popular, drawing a good sized midweek crowd of 8,000. As it turned out, both teams played the game in an exuberant vein, with the ball being moved non-stop around the field with little in the way of stoppages - a tonic for spectators after the old rugby union rules. The final result saw a win to New South Wales 13-10, but the overall honours had been even, with the All Blacks only being denied a win on full-time by a linesman's call.

With four games under their belts, the New Zealanders were starting to get some match fitness. The first ever Rugby League Test between Australia and New Zealand scheduled for Saturday, 11 May, 1908, on the same ground offered an intriguing prospect. The New Zealanders changed their side radically, 'Jum' Turtill, the fullback, being made captain, Wright not playing. Bert Baskiville was on the wing and Bill Tyler, who had played so well in the final two tests against Great Britain, played at inside-centre. Barber, another utility, was at stand-off half. For Adam Lile and Wright in the forwards, in came Con Byrne and Bill Trevarthen, those players being big, fast, impact players and providing a very similar look to the forward pack that had beaten the British. The full teams were:

Australia: Fullback: C Hedley (Glebe). Three-quarters: D McLean (Queensland), HH Messenger (Eastern Suburbs), Devereux (North Sydney), F Cheadle (Newtown). Halves: R Graves (Balmain), AS Hennessy (South Sydney), J Rosewell (South Sydney), T McCabe (Glebe), D Lutge (North Sydney), R Tubman (Queensland), M Dore (Queensland), A Rosenfeld (Eastern Suburbs).

New Zealand: Fullback: HS Turtill. Three-quarters: AH Baskiville, E Wrigley, A Kelly. Five-eighths: W Tyler, J Barber. Half: R Wynyard. Forwards: W Mackrell, C Pearce, W Trevarthen, T Cross, W Johnston, C Byrne. Referee: Mr T Costello.

A crowd of 20,000 was testimony to the enthusiasm for, and interest in, 'The New Rugby'. The inclusion of the three Queenslanders in the Australian side captained by the hugely popular Messenger, added spice to local prejudices. In stark contrast to the two state games just played, the All Blacks took control from the start. The forwards especially, showed great form. Con Byrne, Johnston and Charlie Pearce were prominent and passing like backs. The Australian captain, Hennessy, was injured in the face; Johnston being ordered off, the referee believing a punch caused the incident (Johnston was later exonerated on a touch judge's report).

In this historic first rugby league Test New Zealand completely stunned the Australians from the outset. Wynyard, as had happened numerous times before in Britain, scored first and Baskiville was brought down close to the line. As fate would have it, Baskiville, the key man in organising the tour, now played a remarkable role. He intercepted a pass on halfway, beat two opponents with sheer pace, and scored the try that put New Zealand out to an 8-0 lead, Wrigley converting. When Wynyard scored again, this time in the corner after Wrigley and Pearce both handled the ball, the New Zealanders went to half-time 11-2 up.

Australia recovered well after this initial onslaught, and worked their way back into the game; first McCabe and then Rosewell scored tries, the latter converted by Messenger. At 11-10 to New Zealand, and with 15 minutes left, it was evenly poised and anyone's game. The Sydney Morning Herald captured the moment:

"The excitement was now intense, and as the blues forced their way into the visitors' ground, the roar from the crowd was something to be remembered. Again Australia came, and an All Black kick over the line brought a scrum in their own 25, but New Zealand forced the blues back, and a terrific struggle followed in New Zealand's half. The pace was extraordinary. At the centre, Messenger kicked, and New Zealand forced. There were now only five minutes to go to time. Australia had yet another free kick - this time for shepherding by an All Black - and Messenger just failed. The return was marked by Messenger, and with the ball lying on the halfway chalkmark, he took the kick. From an infringement by the New Zealand forwards, the referee allowed another kick, and New Zealand forced. Full-time." [7]

ABOVE: Stopping a dribbling rush.

BELOW: Copybook tackle.

New Zealand, 11 points; Australia, 10 points.

"The play was hard all through, these games are invariably tough, that is how the New Zealanders have always played, and their opponents, to have hope of success, must do likewise." [8] It was fitting Baskiville played a crucial role in this the first of the many extraordinarily tough tests that were to be played between these two adversaries. He played so well they wrote that: "The new

Match Card 3rd Test. Australia v New Zealand.

three-quarter in the team, usually a forward, was the best back on the ground and was indeed the surprise packet of the day." Quite an accolade when the likes of Messenger, Dick Wynyard and Wrigley were also playing. One newspaper suggested that the New South Wales Rugby League should approach Baskiville with an offer saying: "based on the experience he has gained in the executive position and his knowledge as a player ... Mr Baskiville would be a valuable man." [9] It was also a reflection of this team's pride in itself and in the country they represented that they had won with 12 men.

In something of a precursor to later inter-state rivalry, and the laying of blame with individual players for losses, the Sydney papers attributed defeat almost wholly to the three Queenslanders, MacLean, Dore and Tubman. Dally Messenger was also however severely criticised: "He failed as a goal-kicker on Saturday. He had 14 shots and kicked 2. Yet everything was favourable to kicking." His last kick, they said, brought to the minds of the New Zealanders the game against England where they were beaten by 2 points, there Messenger had a shot at goal right in front of the posts, and missed. [10]

The spectators had certainly got value for money, and the attendance was as good as the most well-attended games played in England. The New South Wales Rugby League's finances looked promising for the tour of Britain the following year. There were still two more tests and three games against Queensland. Added to having the All Blacks touring, a New Zealand Maori Team, arranged by 'Opai' Asher, after a visit from the Australian, O'Farrell, to New Zealand, was about to arrive for a six match programme in two weeks time; further evidence that the emergence of Rugby League in Australia and New Zealand was a co-ordinated venture.

As was the custom the New Zealanders now left Sydney for Queensland by ship. Brisbane, the calm yet vital state capital, had formed a league of its own to play under the Northern Union rules. On the ship, Baskiville caught a chill and when they arrived on the 10 of May in Brisbane he did not feel well. With three days before their Saturday match at the Brisbane Exhibition Ground, they trained hard and also enjoyed the pleasant walks around the gardens and city centre. The New Zealanders felt at home in this city of wooden bungalows, a pleasant change after the large industrial cities of Northern England.

Newspapers carefully explained the new rules to their readers for this the first game against the Queensland state side. Splendid conditions on the day contributed to a good match, with clever passing and fast angled running they won 34-12. Curiously, Hardcastle, one of the opposing players, was a New Zealander and former All Black. The Brisbane Courier thought the new game an improvement on the old one, saying: "The game fulfilled expectations. It was generally anticipated it would be fast and open ... the absence of kicks and of throwing the ball into the lineout from the touchline prevented delays..." [11] and... "another pleasing feature of the game is that the opposition must allow a tackled player to rise and play the ball. This rule in a great degree excludes rough play and free-booting." [12] The good showings and the press coverage, together with the skill of the players involved, gave the code immediate credibility and acceptance. It was as if a breath of fresh air had been breathed into the old Rugby game. Players had long been frustrated by the English Rugby Union's failure to make any changes to the rules.

Baskiville wanted to play, but the day after the Queensland match, and like others before him on the tour, he went down with influenza. Over the next three days he deteriorated badly and pneumonia set in. He was moved to the Victoria Private Hospital. It was the sort of condition that today's antibiotics cure, but medicine had not reached that stage, sulphur drugs only being used. With the game on Wednesday afternoon against the Brisbane Metropolitan side, the players duly took the field. They won the match, but when news came that Bert's condition had deteriorated they raced to the hospital, some still with their football jerseys on. They found Baskiville unconscious and he died late in the afternoon, 20 May 1908, surrounded by his team-mates. They were devastated. It must have seemed unfair that less than a week previously he had played the most important football game of his life in the first test match against Australia. It was said in Sydney: "It was due, in a great way, to his efforts that the All Blacks won." [13]

Reeling from the shock, the whole team wanted to go home, but with two tests and a match against Queensland yet to be played, realistically a return was out of the question. There was little point in calling the tour off; the situation demanded character. They arranged for Baskiville's body to be embalmed and placed in a lead casket. It was then taken to Sydney. From there Harry Palmer and a group of players representing each province accompanied it to New Zealand and after the funeral in Wellington, Bert Baskiville was buried in the

Karori Cemetery. While all this was happening, the grief-stricken remaining members of the side had to play the return game against Queensland, and the two remaining Tests. They drew the state game 12-12, playing with only 12 men against largely the same side that they had defeated by 20 points a week earlier. One of their number, Dick Callus, had only played two games on the whole tour, having originally been taken primarily to assist Baskiville in an administrative capacity. The influenza which had taken their mate, and which had dogged the team now for nine months, shows just how debilitated they were by the constant training and travelling, the changes in climate and the weariness from playing football. It was a circle, the only escape from which was rest, and that is a scarce commodity for a touring side. They now faced playing the second Test only being able to choose a skeleton team. The teams were:

Australia: E Baird (Brisbane), G Watson (Brisbane), H Messenger (Eastern Suburbs), J Devereux (North Sydney), F Cheadle (Newtown), M Dore (Brisbane), A Rosenfeld (Eastern Suburbs), R Graves (Balmain), S Pearce (Eastern Suburbs), A Hennessy (C) (South Sydney), W Hardcastle (Ipswich), J Davis (South Sydney), D Lutge (North Sydney).

New Zealand: E Tyne, H Rowe, J Barber, W Wynyard, W Tyler, E Wrigley, J Wynyard, A Lile, T Cross, W Johnston, W Trevarthen, C Pearce, C Byrne.

The game, played at the Brisbane Exhibition Ground, turned into one of the most decisive Tests New Zealand has ever played. There was no haka before the match. As happened in the Sydney Test, New Zealand dominated early, Harold Rowe scoring, put into space by Dick Wynyard and Bill Tyler. Wrigley converted, beginning a golden day for him. Before half-time Wynyard scored, shortly to be followed by Rowe again, also converted by Wrigley. They were all playing so well it was as if they were playing the game for Baskiville.

By half-time New Zealand led 15-2, Australia's only points coming from a penalty by Messenger. When play resumed, Con Byrne fractured the point of his elbow on the rock-hard surface, but this did nothing to stem the flow of points, Dan Gilchrist, his replacement, being an equally fine hard running forward. Tom Cross scored and Wrigley kicked six goals in all. It was perhaps New Zealand's finest performance. The final score was 24-12 to New Zealand. Australia's points came from tries by Lutge the North Sydney player, and Hardcastle, the former All Black, then playing for Ipswich.

The New Zealanders departed Queensland having given the new code an enormously influential start in the state. Australia had grasped the essence of the Northern Union game and how different it was, or could be, from rugby union. In New Zealand the rebellion against the Rugby Union of which the tour was the most significant manifestation had now started to gather force. At the same time as the All Blacks were preparing for the second test against Australia in

Brisbane, the New Zealand Maoris team had been gathered together by Asher and others acting in the same manner as Baskiville's team. The Maoris landed in Sydney aboard the SS Moana arriving on 29 May, 1908, to a tumultuous welcome that included the New Zealand Government's official representative in Sydney at the time, Mr Montgomery. A flamboyant team, they were accompanied by four tribal elders or 'chiefs' as they were described by the press - Hikurangi Te Whetu, Hekemaru Hamaha, Tehura Hotara and Ranginui Timoti. Resplendent with the rare feathers of the huia adorning their hats, and their shoulders covered by piupiu, they were tremendous favourites with the newspapers and for that matter the rest of Sydney. The Maori side were at the ground supporting the All Blacks during the third Test. This final game of the tour game drew a crowd of 14,000. It was said: "Many were viewing the game for the first time, because of the glowing reports of its quality." A number were disappointed, the game turned into a tight, low-scoring affair; Australia fighting hard to win at least one of these historic first encounters. Some aspects of the old game had not yet died. A reporter wrote: "there followed a series of penalties and line kicking, which for a time made one think he was looking at a Rugby Union game." Three kicks at goal saw Wrigley put New Zealand ahead 6-0 at half-time. Australia scored and then New Zealand again, their most clever player being Dick Wynyard. At 9-3 the match was New Zealand's for the taking; there was an opportunity for a three nil clean sweep in the series. The Australians now inched their way back into the game with Messenger's goalkicking and tries to Graves and Anderson. At 11-9, the result hung in the balance until the end when Jones scored on the final whistle, Australia winning 14-9.

These new professional All Blacks, with their characteristically tough forwards and fast elusive backs, had thrilled the crowds with the Northern Union rules, but equally they had forged a unique place for themselves in sporting history, with test series wins over both Australia and Great Britain on the same tour. They now headed for New Zealand with a new set of rules and a revolutionary message. Just how well those would be accepted at home, and what would happen to rugby in New Zealand if they were, remained unanswered.

1   Letter, Mrs E Stansfield to author.
2   *The Auckland Weekly News*, 26 June, 1908.
3   *The Sydney Mail*, 22 April, 1908.
4   *The Weekly Press*, 11 April, 1908.
5   *The Sun*, 4 May, 1908.
6   *The Sydney Morning Herald*, 4 May, 1908.
7   Ibid, 11 May, 1908.
8   Ibid.
9   *The Arrow*, undated newspaper article, HS Turtill Scrapbook.
10   Ibid.
11   *The Brisbane Courier*, 18 May, 1908.
12   Ibid.
13   *The Town and Country Journal*, 27 May, 1908.

15. SUCCESS AT HOME

There can be no greater contrast than the homecomings of the amateur All Blacks in 1906 and the professional All Blacks in 1908. Both sides had brought tremendous honour to their country; the amateur All Blacks had defeated England, Ireland and Scotland, in one off tests, but had lost to Wales. To mark their achievement a grateful New Zealand Government had paid Gallagher's side their passages home via America, and the New Zealand Rugby Union was able to pocket the £12,000 profit from the tour. Thousands of patriotic New Zealanders had gathered to greet the All Blacks at the wharf in Auckland. The then Prime Minister, Richard Seddon, ever a politician had posed instinctively with the team for photos at the official welcoming function. It had been a rapturous return, a display of national gratitude and pride similar to that given the winners of the Americas Cup many years later.

Equally the tour of the professional All Blacks had been a resounding football success, as well as a being of financial benefit. Baskiville's team had defeated Great Britain in a three-test series playing against the combined might of the greatest professional players from both England and Wales. Then with limited preparation and travelling at their own expense via Australia, they had also beaten Australia in a best of three test series. In being victorious over both these great rugby-playing nations in the same year and on the same tour they established a playing record that no New Zealand team has ever repeated. Yet their return to Wellington was in stark contrast to the wild scenes in Auckland that had greeted the amateurs two years earlier. Not for them bands, bunting, and crowds; and there was no official reception, who could welcome them anyway? The only administrative structure for professional rugby lay within the team itself. The Government saw itself as pro-rugby union and against professionalism and Sir Joseph Ward, the then Prime Minister articulated that position. Speaking later that same year at a Government reception for the Anglo-Welsh team following the game that side played in Wellington he remarked, "amateurism is justly benefited by the visit of the present team" and "if matches were played as played this day there was no fear of professionalism coming into the English and Welsh Rugby Unions." [1] Also with Baskiville's death his detailed reports to the newspapers of the team's affairs, their wins and their losses, and their social engagements had ceased. Those publications, in turn, gave little column space to the team's historic test series' wins. The inevitable consequence was that there were only friends and family to greet them off the ships. The lack of public display and enthusiasm for the team may also possibly be explained by the fact that some members of the party had returned on the SS Monowai with Bert Baskiville's remains a week earlier. However it is difficult to escape the impression that the gulf in the minds of most New Zealanders

The amateur All Blacks had been feted by politicians but the professionals returned unheralded.

between the ideals of amateurism and the practicalities of professionalism was so deep the magnitude of what their fellow countrymen had achieved was hidden from them. All the side could now do was bury their friend, and typically, from their own resources, help the Baskiville family who had been so dependent on him. Bert Baskiville's grave is to be found in the Karori cemetery.

The players while still in Australia had decided to play an exhibition match at Athletic Park, Wellington, to raise funds for Baskiville's relatives and to show the New Zealand public what the new game was like. The proceeds were to be given to Bert's widowed mother. The idea was that they would invite players in Australia and New Zealand who were sympathetic to their cause and to the object of the game to join them in forming two composite teams to play one another. It was hoped Dally Messenger and other players would cross the Tasman with the New Zealanders for the match, but with Messenger selecting the Australian side to tour Britain, and also playing against the New Zealand Maoris, this couldn't happen. The New South Wales Rugby Football League instead decided to share the gate receipts from the New Zealand Maori's first game in Sydney with Mrs Baskiville. This was indicative of the respect in which Baskiville was held in Australia. Earlier, The Sydney Morning Herald had noted local reaction to what had happened saying "The death of Mr Baskiville cast a gloom over all the football grounds, and especially those where league was being played. On all grounds, union and league, flags were being flown at half-mast, and league players wore black bands." [2] Also the New South Wales Rugby Union's kind gesture of calling off all rugby union games so players and others could go to the match, materially assisted the gate. Harry Hoyle, President of the

165

New South Wales Rugby League, publicly thanked the Union or "our friends the enemy", as he called them, for making that decision. [3]

The exhibition match, the first game of rugby league in New Zealand, was played on 13 June, 1908. It attracted a smallish crowd of 8000. It is difficult to know whether this was due to the price of admission being two shillings, or whether it reflected a still strong antipathy towards the players who had turned their backs on the Rugby Union. Whatever the case, the All Golds achieved something tangible for Mrs Baskiville, with the sum of £300 being gifted to her by the players after deducting 50 per cent for hire of Athletic Park from the Park Company. For the record the "Blacks" defeated the "Reds" 55 to 20. Equally importantly, as it was to turn out, a large number of the people who went to the game liked what they saw; they thought the changes made by the Northern Union had speeded the old game up and made it a more interesting spectacle. Newspapers, too, explained the new rules and how they worked; they also had special praise for the high standard of passing the players had brought back from England and for their clean tackling techniques. Many respected authorities thought the game had been improved by the abolition of lineouts, and with possession being paramount, that it had done away with a lot of time being wasted on kicking the ball into touch. For these reasons, they advocated adopting the new rules in some form. There were, of course, other views; those who for one reason or another were not convinced the Northern Union rules made for a better game and they rallied to the cause of the old game with reports that played down the benefits - "The virtues of the Northern game have been greatly exaggerated..." and... "Played in the approved Rugby style, rugby has nothing to fear from the Northern game, particularly if the latter is to develop professionalism." [4] It appeared opinion was divided, even at this early stage, and so it was to prove. After the game, and with the tour now officially at an end, the professional All Blacks, as they were still called, disbursed; the Aucklanders sailing home on the SS Rotoiti, and the Canterbury and Otago players going back to the South Island.

And what of the tour itself, and what of its significance to New Zealand's subsequent sporting history? Jim Gleeson's prediction after the Wigan match that the total receipts could be near £10,000 had been very close. The financial outcome, (see Appendix 3: Receipts and Expenses), with a final payment from both the English and the Australian tours of £300 to each player had been a stunning refutation of the New Zealand Rugby Union's public prediction that a profit could not be made, and that if players went on the tour they would be ruined financially as well as being placed under a life-ban from rugby union. It meant the players had escaped the poverty trap of low wages and little capital. Where before none had existed, they now had choices; the rewards had provided the kind of financial stake with which they could, if they wished, set themselves up in business or purchase a home unencumbered by a mortgage. But it had not been easy - the threats, the uncertainty, the risks and the number of games to be played, the wet conditions in England and the representative fixtures, all these had placed them under strain; and probably none of them had felt those pressures more than Bert Baskiville.

There were also other less tangible, but perhaps more enduring benefits; they had travelled around the world and visited countries most of them could never have otherwise hoped to visit; the high cost of the international travel usually putting this only within reach of the better off. Also the professional rugby clubs and the city fathers in the north of England had given them a tremendous welcome. Baskiville made specific mention of this when writing his last dispatch to the New Zealand newspapers, saying: "I cannot possibly say enough about the way we have been received everywhere. On arriving at each of the cities or big towns we have always been welcomed by the Lord Mayor, or Mayor, as the case may be. Our reception has always been simply magnificent, and the hospitality showered on us has been most lavish." [5]

In a wider context though, and through their individual decisions to go on the tour at their own cost, the players had extended their own personal horizons in terms of what might be achieved, not only through professional football, but also in terms of the various employment and training opportunities open to them. They must have drawn enormous personal confidence from what they had achieved as a team and also individually. In addition to the five players who had stayed on in England at the end of the tour, several of the other players, once they got back to New Zealand, and had time to reassess their affairs, very quickly returned to take up professional contracts offered to them either during the tour, or shortly after. Edgar Wrigley signed with Runcorn for a fee of £400, together with a guarantee of employment in his plumbing trade. Harold Rowe went back to England and played with considerable distinction for Leeds. 'Massa' Johnston accepted a handsome offer from Wigan and, joining Lance Todd there, he played for Wigan until 1910 before being transferred to Warrington and eventually settling in Australia. Others to go back included 'Jum' Turtill to St Helens, only later to be killed in World War 1, Bill Trevarthen, and Arthur Kelly.

The tour had also basically been a happy one; George Smith was later to say that it was the most enjoyable tour he had been associated with. Their success in winning the test series in both England and in Australia could not be questioned; but that in doing so they had also played attractive, open football must have been of immense personal satisfaction. They had also had to accept their defeats, primarily in the tough county matches, these being indicative of just how strong football was at that time in the north of England. Certain individual players had had remarkable personal success. The match statistics from the English leg of the tour show Dick Wynyard had scored 14 tries, and his brother, Billy, 6. Harold Rowe accumulated 10 tries with clever clinical finishing that often had its source in breaks made by Smith, Messenger and Wrigley. Lance Todd had scored 8 tries and his incisive breaks had been the foundation on which several further tries were built. The great George Smith with his 6 tries, and with his defence, had proved a major weapon, his speed to the tackle being a decisive factor in preventing more tries being scored by opponents. Among the forwards 'Massa' Johnston and 'Bumper' Wright topped the scoring with 5 apiece, and significant contributions came from Bill Tyler (3), Con Byrne (2), Joe Lavery (2), Adam Lile (2), Hone Tyne (2) - and Cross, Kelly, Trevarthen and Turtill scored one each.

Heading the goal kicking Dally Messenger's 58 goals were invaluable when added to his 7 tries. Wrigley had kicked 8 and Turtill 3. Wrigley's conversion of Messenger's try in the third Test at Cheltenham with a soaking wet ball from the sideline, with eight minutes to go, and which put them level with Great Britain, and in a position to win the game from there, must rank as one of the crucial moments of the whole tour. Added to this was the magnificent play on their return to Australia, and their determination to win the first two tests ever played between those two countries. In many ways these results forced a change from antipathy to a grudging acceptance in the way the tour was reported in New Zealand. The final outcome meant the side returned home with their heads high, honour satisfied.

The tour provided the Northern Union with an international image, something not possible since their break in 1895; it bestowed credibility on what they were doing. The fact, also, that the New Zealanders had proved so adept at the new game, augured well for the future. That the same team had introduced professional football to Australia was an unexpected bonus, and the Australians' determination to establish the game in their country on a permanent basis mirrored the mood for change that had swept through rugby union. The Australian tour of England commencing in October that same year, 1908, would serve to hammer home the newly found international status of the code.

Of the fact that the team had grown close in what had been almost a year since they had left New Zealand, there can be no doubt. Players who had not previously been known to one another prior to the tour had become lifelong friends. Those who did not go back to England went on to play leading roles in starting rugby league as a game that later was to become widely played in New Zealand. The old issues had not been resolved and widespread unrest among senior provincial players was rife. To many in rugby, something needed to be done if the players were to remain loyal to that code. From within rugby union, calls arose for reform to the rules, and for the financial strictures relating to compensation for players when they were on tour to be relaxed. But generally the calls were lost, the people making them being out-voted on the various rugby unions.

In Canterbury, that province had had considerable difficulty the previous season in getting the full representative side together for a tour. Players had refused to go because they would be off work for two weeks and could not afford the loss of wages involved. In May 1908, a member of the Canterbury Rugby Union, Mr SF Wilson, moved a motion that representative players who lost

Commemorative stamp of George Smith and Albert Baskiville,
eighty-nine years after the tour took place.

wages whilst on tour should be paid for the time lost. He was supported by the Chairman, GH Mason, who likened it to a workman being paid overtime. They knew that it was on this exact issue that the Northern Union had split away. While the supporters of the proposal did not think it was professionalism, clearly the other committee members saw it heralding the breakdown of amateurism if allowed to proceed. The motion for the matter to be forwarded as a remit for the New Zealand Rugby Union's conference that year was lost by a margin of 7 to 3. [6] The Canterbury Times also carried a report from Wellington about player discontent saying: "Should the Northern Union Rugby code establish itself in this city, the members of two senior clubs are understood to have made up their minds to overthrow the present amateur body." [7] The two clubs were Petone and Melrose.

When the All Golds returned bringing with them the Northern Union game, and as the one game played in Wellington had impressed many rugby players and followers, there was now an alternative game to rugby union, but it lacked any administrative structure. That there was however already interest in the new code is confirmed by the fact that the first game played after the exhibition game in Wellington, was played, not in either Auckland or Wellington, where most of the players had come from, but in Southland, at Bluff. That game, as reported from Dunedin on 22 July, 1908, just five weeks after the All Golds' return, was between the Britannia Club and Pirates (Invercargill). [8] Northern Union rule books brought back to New Zealand by the professional players were sent down to Invercargill for the match.

With the All Golds having been disqualified by the New Zealand Rugby Union, and with other players, some of whom had wanted to go with them, still being frustrated by the lack of any significant change in rugby union, the All Golds seized the initiative, and other players joined them in playing Northern Union on a provincial basis. The first provincial rugby league match was played between Auckland and Wellington on 24 August, 1908. With Dan Fraser now taking Baskiville's place as their organising secretary, thirteen All Golds and thirteen other top players took part in the game, won 16-14 by the Auckland side captained by Dick Wynyard. Wellington scored four tries to Auckland's two, which gives some idea of their strength. It was that versatile and well-performed All Gold, Bill Tyler, fresh from the tour of England where he had played a vital role in the final two test matches, who won the game for Auckland with two conversions, two penalty kicks and two kicks from marks. The Wellington All Golds players had been joined by a number of other very prominent players, including the then current amateur All Black fullback, George Spencer, and his brother, also an All Black who played in the forwards. After this match, which had been played on Victoria Park before a crowd of 8000, the two sides were entertained at the Grosvenor Hotel in Hobson Street. The All Gold, Bill Mackrell, speaking at that function, outlined what they were doing and why, saying: "It was not intended that any players should live on the game, any such suggestion should be discouraged, but the new game did undertake to compensate players for any loss of time while on tour." [9] In the return match played in Petone on 12 September, 1908, and drawn 13 points all, the Wellington side included 'Bumper' Wright and 'Hone' Tyne who had missed the game in Auckland. The enthusiasm for change, however, meant that if it were to survive there would need to be a general push to formally establish the Northern Rules game.

There was now an element of urgency about what should be done. A complicated debate took place in Christchurch rugby circles, and at a meeting of 150 players they discussed whether to adopt the new game. W Moyle, who some years later became important to the founding of rugby league in Canterbury, was a leading advocate for change and for adopting the new game. Rugby was at a crossroads as it faced the issue of whether to adopt the new rules in some form and also whether to move towards compensating provincial and national players (All Blacks), and thereby ward off any formal split in the game that would come from the establishment of a rival code. The alternative was to set its face against change, remain loyal to the English Rugby Union, and hope that the threat of life-bans for playing the new code would be a sufficient deterrent to its formal establishment.

It was a motion from the Otago Rugby Union on the question of compensation that was eventually discussed by the New Zealand Rugby Union at its conference in October 1908 in Wellington. In a full debate on this issue,

Auckland proved in favour of compensation, and they were not alone. Some delegates in support of compensation recounted their own experiences - of not being able to represent their country because of the loss of wages while on tour, and of the embarrassment associated with receiving gifts of money from their union. Others opposed compensation to players in any shape or form - "professionalism is mere white slavery"... and: "There are very few single men who could not afford to tour. No married man should play football." The motion on compensation at this conference was subsequently defeated by a wide margin.

Steps were also taken to try to have the rules of the game altered, primarily because, as one delegate said: "The players are clamouring for the Northern Union game in some shape or form." [10] On July 10, 1908, the New Zealand Rugby Union had before it various recommendations to reform the rules and make it more like Northern Union football. These included reducing the number of players to 14, that a try be allowed for a player falling on the ball instead of touching it down with his hands, that dropouts be taken from the goal-line - but they rejected them. The hopes of many that a compromise could be found were dashed. The debate on compensation and rule changes, as well as the autocratic administration of the Rugby Union, now quickly widened in the footballing community to the point where one administrator said: "The gloves were off and it would be a fight to the finish".

When the Rugby Union rejected reform, many players and administrators became disillusioned and gradually left the game, setting up their own organisations and clubs to play Northern Union - rugby league - but on what they saw as an amateur basis - the only payments being to players when away on tour. Rugby in New Zealand was splitting gradually in two, not, as had happened in Sydney, with one momentous meeting, but being split it definitely was.

Later that same year, on 3 October, 1908, the South Island hosted its first provincial rugby league game - Otago played Southland in Dunedin, where that city's Mayor had become the patron of the Northern Union Amateur Rugby League (Otago Centre). That organisation had, even by then, properly constituted itself and had rented the Otago Rugby Football Union's goalposts for the match at the Caledonian Ground in Dunedin for two guineas. There was a return match in Invercargill on 7 October, 1908. All except one of the Otago team were members of senior rugby union club teams in Dunedin. The All Black, Ned Hughes, played for the Southland team (and also later the New Zealand Rugby League team in 1910 against the British). The Otago Rugby Union was told by the New Zealand Union to forward the names of those who took part in the Northern Union match; they were given the almost mandatory sentence of disqualification for life. The same pattern soon began to emerge in other centres, with games being undertaken by returning players teaching their clubmates the new game, games being played and bannings for life being imposed. The battle lines were being drawn for what was to be one of the most

Inter-provincial Rugby League Match 1908.
Taranaki defeated Auckland at Victoria Park. Auckland was captained by Dick Wynyard.

acrimonious periods in the history of New Zealand sport.

So, gradually during the latter part of 1908, and then in 1909, rugby league was played among groups of provincial representative rugby players throughout the country as a precursor to the establishment of rugby league clubs. The revolt was being led by the All Golds backed by provincial players, and even before the first club games were played on a regular basis in Auckland, commencing in 1910, the players selected a New Zealand team to tour Australia in 1909. The All Golds players in the New Zealand side were Adam Lile, Con Byrne, Bill Trevarthen, J Barber (captain) and Harold Rowe; Dan Fraser, who had been one of Baskiville's assistants on the tour of England was the Manager. That tour sprang from their discussions with the New South Wales Rugby League, which had arranged for its vice-president, Mr CH Ford, to visit New Zealand. Ford arrived in Wellington aboard the SS Moeraki in May 1909. Once Ford completed those discussions he went up to Rotorua to arrange for a New Zealand Maoris team to also visit Australia that year. During this period of eighteen months, starting from when the All Golds had returned, players, and well known rugby administrators like Duncan W McLean in Auckland, who was on the Auckland Rugby Union Management Committee, and who later became the first Chairman of the New Zealand Rugby League, were having to decide which form of rugby they wanted to be associated with. The time immediately leading up to the two tours of Australia in 1909 heralded a frantic period of activity at an administrative level and, nine days before the Maoris left for Australia, the first official steps were taken to form a national governing body in Auckland at a meeting on 19 July, 1909, at the Chamber of Commerce boardroom. As it turned out, the New Zealand Maoris, led by Nirai Whareure (McCrae), had greater success than the New Zealand side this time, and, managed by John T Hetet, of

Te Kuiti, they went on to defeat Australia 20-16. The Maoris played with such skill and enthusiasm the crowd of 45,000 carried these victors over their own countrymen shoulder high from the field.

The All Golds also played a role in establishing rugby league clubs. In Auckland Dick and Bill Wynyard helped found the North Shore Albions Club breaking away from one of the oldest rugby clubs in Auckland - North Shore. Those two clubs were at loggerheads over the use of grounds and clubrooms for a long time. Such fledgling organisations, without the business sponsorhip available today, could not afford to pay players even if they wished to, which appears not to have been the case anyway. The All Golds, drawing on their experience gained in England also coached their clubmates in the new game. Even as late as the 1930s, Dick Wynyard's coaching tips on how to play the game were being used in rugby league publications. The Auckland Rugby League Gazette, 28 May 1938, quoted him as saying: "In good company, indiscriminate kicking is considered poor league, since it merely gives possession to the other side. Passing the ball, with continuous backing-up, should be aimed at." Bill Mackrell and Charlie Dunning, too, were influential in forming the Ponsonby and Newton Rugby League Clubs and, from the New Zealand Maoris' side to Australia in 1909, Opai and Ernie Asher were instrumental in setting up the City Rovers Rugby League Club in Auckland. In an interesting twist to history, the name given to Northcote Rugby League Club when it was first formed in 1910 was 'The Warriors'.

Further south, Adam Lile had returned to Taranaki and assisted in the establishment of league there. It is reported that: "fresh from his experience with the All Golds, he was all energy," and that this "well known and respected sportsman duly arranged practice games on the old Kukupa ground." His enthusiasm must have had some effect if we are to be guided by the results of Teriyaki's first inter-provincial games played in 1909. They defeated the strong Wellington side 22-18, which included among its players Tom Cross, Wright, Con Byrne, and Dan Gilchrist, all returned All Golds. They then played Auckland, which had players like Dick Wynyard, Bill Mackrell and Charlie Dunning. At Victoria Park, Auckland, before a crowd of 5,700, Taranaki won 5-3 in what was a shock result. That particular match was refereed by Lance Todd, who had returned home for a short spell in the off-season from Wigan. Todd then returned to Wigan taking with him the Canterbury representative rugby union three-quarter David Michael, who was also at the time the Canterbury 100 yards sprint champion.

The New Zealand Rugby Football League was formally constituted on 25 April, 1910, and Billy Wynyard who had played so well with his brother, Dick Wynyard, on Baskiville's tour was on the New Zealand Council, later being joined there by Jim Gleeson, back from England having completed his legal training there. Of the other players on Baskiville's tour, Con Byrne went to Sydney and played for the North Sydney club and after that was granted a transfer to play in England. Charlie Dunning captained the New Zealand Test team against Great Britain during their tour in 1910 of Australia and New Zealand and Charlie Pearce captained the Canterbury Rugby League team when league was formed in Christchurch. Jim Gleeson and 'Hone' Tyne were significant in starting rugby league in the Hawkes Bay. The first game was played on the old Recreation Ground against Auckland. Four clubs were playing in 1911 when the Hawkes Bay Rugby League was formed. It appears most, if not all, of Baskiville's team either contributed in a tangible way to the development of rugby league in New Zealand, or played further afield in England or Australia. The timing of their involvement in the new game, and the sheer level of their commitment to it, together with Baskiville's public statements of what they would do when they returned, if nothing else, points to them at some point on their tour deciding to establish the game in New Zealand. There was also their clear conviction that the Northern Union's rules made for a better game, their life-long disqualification from Rugby Union, and the fact that while in England they had asked the Northern Union about having a Great Britain team visit New Zealand and Australia in 1909. It appears that 1909 may have been too early but that the tour took place once the administrative structures necessary for such an undertaking were in place in 1910. The evidence is persuasive that the formation of Rugby League in New Zealand was planned by the returned All Golds with the same foresight that Baskiville had brought to the formation of the touring team in 1907, and that his side must be viewed in the context of an overall rejection of rugby union among many players and administrators in New Zealand at that time. This would also explain why rugby league gathered strength so quickly, to the point in Auckland, in 1912, where its public profile tended to overshadow rugby union, and also why it met with such a ready acceptance throughout the country, including many smaller areas like Nelson and Wanaque, to mention but a few, prior to World War One.

The independent paths chosen by the All Golds were soon followed by many other outstanding footballers of the Edwardian era, some of whom, like George Gillett, AH Francis, William Curran, and Charlie Seeling, who joined his Auckland team-mate Lance Todd at Wigan, also went on to fashion outstanding professional careers. Todd played for Wigan until 1914 when he was transferred to Dewsbury, much to the dissatisfaction of many Wigan supporters. Later, when managing Salford, Todd did much to make that club a power in rugby league, and as a BBC commentator he introduced many people to the game. As long ago as 1937, and before the days when games could be floodlit, the perceptive and knowledgeable Todd strongly advocated that rugby league in Britain was a game that needed to be played in summer, when games would be less likely to be affected by weather and bad light.

It remains finally to consider Albert Baskiville, his achievements and the significance of his contribution to sporting, and therefore social history. The idea of the Professional All Black Team was his, and he also played the most important role in its realisation. Intrinsic to the success of the tour was their complete confidence in him. Of the fact that this trust was not misplaced we can be certain; the Public Trustee's summary of Baskiville's assets valued his total estate at less than £250. For its part the team had given him the necessary discretion to accomplish what they set out to do. Of this 'Massa' Johnston said: "We were under very strict management, as a professional combination has to be, and to Mr Palmer - 'the boss' as we called him - even such little things as our comings and goings in the evenings had to be submitted. But Albert Baskiville was always considered to be the exception outside the rule. No one ever thought of questioning what he did or when he came and went." Baskiville, too, seems to have enjoyed his new role. He was respected by Northern Union officials and he also had an engaging way of "getting an entree into very exclusive circles in England." Like many who, for financial reasons are not able to advance to higher education, he had an insatiable appetite for information about many things. England was new to him and it was his original intention to stay on there for a short time after the tour to see more of what it offered; but he decided against that when the Australian tour was agreed to.

It was perhaps sad that, because he was organising the tour, he played so few games. Speaking about this Johnston said: "It was not until the St Helens match that he was asked to put on a jersey. In that match he gave a fine exhibition of three-quarter play and scored two tries." He played so well in fact that he played his way into the top side with that one game. In the Test he played in Sydney against Australia there can be no doubt that he was vital to the winning of that game and the series. He had strength, stamina and speed, combined with a desire for, and an ability to seize, scoring opportunities; he had in fact all the attributes necessary for an outstanding career.

In matters relating to team finances he was untiring, frequently going out to grounds on which they were to play as early as 12 o'clock to check the turnstiles and to see to all the incidental arrangements. When the first balance sheet was made out (at Manchester) complimentary reference was made by the auditors to the business-like manner in which the books had been kept. But Baskiville had possibly taken on more than he should have. Johnston's view on this is instructive. He said: "When it was all over, and the boys were on the boat leaving England, he just seemed like an old man who had lost interest in the past and was looking far into the future. He told us he already considered the tour a success, and that he was already looking forward to taking a team to America - that was to be his next achievement, if he could manage it." [11]

On a more personal basis, the Wellington weekly "The Times" said of Baskiville: "Bert was a young fellow of many sterling qualities. Amongst his companions both on and off the field he was a warm favourite, but behind all of this there was a real nobility of character that endeared him to his intimates. As a runner, he was a most generous opponent as well as a desperate finisher, his best performances being over middle distances. In the Oriental Rugby Club he made many good friends and among his opponents he was highly esteemed for the good-tempered way he played the game." At his funeral friends noted that both the Queensland and New South Wales Rugby Unions had sent wreaths and they were disappointed that the Wellington Rugby Union did not offer the family its condolences.

Yet, despite all Baskiville's achievements, as a writer, athlete, and footballer, it is as the organiser of the first Professional All Black team's tour to England with its series win there, and as the person who introduced professional rugby and rugby league to Australia, and then, through the team he had organised, rugby league to New Zealand, that he is of historical sporting significance. The legacy he and his side left in both Australia and New Zealand is the rugby league game, and all that it means to those people.

It is perhaps ironic that Baskiville, so vilified by the New Zealand Rugby Union for challenging its authority, died at such a young age, but that the rugby league game, which he adopted, and which he and his team played so well, was to survive and prosper. Where previously it was considered anathema by many, because of their focus on rugby union, television was, by 1994, taking it into many New Zealand households for the first time, on a regular basis, and it changed the public's perception. Rugby League's success in attracting players and audiences was so great, rugby union could no longer resist the players' demands for compensation. It quickly cast off the facade of being amateur. That momentous decision was taken precisely one hundred years to the month since the Northern Union had broken away from the English Rugby Union in September 1895.

1   *The Sydney Morning Herald*, 25 May, 1908.
2   Ibid.
3   *The Auckland Weekly News*, 25 June, 1908.
4   *The New Zealand Herald*, 15 June, 1908.
5   *The Weekly Press*, 1 April, 1908.
6   *Lyttelton Times*, 7 May, 1908.
7   *Canterbury Times*, 27 May, 1908.
8   *The Weekly Press*, 22 July, 1908.
9   Davidson, W. Rugby League, 1939 p.12.
10   Ibid p12.
11   Undated newspaper article, HS Turtill Scrapbook.

APPENDIX 1

Football

(From the Pall Mall Gazette, Nov 14 1867)

Football is, a par excellence, the winter sport of English youth, and frozen-out cricket and rowing clubs gladly welcome a game which the cold renders only more enjoyable. The exercise however, is the exclusive monopoly of the young. At cricket a steady wrist and unerring eye may counterbalance years, and a rowing man may be in the height of his powers on the wrong side of thirty, but the elasticity and activity required at football are to be found only in frames still growing or unset. In later life, to say nothing of stiffness and other disadvantages, limbs are more brittle, and bodies too heavy to endure the shock of "spills" and "charges" with safety. The game itself though practised in season by all schools differs in relative importance in most of them. With Eton, Westminster, and Radley the "eight" is the leading feature; with Harrow and Winchester the "eleven". In these schools football, though the predominant winter game, is adopted only for want of something better to do; but at Rugby the case is different: football is there the game of the place. Cricket, though brought to great perfection, is only tolerated when the season will no longer permit of the favourite amusement. Marlborough, an offshoot from Rugby, shares its predilection of the game, but in a minor degree, and allows an equal rank to cricket.

A great drawback to a more popular appreciation of football is that it is not regulated by any uniform code of laws. Each school plays its own peculiar game, governed by traditional contingencies of numbers, shape of ground etc. Some good may possibly be extracted from the variety of rules. At present, however, the multiplicity of systems prevents many schools from competing with each other, and also embarrasses the game at the universities. If one side submits to the rules of the other side, it does so obviously to its own disadvantage; if both sides share all the privileges allowed by their codes there will be little discipline left, while if the joint restrictions are enforced, there will be hardly any chance of touching the ball at all. At Oxford the programme is arranged with a view to mutual accommodation for a Harrow, Rugby, Eton, or Winchester game, as the case may be. At Cambridge a modified code of rules has been drawn up and adopted; and in the neighbourhood of London also local clubs have formed a "Football Association", and prepared rules to suit, as supposed, all exigencies of the game and all local prejudices. What is wanted is a supreme body like the MCC at Lord's, which should legislate by the weight of its own prestige for all the votaries of the game. It is to be feared, however, that mutual prejudices and jealousies are too rife among the football clubs to permit much hope of such a result.

There are certain principles common, from their simplicity, to all phases of the game. It is played with sides in a "ground" marked out or enclosed; the object in all is eventually to drive the ball through the "goal" to the opposing side. The ball is "out of play" or "dead" if driven out of the ground, yet not through the goal, and has to be brought back to its place of exit. "Off side", "sneaking", "poaching", "tagging" etc which describe the offence of unfairly passing on the ball from one to another on the same side, are universally forbidden; but beyond these few "common measures" there is a perplexing variety in the different games.

Although the ground is always of an oblong shape, the "goal" varies. In the Winchester game the ground is bounded by canvas screens and ropes, is proportionately narrower than other grounds, and the whole width of either extremity constitutes "goal". In most other games a narrower central space, defined by flags, at either end of the ground is goal; if the ball passes this line of flags without going between them it is "behind", and no goal is won. The Rugbeian system requires the ball to be kicked not only between the goals, but also over a bar, at a certain height from the ground to win the game. Etonian laws compel the ball to go under a similar line. Most other rules recognise a victory when the ball passes between the flags, at any height from the ground. Next there is a choice of balls. The Etonian ball is small and light, suitable for being kept on the ground, and "bullied" through the forest of legs, where a larger orb might find difficulty in passing. The Harrow ball is about the largest. That used in the Rugbeian style of games is more oval than round, which renders it a favourite where long kicking is practised. As to the numbers employed in a game, eleven or fifteen suffice at Eton and Winchester; tens or even hundreds may engage at Rugby in the great matches, but twenty a side is the usual array. In commencing the game at Harrow and Rugby the ball is "kicked off" from the middle of the ground; at Eton and Winchester the commencement is a "bully" or "hot" - all the players en masse, shoulder to shoulder - in the centre of the ground.

"Handing" or "holding" is altogether prohibited by Etonians. The hands may never be used by them except to stop the ball, keep it down to the feet, or touch in a "rouge". The Rubgeian code - the opposite extreme - by a new rule allows the ball to be held even when picked up off the ground; he who has it may, at his peril, run with it into the opposite base, with a view to "touch" and "try at goal", hereafter to be explained. Harrovians permit a "fair catch" if the ball is killed, ie. driven from below the knee, though in its passage it may glance off any other part of the body, provided it does not touch ground. He who catches may claim a "free kick" if he calls at once "three yards", otherwise he is liable to have his prey knocked out of his hands. Wykehamists allow a "free" kick from a fair catch, if it can be got; hence in the case they suspend their rule disallowing running with the ball, so far as to afford the catcher the power of getting his kick with a three yards run, if he can, and also allow "holding" to stop him for the moment, but the instant he has his course clear, or the ball has been kicked, further privileges of holding or running come to an end. "Shinning" or "hacking" is variously allowed or disallowed. The Rugby school of players uphold and countenance it, as a necessary means of forcing the ball through the dense masses that play in such games, and one who runs with the ball may be hacked ad lib., but most other schools taboo it, as unsatisfactory and unnecessary. Many other differences in the mode of play might be enumerated; and these of course have all their effect upon the length of time occupied in each game. Three days may elapse in a great Rugby match before a goal is won. Etonian and Harrovian games are more rapid, and two or three may be played in an afternoon. Winchester games occasionally last only a few minutes; or a dozen can be sometimes played in one match.

We cannot attempt to strike a balance in favour of any one system. It is plain that there are advantages and imperfections in all. The absolute condemnation of "hands", even to the extent of a "fair catch", as in the Etonian game, seems, for instance, rather an extreme measure, though the principle of invariably keeping the ball down is in the spirit of true sport; "rouges", though unique in one way, correspond very much to the Rugbeian "touch" and "try", and have the advantage of being of value in weighting in an otherwise undecided game. The imperfection of the Rugbeian system, and the plan of "touch" behind goals, is that it tends to draw the game systematically to a corner, instead of to the centre of the ground. High kicking also tends to keep the game for a time very much in the hands of a few. The "running in", though cherished and traditional, is contradictory in a great extent to the title of the game, though it gives scope for the display of skill of another kind.

But the great evil is the recognised legality of "hacking". Where usage of law, and the chances are the same for all, it may not appear fair to those used to it, but to an external observer there is much in it that is objectionable. There is something brutal in deliberately "hacking" the shins of fellow creature in cold blood, while hot blood, that might extenuate the seed, is the first evil to be avoided. Barked shins, and occasionally broken limbs occur in almost all forms of football, but the knowledge that they are due to accident is at least some consolation to the sufferer. In fact, in an eleven-a-side game with the ball in perpetual motion, plenty of room for full play of legs, and no crowd, there are often more casualties, though purely accidental, than in a "hundred-a-side" game. Pluck, therefore in codes other than Rugbeian, is equally called into play. It may be remarked that, as a rule, when a leg is broken in a charge between two players, it rises from the fact that one of them, not the sufferer, has flinched or widely missed the ball, at the moment of collision, kicking his opponent instead. No accident can happen if both kick fairly and with good aim at the ball; and if the ball is then missed, or only half struck, the foot or ankle only suffers, not the upper part of the shin, which is the dangerous spot; if, however, one player happens to be double the weight of another, an ankle might be twisted. But as a rule such casualties are not common.

APPENDIX 2

Evolution of the Tour
Otago Daily Times, 10 Dec 1907. By A H Baskiville

Colombo, September 11.

The possession of some money and a love of adventure and an article appearing in a London daily paper are in the first place responsible for a team of New Zealand Rugby footballers visiting Great Britain and playing combinations affiliated to the English Northern Rugby Union. The article written by F W Cooper, a Northern Union enthusiast, indicated that there existed in the North of England a keen desire to see their clubs or players try conclusions with a team of New Zealanders. The following extract proves this:- "What many old players like myself would like to see would be a match between a picked Northern Union team and the colonials. I have no hesitation in saying that I would pick 15 players who would willingly give their services to play such a match, the proceeds of which could be devoted to charity, and I have little doubt that my side would achieve victory. The wearers of the silver fern have not been defeated, but they have not played the cream of English football. Such men play under the banner of the Northern Union. The men who opposed New Zealand at Headingley are the weakest lot who ever donned Yorkshire jerseys, and the visitors did not achieve anything out of the common when they beat them. I may add that Jack Toothill, the famous international, and Albert Goldthorpe, prince of goal droppers, are in accord with my views."

From a conversation with a returned 1905 "All Black" I gleaned that the Northern Union authorities had actually held out a substantial gate guarantee for a match with the New Zealanders, but of course this proposal could not be entertained then. This set me thinking why shouldn't a New Zealand team play the Northern Unionists? Strict amateur supporters will answer: "Because some of their players are professionals". This argument seems weak if we keep in view the fact that in the sister Association code amateurs and professionals often play on the same side and frequently against each other. A representative fixture, Amateurs versus Professionals, is sometimes played in England. People in the colonies would not demur if an Association team were to travel to New Zealand and play the principal British clubs, which are nearly all professionals; therefore, why should an outcry be raised if a Rugby team did likewise? It was thought that perhaps friends would consider a player mercenary, and regard him in an unfavourable light, if he formed one of a team to go Home and share in the pleasures and profits, if any of a British Northern Union tour; but all doubts on this point were set at rest by their expressing an opinion, when sounded, that it would be a shrewd and rather sensible idea. In fact, they all seemed to rather like the scheme. Guarded conversations with prominent New Zealand players elicited the information that, with few exceptions, they would be willing to join a team if one was formed with that purpose in view; so I set to work. The Northern Union clubs were circularised, and an offer of 70 per cent of the gross gates obtained, also a guarantee of £3000 for a series of matches in the 1907-08 season. The guarantee was for a New Zealand team, not, as was reported in some papers, for a team that has to contain a certain number of New Zealand representative players. A free hand was given in the matter of selecting a team. Once the scheme was fairly started and advertised gratuitiously by the different Rugby Unions, no difficulty was experienced in getting together a strong combination. The trouble was the selecting of a team from the numerous applicants for positions in it. Of course, one could not hope to get absolutely the best team that New Zealand could produce to break away and run the risk of permanent disqualification from playing the amateur game. Yet, strange to say, a number of people thought this actually possible. They wanted to see the best team go Home, and they were disappointed because their hopes were not realised.

Before proceeding further, it should be mentioned now that if a capitalist had promoted the tour with an idea of making money he could have secured a team that would have satisfied many others by taking Home a few very prominent players as professionals - that is, by paying them a certain sum of money and their expenses. But this would have spoiled the whole groundwork of the scheme. Our idea was to get players to travel Home as amateurs - this is, to pay their own expenses and divide the gate proceeds equally, as the Australian cricketers do. We hold that we are still amateur footballers because we do not, nor do we intend to, gain a living by playing football. We are making a trip to England at our own expense. The mere fact of our playing against teams which play a few professionals does not alter our status one jot. The Australian press, upon becoming acquainted with the idea of our tour, in most cases, cut out the word "professional" altogether, when discussing the All Black play or players. It was better acquainted with conditions of this sort than the New Zealand press.

Selecting a Team

In selecting a team to represent New Zealand against the Northern Unionists a number of conditions had to be taken into consideration which a majority of people although well acquainted with amateur Rugby points, knew very little of. The thirteen-aside game and the recent amendments in the old Rugby rules by the Northern Union had, according to newspaper reports of matches, altered the style of play considerably. One radical change, for instance - the abolishment of the line out and the substitution of a scrum 10 yards in the field as a means of bringing the ball into play after going into touch - made a great difference. Some New Zealand forwards are noted for their cleverness on the lineout and are included in the representative teams sometimes because of their skills in this direction, apart from other qualifications. Of course these would not be ideal men for our purpose. Again, it seems that another new Northern Union rule should result in the ball being centred more when returning it, instead of being invariably kicked into touch, as in the New Zealand amateur game. It is easily seen that this should result in the play being faster and more open, so that a speedy man, providing he is a good scrummager, should be our ideal. A slow, heavy-weight would be at a great disadvantage at once, even if he was a good line-out man and scrummager in New Zealand. Another thing had to be considered in selecting the forwards. There should be a big proportion of hookers or frontrow men included. The thirteen-aside rule will probably necessitate a reduction in the number of pack men, so that it is likely the three-two-one formation will be adopted in the scrum if it is found that five New Zealand forwards, packed their own way (two-three) are incapable of holding six Northern Unionists. It is also understood that the packs in the North of England have to be formed very quickly and this might necessitate our forwards packing in on the first up first down principle - that is, the first two or three men to arrive at the scene of operating the scrum go in the front row, and the remainder back in behind, irrespective of their New Zealand scrum merits or qualifications. So, keeping this in view, good all-round forwards such as Trevarthen (Auckland) and Gilchrist (Wellington), who can also play in the front row in New Zealand, were preferred. Tyler, whose brilliance in open play is well known in Auckland, was included on this score, and also because it was known that he could play in the front-row position if required. The other regular hookers (New Zealand formation) included are Dunning and Mackrell (Auckland), and Watkins, Callum, and Baskerville (Wellington). Some of the latter can also play in other positions in the scrum if required.

Turning now to the lock position in the scrum, we are confronted with a problem. A lock may not be required at all. However, Wright (Wellington) was not included solely because of his lock qualifications. He can play well anywhere in the scrum. The remaining forwards chosen - Johnston (Otago), Pearce (Canterbury), and Cross, Byrne and Lile (Wellington) - are all good scrummagers, and can also hold their own with the best of the colony in the open field. Many other New Zealand forwards with good local reputations, no doubt excellent men if tried in a good team, applied for positions, but they were passed over, in some cases reluctantly, by us because we could not see them play or give an exhibition of their prowess.

The selection of half backs presented another difficulty, as we were a little uncertain as to the requirements of the players in that position. A Northern Union rule practically eliminates the wing forward of the New Zealand game rendering him useless. It prevents a half back (or wing forward) advancing around the scrum when his opponents have secured possession by hooking, even in front of his own back row forwards, until the ball is heeled absolutely clear of that scrum. This rule gives an attacking scrum half back a clear start if he is dexterous in snapping up the ball. One should therefore, for scrum purposes be quick off the mark, fairly fast and good giver of passes. For defensive purposes in the open field he must be a good tackler and rush stopper. Our half backs - Kelly and Tyne (Wellington) and Gleeson (Hawkes Bay) - performed well in the Sydney matches, and justified their inclusion, although they were not quite up to the high standard set by our recognised New Zealand representative in that position. F Roberts will long remain a model half-back for colonial players to educate themselves up to. Other New Zealand half-backs were anxious to come Home with us, and would perhaps have been included if an opportunity had existed of seeing them play. The five-eighths chosen are all well-known men in New Zealand football. Todd and R Wynyard were nominated from Auckland; no doubt for these positions in this year's North Island team. W Wynyard, a brother to the other of that name, is considered by some Auckland critics to be his equal on the field. Wrigley, the sole Wairarapa representative in the team, will fill a five-eighths position, although, like McGregor, he can also play in the three-quarter line. Other three quarters besides the latter two players mentioned are Smith and Rowe (Auckland) and Lavery (Canterbury). Messenger, the Australian star player, will most likely fill the centre three-quarter position, although he is quite at home on the wing. He can also play five-eighths if required. Turtill, who represented New Zealand against New South Wales on the occasion of their last visit to New Zealand, and the South Island this year, was given the full-back position. Rowe, though nominally a centre three-quarter, will act as emergency full-back. D Fraser, of Petone (Wellington) Club forward, visited Sydney with the team, and was included over there. Besides rendering assistance (clerical or otherwise) in conducting the tour, he can play if required.

The team, regarded collectively, should do well in England. There are a number of young players included, but in most cases they are tried men. The leaven of old players should soon teach them the finer points of the game and bring out any dormant football that is in them. Some people may not consider certain players good enough. It is submitted that these might not be quite up to New Zealand representative form now, but they will improve considerably when on tour and when they reap the benefit of the experience that the older hands will impart to them. The material is there at any rate, and it is very promising at that. Again, when the scheme of organising a team was first mooted people had no idea that such a strong combination would be obtained. Certain players were promised the tour, and because they made considerable preparation and looked forward to it so enthusiastically, one could not turn around and disappoint them, even if they had lost form to an extent, because better players come forward at the eleventh hour and offered their services. Wright (Petone) has been elected captain and Smith (Auckland), vice-captain, and these two and Johnson will form the Selection Committee.

APPENDIX 3

The Agreement

AGREEMENT made this twenty fourth day of August in the year one thousand nine hundred and seven **WHEREBY George William Smith, Charles Dunning, William Thomas Wynyard, William Thomas Tyler, James Gleeson, Albert Henry Baskiville, Charles Pearce, Harry John Palmer, John Richard Wynyard, Arthur Callum, Arthur Frederick Kelly, Duncan McGregor, William Johnston, Edgar Wrigley, Eric Leslie Watkins, Hercules Richard Wright, Hubert Sydney Turtill, Conrad Byrne, Joseph Aloysius Lavery, Harold Francis Rowe, William Henry Mackrell, William MacVay Trevarthen, Thomas William Cross, Daniel George Fraser, Adam Lile, Edward Tyne, Daniel Gilchrist, Lancelot Beaumont Todd,** all of the Colony of New Zealand and **Herbert Henry Messenger** of the State of New South Wales **MUTUALLY CONVENANT AND AGREE** with each other as follows:

1. The said parties hereto shall form themselves into be constituted as from the date hereof a combination known as the "New Zealand All Black Rugby Football Team".

2. The objects of the said combination or team shall be to play, engage and take part in Football matches against professional rugby football teams or other teams affiliated to the English Rugby Union in the British Isles during a tour of the British Isles or such other countries or places as the Management Committee hereinafter mentioned may deem fit to substitute in lieu of or in addition to the British Isles.

3. The affairs of the combination shall be managed by a Committee of Management (hereinafter called the Management Committee) consisting of the following persons: James Collins Gleeson, Harry John Palmer, Albert Henry Baskerville, William Johnston, Lancelot Beaumont Todd, Hercules Richard Wright and Duncan McGregor all of New Zealand who shall have the sole and absolute government of the said Combination and all business transactions in connection with same or the tour of the said Combination.

4. Each member of the said combination shall pay into the fund of the said Combination to meet the initial expenses of the said tour the sum of **fifty pounds** provided that any member may subscribe a less sum than the said sum of fifty pounds on condition that he shall pay interest as hereinafter provided upon the deficiency between the amount so subscribed and the sum of fifty pounds.

5. Each member of the Combination shall diligently and faithfully devote his exclusive services for the purposes and objects of the Combination for the said tour commencing in Sydney on or about the twenty fourth day of August 1907 and extending over a professional football tour through the British Isles terminating at the end of the ensuing football season in the said British Isles.

6. Each of the parties hereto agrees to play football matches for the said Combination during the said tour in all things according to the best of his ability skill and judgement at such times and in such places as the said Management Committee may designate during the said tour and to conform to and accept as binding all Rules regulations orders decisions directions commands and judgements of the said Management Committee.

7. Each of the said parties hereto agree to faithfully diligently and loyally obey the orders directions instructions and commands of the said Management Committee or any person or person such Management Committee may appoint with regard to the duties each member of the Combination will be required to perform whether on or off the football field appertaining to or respecting the regulations of the said tour.

8. Each member of the said Combination hereby agrees to conduct and demean himself in all respects in a respectable and proper manner at all times and agrees to uphold the dignity and reputation of the said Combination by respectability sobriety honesty and uprightness and by the payment of his just debts during the continuance of this Agreement.

9. Each member of the team agrees to attend all Meetings for the purpose of training and preparing for matches and all practice and other matches authorised or appointed by the said Management Committee or any person or persons the said Management Committee may appoint except when a member of the said Combination in incapacitated from so doing by sickness or injury in which case the said member must produce if called upon a Medical Certificate showing his inability to attend such meetings or play in such matches and it shall be at the option of the Management Committee or their representative to send a Doctor to such member and a report of such Doctor shall be final.

10. If at any time during the continuance of this agreement the conduct of any member of the

Combination shall in the opinion of the said Management Committee be such as to render him unworthy undesirable or unfit to remain a member of the said Combination of which matters the said Management Committee shall be the sole and absolute judges such member shall be liable to expulsion from the Combination and shall forfeit all moneys payable to him out of the funds of the said Combination and all his rights and privileges under this Agreement and shall have no claim or demand whatsoever against the said Combination in respect of such moneys or in respect of any other cause matter or thing whatsoever and such moneys so forfeited shall be the absolute property of the said Combination.

11. **If** any member of the said Combination shall refuse to obey the commands orders or directions of the said Management Committee or any other person or persons the Management Committee may appoint or misconduct himself in any manner whether on or off the football field of which misconduct the said Management Committee shall be the sole and absolute judges and in case such Management Committee shall deem his misconduct of not so aggravated a character as to warrant his expulsion from the team be liable to a fine not exceeding ten pounds **and** we and each of us expressly authorise and empower the said Management Committee to impose such fine or make such expulsion referred to in clause ten hereof as aforesaid.

12. **The** inability of any member to attend to his duties in connection with the said tour or to play in any such football matches or to appear at such training meetings whether arising from illness or any other cause must be communicated at once to the Management Committee by such member by notice in writing and in the case of illness such notice shall truly state the nature of such illness and if in the opinion of the said Management Committee they shall deem it so advisable the medical and surgical fees or other fees and expenses in connection with the illness or such member may be paid out of the funds of the said Combination.

13. **Each** member who faithfully carries out all the covenants and agreements herein on his part contained shall be entitled to receive the sum or allowance of one pound per week out of the funds of the said Combination such payment to be computed from the date of the arrival of the said Combination in the British Isles and be paid within one week after arrival of the said Combination in the British Isles.

14. **Each** member who faithfully performs the agreement herein on his part contained shall be entitled to receive and be paid out of the funds of the said Combination all usual travelling and hotel expenses and the said Combination shall find and provide all football uniforms and other usual expenses incurred in the conduct of a football tour.

15. **If** in the opinion of the said Management Committee the financial position of the funds of the said Combination so warrants it the said Management Committee may upon receipt of a requisition from any member in their discretion advance such member any sum not exceeding the sum of five pounds which sum shall be a debt to the Combination until the liquidation of such debt and may be deducted from any moneys other than the said weekly allowance of one pound to which such member shall become entitled to receive from the funds of the Combination.

16. **Subject** to clause eighteen hereof should any member of the combination be desirous of obtaining an advance from the funds of the Combination to forward to his family or relatives it shall be in the discretion of the Management Committee on application to them by such member to pay a Bank Draft on any Bank of New Zealand or the Bank of New South Wales for such amount as the Management Committee in their descretion shall decide to advance such member and such allowance shall be a debt from such member to the Combination and all moneys which any member shall be entitled to receive from the funds of the Combination shall be debited and chargeable which such advance.

17. **The** said Management Committee shall have full control over all moneys received in connection with tour of the said team and have full power in their discretion to invest same either on deposit at interest or on current account in any Bank in Great Britain or Ireland or in any other manner they may deem advisable.

18. **No** money other than those mentioned in clauses fourteen and fifteen shall be advanced to any member of the Combination unless and until the Reserve Fund hereinafter mentioned of the said Combination shall reach in the aggregate the amount of the moneys paid into the funds of the said Combination by the Members thereof together with the amount necessary to provide and procure at the least a third class return ticket from where this agreement shall need to the nearest port in the Colony of New Zealand or the State of New South Wales for each Member of the Combination.

19. **The** said Management Committee shall after deducting thereout all incidental expenses and outgoings and moneys paid to the said Members of the Combination by way of allowance for travelling and other expenses of the said tour pay all moneys received by them in connection with the said tour in and towards the establishment of a Reserve Fund to repay the members of the said Combination all moneys advanced by them to the said Combination and to secure the purchase and provision of at least a third class return ticket or passage for each member of the Combination from the place where this agreement shall end to the nearest port in the Colony of New Zealand or the State of New South Wales.

20. The said tour of the said Combination shall terminate at the close of the ensuing football season in Great Britain and Ireland.

21. Such Management Committee shall keep or cause to be kept proper books of account showing all transactions in connection with tour of the said Combination and all receipt and disbursements in connection therewith and each member of the Combination shall have the right of access to and inspection of the said books at all reasonable times.

22. All Promissory Notes Bills of Exchange Cheques and Drafts shall be drawn by the Manager and countersigned by the Secretary and Treasurer appointed as hereinafter mentioned.

23. On the determination of the said tour the assets of the said Combination shall be realised and applied first in payment of the debts and liabilities of the Combination secondly in paying to the members of the Combination the respective amounts advanced by them to the funds of the Combination and in estimating the amount to be paid all such respective sums so advanced by the respective members to the Combination all members who have advanced less than fifty pounds shall be charged interest at the rate of twenty pounds per centum per annum on the deficiency between the amount advanced by them respectively and the sum of fifty pounds which said interest shall be placed to the credit of the said Combination and the surplus if any of the funds of the said Combination shall then be divided between the members of the Combination or their representatives in equal shares.

24. Should any member or members of the said Management Committee at any time or times die or desire to be discharged from or become unfit or incapable to act as a member of such Management Committee the remaining members of the said Management Committee may appoint from among the members of the said Combination a member or members to take the place of the member or members of the said Management Committee so dying or desiring to be-discharged or becoming unfit or incapable to act as aforesaid **and** such members so appointed shall have the same powers authorities and discretions and shall in all respects act as if he or they had been originally a member or members of the said Management Committee.

25. The said Management Committee shall appoint from among their number a Manager of the said team and Secretary and Treasurer of the Combination.

26. Should any member of the said Combination be dissatisfied with any directions orders or decisions given by the said Manager Secretary or Treasurer then such Member shall have the right to appeal to the Management Committee and its decision shall be final and conclusive and not subject to any appeal either at law or in equity.

27. Any four members of the said Management Committee shall form a quorum and at all meetings of the said Management Committee the Manager shall be the Chairman and in his absence from any meeting such member of the said Management Committee as the Members of the said Management Committee present at any such meeting shall appoint. **In** all matters of difference the Chairman shall have a casting vote.

28. It is agreed between the parties hereto that all conditions stipulation's and agreements contained in this Agreement shall be observable and duly observed in the United Kingdom of Great Britain and Ireland and in the Colony of New Zealand or such other countries or places hereinbefore mentioned and subject to the laws of the said United Kingdom of Great Britain and Ireland and the Colony of New Zealand or such other countries or places without further Contract Agreement or special clause should such appear to be necessitated by any special procedure or enactment of the United Kingdom of Great Britain and Ireland or the Colony of New Zealand or such other countries or places precisely as if this agreement had been made and executed in and within the jurisdiction of any one of such countries of the United Kingdom of Great Britain and Ireland and the Colony of New Zealand or such other countries or places or in the identical country State or places in which any disputes as to this agreement may arise.

29. And lastly it is hereby agreed and declared by and between the parties hereto that nothing herein contained shall be held of construed to form or be a partnership between them.

In Witness whereof the said parties to these presents have hereunto set their hands the day and year first above written.

APPENDIX 4

Income and Expenditure

Receipts

Gate Receipts	£	*s*	*d*
Sydney	427	11	1
Ceylon	50	0	0
England and Wales	8838	2	4
Acrobat	4	0	0
Fines from members	32	0	0
Interest on unpaid contributions to capital bank account	114	0	0
Bank interest, less charges	27	16	10
	£9493	10	3

Expenses

Ocean Travelling	1125	4	7
Railway Travelling	429	3	0
Hotel Expenses	1371	14	0
Gratuities	63	9	3
Uniform, gears, etc	64	2	1
Medical attendance	74	7	1
Organising expenses	40	0	0
Cables, postage etc	36	4	3
Sundry payments	5	17	6
Auditor's fees	4	4	0
Weekly allowance to members (22 weeks at £29 per week)	638	0	0
Divisible profit	**5641**	**4**	**6**
	£9493	**10**	**3**

APPENDIX 5

The 1907-08 New Zealand Team in Australia, England, Wales and Ceylon
Captain: H R Wright (Wellington)

August

17	1907	v	New South Wales	Won 12-8 (Under Rugby Union Rules)
21	1907	v	New South Wales	Won 19-5 (Under Rugby Union Rules)
24	1907	v	New South Wales	Won 5-3 (Under Rugby Union Rules)

September

12	1907	v	Ceylon	Won 33-6 (Under Rugby Union Rules)

October

9	1907	v	Bramley	Won 25-6
12	1907	v	Huddersfield	Won 19-8
16	1907	v	Widnes	Won 26-11
19	1907	v	Broughton Rangers	Won 20-14
23	1907	v	Wakefield Trinity	Drew 5-5
26	1907	v	Leeds	Won 8-2
30	1907	v	St Helens	Won 24-5

November

2	1907	v	Merthyr Tydvil	Won 27-9
5	1907	v	Keighley	Won 9-7
9	1907	v	Wigan	Lost 8-12
13	1907	v	Barrow	Lost 3-6
16	1907	v	Hull	Won 18-13
20	1907	v	Leigh	Lost 9-15
23	1907	v	Oldham	Lost 7-8
27	1907	v	Runcorn	Lost 0-9
30	1907	v	Dewsbury and Batley	Won 18-8

December

4	1907	v	Swinton	Won 11-2
7	1907	v	Rochdale Hornets	Won 19-0
10	1907	v	Bradford	Lost 2-7
14	1907	v	Halifax	Lost 4-9
18	1907	v	Yorkshire	Won 23-4
21	1907	v	Warrington	Lost 7-8
26	1907	v	Hunslet	Drew 11-11
28	1907	v	Salford	Won 9-2

January

1	1908	v	Wales	Lost 8-9 (Aberdare)
4	1908	v	Hull Kingston Rovers	Won 6-3
8	1908	v	Cumberland	Lost 9-21
11	1908	v	England XIII	Lost 16-18 (Wigan)
18	1908	v	Lancashire	Lost 4-20
25	1908	v	Northern Union	Lost 6-14 (Leeds)
29	1908	v	York	Lost 3-5

February

1	1908	v	Ebbw Vale	Won 3-2
8	1908	v	Northern Union	Won 18-6 (Chelsea, London)
15	1908	. v	Northern Union	Won 8-5 (Cheltenham)
22	1908	v	St Helens	Won 21-10

April

| 22 | 1908 | v | Newcastle | Won 53-6 (Under Rugby Union Rules) |
| 25 | 1908 | v | Northern Districts | Won 37-8 |

May

2	1908	v	New South Wales	Lost 10-18
6	1908	v	New South Wales	Lost 10-13
9	1908	v	Australia	Won 11-10 (Sydney)
16	1908	v	Queensland	Won 34-12
20	1908	v	Brisbane	Won 43-10
23	1908	v	Queensland	Drew 12-12
30	1908	v	Australia	Won 24-12 (Brisbane)

June

| 6 | 1908 | v | Australia | Lost 9-14 (Sydney) |

NEW ZEALAND ALL BLACK RUGBY FOOTBALL TEAM 1907-08
Back row: W M Trevarthen, H R Wright, W Johnston, T W Cross, A Lile, C J Pearce,
D G Fraser. *Third row:* H F Rowe, G W Smith, W H Mackrell, E Wrigley, J A Lavery,
C Byrne, D Gilchrist, E Watkins, W T Tyler.

Second row: J R Wynyard, C Dunning, L B Todd, D McGregor, H J Palmer (Manager),
H S Turtill, J C Gleeson (Treasurer), W T Wynyard.
Front row: A Callum, E Tyne, A H Baskiville (Promoter and Secretary),
H H Messenger, A F Kelly.